Trammell

ALSO BY TODD MASTERS

*The 1972 Detroit Tigers: Billy Martin and
the Half-Game Champs* (McFarland, 2010)

TRAMMELL
Detroit's Iconic Shortstop

Todd Masters

McFarland & Company, Inc., Publishers
Jefferson, North Carolina

LIBRARY OF CONGRESS CATALOGUING-IN-PUBLICATION DATA

Names: Masters, Todd, author.
Title: Trammell : Detroit's iconic shortstop / Todd Masters.
Description: Jefferson, North Carolina : McFarland & Company, Inc., Publishers, 2017 | Includes bibliographical references and index.
Identifiers: LCCN 2016048728 | ISBN 9781476666600 (softcover : acid free paper) ∞
Subjects: LCSH: Trammell, Alan, 1958– | Baseball players—United States—Biography. | Detroit Tigers (Baseball team)—History. | Shortstop (Baseball)—History.
Classification: LCC GV865.T68 M37 2017 | DDC 796.357092 [B]—dc23
LC record available at https://lccn.loc.gov/2016048728

BRITISH LIBRARY CATALOGUING DATA ARE AVAILABLE

ISBN (print) 978-1-4766-6660-0
ISBN (ebook) 978-1-4766-2579-9

© 2017 Todd Masters. All rights reserved

No part of this book may be reproduced or transmitted in any form or by any means, electronic or mechanical, including photocopying or recording, or by any information storage and retrieval system, without permission in writing from the publisher.

Front cover: Detroit Tigers shortstop Alan Trammell at bat (National Baseball Hall of Fame Library, Cooperstown, New York)

Printed in the United States of America

McFarland & Company, Inc., Publishers
Box 611, Jefferson, North Carolina 28640
www.mcfarlandpub.com

Table of Contents

Acknowledgments vii
Preface 1
Introduction 5

1. San Diego 11
2. Minor League Days 20
3. Rookie Sensation 36
4. Sparky 47
5. Breakthrough 64
6. "Bless You Boys" 77
7. MVP 93
8. Back to Earth 108
9. 1987 118
10. Race to the Finish 130
11. Disappointment × 2 143
12. End of the 80s 149
13. Lost Seasons 158
14. The Long Goodbye 171
15. "Bringing Back a Hero" 186
16. Legacy 197
17. Hall of Fame Bound? 205

Appendix: Career Statistics 215
Chapter Notes 217
Bibliography 225
Index 227

Acknowledgments

There are many people I would like to thank for their help on this project along the way. First, many thanks must go to the quality writers that covered Alan Trammell's career on a daily basis over more than two decades. Writers for the *Detroit Free Press* and *Detroit News* that included the likes of Jim Hawkins, Tom Gage, Joe Falls, Jerry Green, Charlie Vincent, Brian Bragg, Lynn Henning, John Lowe, and many others—created a ton of quality material while covering the Detroit Tigers from the 1970s and into the 2000s, which then became a wealth of information as I researched for this book. The same is true of writers for publications such as *The Sporting News* and *Sports Illustrated*, which did a number of feature articles on Trammell and the Tigers over the season's he played in.

Special thanks go out to those who helped me piece together the story of Trammell's life before he became a public figure in Major League Baseball. Bruce Ward and Steve Grooms got me started with background information and contacts concerning the prep powerhouse that was San Diego's Kearny High School in the mid–1970s. Hugh McMillan, who was Kearny's junior varsity and then assistant varsity baseball coach during the years Trammell played at those levels, was an invaluable resource, as was fellow school administrator, Brad Griffiths. Their insights about Trammell in both baseball and basketball were remarkable. Nick Canepa, who worked at the *San Diego Evening Tribune* during that period, gave me his remembrances from covering Trammell the high school basketball star. John Maffei of the *Union Tribune* similarly gave me his recollections from covering the local prep sports during that period.

Larry Corr and Terry Lynch, teammates of Trammell's in the Detroit Tigers' minor league system at Bristol and Montgomery, were very generous with their time and supportive of my efforts. The information and stories they shared were priceless. Lori Webb, current president of the Double-A Southern League, was very helpful in feeding me articles from those long ago minor league playoff battles in the Deep South.

Dick Tracewski, who played eight seasons in the major leagues and then served as a Tigers coach for 24 seasons under managers Billy Martin, Ralph Houk, Les Moss, and Sparky Anderson, was again a great friend to me on this project. Mr. Tracewski played an integral part in the progression of Trammell's career, serving as a coach for all but his last season.

I would like to thank the friendly staffs and comfortable settings at both the Michigan State University Library where I did most of my research of newspaper microfilms, and at the Cascade branch of the Kent District Library in Grand Rapids, Michigan, where I did most of my writing. I am much in debt to the help I was given by Ken Roussey, photo archivist at the National Baseball Hall of Fame Library, who did so much digging for me while finding the terrific photos that are part of this book. He is great to work with.

Finally, much appreciation goes out to my friends and family that listened to my idea and supported me through the nearly three years it took to complete this. That is especially true of my wife, Diane, and sons Nicholas and Peyton, who showed patience while I was hurrying out the door on so many Saturday mornings. I love you all.

Preface

"Why Alan Trammell?" I've been asked that question quite a few times while writing this book. I knew for my next project that I wanted to marry two of my personal passions: a love of books, especially the genre of biography, and my deep-rooted interest in baseball, and in particular the great teams and players of the past. The year 2014 marked the 30th anniversary of the Detroit Tigers 1984 World Series title team, a beloved team among Tiger fans like me.

The summer of 1984 was where all things in my life aligned. It was *the* summer that someone of my generation will never forget. For me, it happened at the right time and at the right age, where I could fully appreciate and eventually savor what happened that season. My childhood had been filled with tales and reverence for the Tigers 1968 World Series-winning club, a legendary team in Detroit's history. But I was too young to really understand or appreciate that team. That was the team of my father's generation. I grew up watching the painful transition as those post-'68 Tiger teams faded into terrible teams, which was then followed by several years of terrible Tiger teams evolving into mediocre teams. Fans like me suffered through the many false-starts and disappointments that inevitably go into the long building process that used to take place before a championship was even possible. By the time the "Bless You Boys" of 1984 took flight, I was old enough to appreciate what it took to get there, yet still young enough to revel in the exuberance that came with that victorious campaign.

So why Alan Trammell? Libraries are void of books profiling the stars from the Detroit Tigers teams of the 1980s, even though the 1984 team put together the greatest single-season witnessed over the second half of the twentieth century. There were certainly others from that team that could have been written about. Jack Morris and Kirk Gibson were arguably more electric talents on the field, and certainly more polarizing personalities off the field. Lou Whitaker, Lance Parrish, Darrell Evans, and Chet Lemon were all very accomplished and brought a quiet excellence to the sport.

But it was Trammell that embodied that era of baseball in Detroit, something he did well for 20 seasons as a player and has continued to do in the quarter-century since, serving as a beloved symbol of those treasured seasons.

He was the quiet, unassuming kid from California that came to work each day in the blue-collar city of Detroit, playing shortstop for the Detroit Tigers. To appreciate him in full, you had to watch him play every day. He didn't have muscles like Lance Parrish or Mark McGuire, and he didn't run like Willie Wilson or Rickey Henderson. He wasn't touted as "the next Mickey Mantle." Trammell entered the professional ranks pegged as the prototypical good-glove, weak-hitting shortstop common to those times, yet by the time he was a year past the legal drinking age, he had become a centerpiece for Detroit's building of an eventual championship team. He won Gold Gloves, accumulated lifetime offensive totals that rivaled almost any previous shortstop in history, and won the respect of all of those who played with or against him.

That is what this work tries to capture. Alan Trammell's life and baseball career is one worthy of closer examination and commemoration. From his days as a multi-sport prep star in talent-rich Southern California, continuing through his quick ascension up the Tigers' minor league system, and finally through his 20 seasons in the major leagues and beyond, Trammell has managed to endear fans and admirers in a lasting fashion that still exists today.

Along the way he proved doubters wrong, overcame a mid-career injury crisis, and made a remarkable on-field transformation as a player. While his playing career was beyond reproach and void of controversy, more speculation and discussion has surrounded him in the three decades since he retired than ever existed while he played. A failed managerial reign, begging questions about whether he was in over his head or had been simply a ceremonial hire, still exists, as does the continued controversy regarding his Baseball Hall of Fame worthiness, a debate that stirs both provincial and national passion.

Trammell also played during an extraordinary era in baseball history. It was a time of great change, where greed over money between owners and players resulted in significant interruption of games on two different occasions, and the pendulum of power swung firmly towards the players. The peak of his career was played during one of baseball's golden ages, especially in the American League's Eastern Division, where six cities took turns putting juggernauts on the field, whose greatest challenges often came in just trying to win their own division. He played with, and against, some of the biggest stars of the past forty years, cutting his teeth against great players from the 1970s and ending his career against personalities that would be present well into the second decade of the 2000s.

Over the past twenty years, many of the biggest stars in baseball have been shortstops-players such as Alex Rodriguez, Derek Jeter, Barry Larkin, and Nomar Garciaparra. And while in all sports there is no doubting that the athletes of today are bigger, stronger, and faster than their predecessors from previous generations, many of the all-around games of shortstops today resemble that which was played so well by Alan Trammell.

Introduction

The roars cascaded down from the double-decked stadium until the light towers nearly shook, before quickly lessening to hushed murmurs seconds afterwards. Those alternating outputs of sound and then near silence, at opposite ends of the audible spectrum, were not the unintelligible shouts and cries of a rowdy, beer-fueled crowd out on a Friday night at the ballpark. No, these sounds, although genuinely and loudly passionate, were full of reverence and appreciation.

The date was Monday, September 27, 1999, and the 43,356 souls fortunate enough to have found their way into the ballpark that afternoon and early evening were there to see more than just a baseball game between two American League Central Division also-rans finishing out the schedule. The Detroit Tigers had just defeated the Kansas City Royals 8–2 in the final game of the 1999 season. Of greater interest to the patrons who had stayed more than a half-hour after the game's final out, was the ceremony taking place before them.

The game that day had been the final one in the 88-year history of Tiger Stadium, one of the last and most celebrated of the classic ballparks still in existence at the close of the twentieth century. No one had left as the Detroit Tiger organization closed out the stadium's final official event with a fitting celebration of the team's history. Appearing one-by-one, Tiger players from generations dating back nearly seventy years entered the field through the gate in deep center field adorned in full uniform. Playing on the theme and music from the heart-tugging baseball movie from a decade earlier, *Field of Dreams*, the former players crossed onto the turf before making their way towards their traditional defensive positions around the diamond.

While many of the more elderly representatives could manage only a slow, deliberate walk towards the infield, and others had to be transported in golf carts, some former players still looked natural in uniform and ran with an athletic grace the 75–100 yards it took to meet their positional counterparts. Most waved their caps while soaking in the enthusiastic cheers of a reminiscing crowd. A hush would then follow as fans eagerly anticipated the next symbol of Detroit's baseball past to appear through the centerfield gate. Respectful ovations were given to players such as 89-year-old Eldon Auker, and his 84-year-old former teammate, Billy Rogell, key members of the Tigers' 1934 and 1935 pennant-winning teams which ruled long before most in attendance that day had even been born. But the most fervent cheers were directed towards more recognizable players, especially those from Detroit's most recent World Series championship teams from 1968 and 1984.

George Kell, Jim Bunning, Reno Bertoia, Cecil Fielder, Aurelio Rodriguez, Frank Tanana, Steve Kemp, Jason Thompson, Ron LeFlore, and Mark "The Bird" Fidrych were just some of the favorites that fans got to see one final time in Tiger Stadium. From the 1968 team was Bill Freehan, Mickey Lolich, Jim Northrup, Dick McAuliffe, Mickey Stanley, Gates Brown, and Willie Horton among others. The 1984 championship club was also well represented with Tom Brookens, Dave Rozema, Darrell Evans, Larry Herndon, Dan Petry, Willie Hernandez, Chet Lemon, Lance Parrish, and Jack Morris taking their bows before the adoring crowd. Like a fireworks finale, the last entrances were reserved for those players that would receive the loudest ovations as the ceremony reached its crescendo.

Kirk Gibson, the local product and fiery outfielder from the great 1980s teams, re-enacted the hands-raised leap he had made after his Game Five clinching home run in the 1984 World Series, as he entered the turf and loped over to right field. Before the noise had even abated from Gibson's appearance, Al Kaline walked through the gate and doffed his cap before gracefully jogging over to the grass in right field, the area that had been his workplace for over 20 years. No celebration of Detroit Tigers history from the last half-century would have been complete without recognition of Kaline, who had been such a graceful and elegant player between the early 1950s and mid–1970s, described as "The Joe DiMaggio" of the Tigers.

Most would have thought that the silver-haired Kaline would have been the final player introduced to close out the ceremony. He had truly symbolized Detroit baseball in the post–World War II era, and was "Mr. Tiger" to most people. But as one Tigers' legend reached his spot in right field, even louder cheers flowed down from the crowd as two distinctly recognizable figures walked out together from under the center field stands and made their appearance. Alan Trammell and Lou Whitaker, the beloved shortstop-second base combination for nearly two decades from the late-1970s until the mid–1990s, waved their caps and then ran in tandem towards the middle of the infield as the customary "Loooooouuuuuu …" call from the crowd poured down over them. As they reached second base, the two exchanged a brief shake of the hands and then broke away to their respective spots on the diamond.

That two middle-infielders held the respect and popularity displayed by the Detroit organization and its fans, and would be introduced last from among all of the generations of former Tiger players that appeared on the field that evening is indicative of the esteem they hold in team history. But while Whitaker was the recipient of the distinctive call from the crowd each time he appeared at the plate or made another of his slick plays in the field, it is Trammell who comes closest to the legendary status that is held by Kaline. Like his predecessor had done in the quarter-century since his retirement, Trammell still wore the uniform like it was part of him, with style that separates him from most of the other former players. As he stood on the familiar infield dirt in Tiger Stadium that evening, the bright lights shone down one final time on Alan Trammell in the place where he had spent much of his adult life.

He played 20 seasons in a Detroit uniform, one of only three players ever to have done so in the nearly 120-year history of the franchise—with Kaline and the immortal Ty Cobb being the others. He grew up in Southern California, land of year-round sunshine, warm temperatures and beaches; rights-of-birth that could make someone immediately unlikeable to natives of Rustbelt cities like Detroit. Yet, Trammell would become one of the grittiest performers the club has ever had, symbolizing the honest effort and work ethic that Midwesterners pride themselves for being known for.

Trammell arrived in Detroit as a teenager, having spent barely more than a year playing professional ball in the minor leagues. It was 1977, the first year of Jimmy Carter's presidency, and he would not leave the game as a player until the midway point of Bill Clinton's administration. When he came to the Tigers, the premier teams in the American League were the New York Yankees and Boston Red Sox, big market franchises that would spend extravagantly in order to dominate their competition. When he retired as a player, the premier teams in the American League were still the New York Yankees and Boston Red Sox, big market franchises that continued to spend extravagantly in order to dominate their competition. The principal difference over that time was that the average salary in baseball had increased from $74,000 when Trammell debuted, to over $1.1 million when he departed in 1996.

He entered professional baseball with the label of being an exceptional prospect with the glove, but serious doubts existed as to whether he would hit well enough to be a regular in the big leagues. He was slight of build with below average strength, and appeared to be the typical "good field, no-hit" middle infielder that populated most professional rosters in the mid–1970s.

By the half-way point of his Major League career, however, he was one of the most respected hitters in the game, playing a significant role offensively on some of the best teams of the 1980s. He could hit for average and also with surprising power. He scored runs, stole bases, and rarely struck out. He had lightning quick hands and could turn with authority on an inside fastball, but was equally adept at punching the ball into the opposite field. The only offensive category he ever led the league in was sacrifice bunts, which he did twice. Yet, he showed his versatility by batting clean-up one season on the highest-scoring team the game had seen in more than a quarter century. The more crucial the situation, the more dangerous a player he became. He put on an MVP performance in the 1984 World Series, where he batted .450, scored five runs, and most notably belted two home runs in the fourth game, while leading the Tigers to a World Championship.

It was in the field playing shortstop, however, that Trammell made his most indelible impression. He was a textbook standard of how to play the position. Whether he was fielding the baseball in his sure-handed manner or throwing with his quick overhand release, his technique was above reproach. His footwork around the bag and positioning within the infield was incomparable. He didn't take shortcuts and meticulously worked and honed his fundamental skills religiously. Tony La Russa, the Hall of Fame manager of 33 years in the big leagues with three World Series titles and six pennants to his credit, once said that "watching Trammell take infield practice was as good as watching Mark McGuire take batting practice."[1]

"He was a clinic as far as making the plays," said Dick Tracewski, a Detroit coach for 19 of the 20 years Trammell played. "Charging the ball, playing the proper hop, making strong overhand throws, he did it all. He was also a take-charge guy in the infield."[2]

"I always liked him," said Whitey Herzog who managed Kansas City early in Trammell's career. "I always thought Alan was as good on defense as anybody I had ever seen."[3]

With Whitaker, his keystone partner for nineteen seasons in Detroit, Trammell formed the longest-running double-play combination in Major League Baseball history, and also arguably the best. The duo was about much more than just the pairing of a shortstop and second baseman with physical skills. They possessed chemistry and a shared understanding of how the game was to be played in the middle of the diamond. With an innate sense of where the other would be, knowing where and how to deliver the ball at the bag, the two pulled many a Tigers pitcher out of an uncountable number of jams with a slickly turned 6–4–3 or 4–6–3 double-play.

Introduction

Trammell came to Detroit during one of the darkest periods in the city's history. Not only was the ball club struggling through a painful rebuilding phase on the field, having averaged over 90 losses per season in the four years prior to his full-time arrival in Detroit, but the city was suffering from severe economic woes, fueled primarily by a downturn in the domestic auto industry, where an increased number of foreign models flooded the marketplace. Unemployment, urban decay, and high crime rates had become synonymous with Detroit.

But a skinny, fuzzy-cheeked kid from San Diego helped to turn the hopes of the once great city. Once he was inserted as Detroit's full-time shortstop, Trammell, along with a core group of other talented young players, helped turnaround a centerpiece of blue-collar Detroit's culture. The Tigers reversed the four-straight losing seasons prior to his arrival, and instead turned that into eleven-consecutive winning seasons, including a summer in 1984 that no one in Detroit or across the state of Michigan would ever forget. The Tigers became a source of pride for the people of Detroit and created an excitement and energy that hadn't been matched in some time.

Fast-forward fifteen years from the emotional closing ceremony on Tiger Stadium's last night. It is the evening of June 30, 2014, in spacious Comerica Park, the new home of Detroit's baseball team for more than fifteen seasons. Another ceremony is taking place. This time it is before a game with the visiting Oakland A's. Taking seats upon chairs placed on a platform between home plate and the mound are members of the 1984 Detroit Tigers. Most have gained a few pounds and their hair is much grayer. Like Tiger Stadium, a few team members, including manager Sparky Anderson, have passed on way too early. The ceremony is brief with short introductions of each of the former players and coaches in attendance. The highlight is a faux double-play turned by Whitaker and Trammell, in lieu of a traditional first pitch. But on a night where some of the biggest names on one of the greatest teams in Detroit Tigers history are together once again, there is one person that represents them.

Alan Trammell, whose thinned, gray hair is the only concession to his otherwise youthful-appearing 56 years of age, gives what appears to be an ad-libbed, but heartfelt address to the appreciative crowd. He describes the championship won three decades earlier as the highlight of his baseball career, but humbly deflects any personal credit for the great accomplishment. However, the response he received from those in attendance that evening refuted any such modest appraisals. His introduction was met with rapidly building applause as emcee Dan Dickerson exhorted "Tigers' shortstop for twenty years. He defined what it is to be a Detroit Tiger and a

World Champion." The rest of the introduction was soon drowned out by the loudest roar of the evening. The kid who once said "playing baseball is the only thing I ever really wanted to do" and was described by Sparky Anderson as "Huck Finn in a baseball uniform" was being remembered as one of the greats in a celebrated franchise's history. He is part of Detroit Tigers royalty. He is Alan Trammell.

1

San Diego

Some believe it to be the first European settlement in what is now present-day California. Settled originally as a mission fort in 1769 on Presidio Hill, with a sweeping command of the bay leading out to the Pacific Ocean, the Spanish mariner, Sebastian Vizcaino, named the beautiful area for the Catholic saint San Diego de Alcala. Over the next 200 years San Diego grew from a tiny fort into one of the iconic locales in the southwest, becoming a major U.S. city and home to research firms, technology companies, and the largest naval base in the world.

It is San Diego's weather, however, that eventually gained the city fame and attracted tourists. Blue skies and bright sunshine, beaches, amusement parks, and a world-class zoo are synonymous with the area's third largest industry, enjoyed in the closest thing to a guarantee that Mother Nature will ever issue. Nestled against the Cuyamaca and Laguna Mountains to the east, and the Pacific Ocean to the west, San Diego enjoys some of the most mild and favorable weather on Earth. With the average high temperature residing between 65 and 77 degrees Fahrenheit year-round and only about ten inches of rainfall annually, the hilly terrain and urban canyons that constitute much of San Diego are an outdoor enthusiast's dream. It is in such a perfect environment that a high-energy boy with uncommon athletic ability, a strong inner drive, and the eagerness to be coached by willing and able instructors, has abundant opportunity to fully develop his talents.

Alan Stuart Trammell was born on February 21, 1958, in Garden Grove, California, some one hundred miles further north, near Long Beach. However, it was in San Diego that the young Trammell grew up. Born to Forrest and Anne Trammell, Alan grew up in an idyllic childhood he later termed as "a happy one."[1] His father's surname is of English decent, with ancestors likely from the rugged coastal area of southwestern England known as Cornwall. Anne Trammell was of Polish decent with the maiden name of "Panczak." Her parents were immigrants from Poland, having settled in Bridgeport, Pennsylvania, where she was later born. Forrest was an insurance salesman and provided a moderately well-to-do income level for his family.[2]

Alan gravitated to athletics at an early age, the rigorous activity being the perfect outlet for his high energy level. "Ever since I can remember, everything I've ever done in life involves sports,"[3] Trammell said much later about his formative years. He developed a strong work ethic early in life, especially as it applied to the sports he loved most, basketball and baseball. He was the stereotypical gym rat, shooting baskets, working on his game, while always looking for a pickup game wherever it might exist. He spent hours rifling a tennis ball off of the family's garage door or the fireplace chimney on the back of the house, fielding the ball as it ricocheted back at him. He drew a strike zone and zipped ball after ball at his target. It was there that he first developed the direct overhand throwing motion that he would one day be known for, and that would serve him so well. "I used to wear out our garage door with a tennis ball."[4]

Alan showed all of the outward signs that could be expected of a kid with his emerging talent and passion for sports. As a young boy, he was a standout in all sports, but especially stood out as a Little League player on the diamond where he displayed an intensity level and will to win that was well beyond that held by most of his peers. Years later, he would recall a grand slam home run he belted in Little League as one of the most memorable moments of his sports career. It was also during those early days learning the game that he first gravitated to the spot on the diamond that would best utilize his skills and become his future home. "When I was a little kid, they put me at shortstop," Trammell recalled years later. "Anybody with a strong arm, they stick you there. People think catching is hardest, but I think shortstop is just as tough. It's challenging to take away a hit from somebody, and you've got to be a take-charge guy."[5]

The only limitation he had to learn to accommodate was the rather scrawny body he possessed, which he pushed mercilessly to its boundaries. The limitations of his less-talented or semi-engaged teammates would prove to be another source of frustration to the ultra-competitive Alan, who always wanted to win. However, that early discrepancy in passion and ability turned into the source for a life-molding lesson from his mother. Anne Trammell had been a St. Louis Cardinals fan as a young girl, with her favorite player being the Redbirds' Stan Musial. She regaled young Alan with tales about the classy Cardinal star and his humble demeanor, and tried to instill those qualities into her talented son, using Musial as a role model.[6]

Others also began to recognize Trammell's talent and passion for sports at an early age. As a ten-year-old he was assigned by his teacher to watch the deciding Game Seven of the 1968 World Series on a television setup in the back of the classroom.[7] In an age when the World Series was the premiere sporting event in the country, and with all games still played during the daytime hours, Trammell was expected to report at regular intervals to the rest of the class on the happenings of such a newsworthy event. The irony of the October 10, 1968, game being won by the Detroit Tigers wouldn't be realized until nearly a decade later.

Trammell's middle school years were spent at Montgomery Junior High, during which he continued to develop an industrious work ethic both on and off the playgrounds and playing fields. He worked at a young age as a vendor at San Diego's Jack Murphy Stadium where professional baseball, football, and soccer was played, selling soft drinks and other snack items during games. The stadium was located only three miles from the Trammell household. Although back-breaking at times, the commission-based vendor work provided a source of spending money for the young teen.

The year 1969 saw an important event in Trammell's childhood as the city of San Diego was awarded a major league baseball team that began play that spring. The Padres were an expansion club, but brought a major league presence to what had been a long-time minor league city. For Trammell, it provided an up-close glimpse into life in professional baseball at its highest level. Although they were a perennial 100-loss team, the Padres would provide a major league club to follow during Trammell's formative early teens as the sad-sack Padres rolled out early stars like Nate Colbert, Enzo Hernandez, Cito Gason, and his personal favorite, third baseman Ed Spezio.

He and a group of friends developed tactics for finagling their way into the stadium to watch the hometown Padres' games for free. In the days long before worries over "Homeland Security" and "locking down" a venue became a matter addressed in a serious nature and by sophisticated means, a large stadium such as Jack Murphy was an inviting target waiting to be invaded by a pack of mischievous schoolboys. "It was starting in junior high school in the seventh grade," Trammell remembered years later. "Right after school we'd go directly to the ballpark. We got there so early before the ball games; two or three gates were always open."[8]

They gained entrance through unattended gates, freight entrances, or other loosely secured ports hours before a San Diego home game. If all else failed, Trammell and his friends "were so skinny at the time, we could go to center field and slide under the fence." The boys would then spend hours inside the cavernous structure roaming around, killing time until the game began. They even had contingency plans in case the legitimacy of their presence came into question. "We'd have an old general-admission ticket that didn't have any date on it. We could show it to the ushers if they ever stopped us."[9]

To the stadium workers and even the players and coaches in uniform, the boys were more of an annoyance than a danger, pestering players for autographs or to let them come on the field during batting practice. For a Padre franchise that was mired in last place most seasons, and struggled to draw even a million fans to its home games annually, the specter of a few young kids *wanting* to sneak into their games, was probably a welcome one. Those hijinks are fondly recalled by Trammell, even well into adulthood. "I know I got to be a pain in the butt sometimes, bothered the ballplayers," he recalled a decade later, knowing full well at that point what preparations were necessary to be competitive each night at the major league level. "Maybe they were happy to have us there. We didn't pay for the tickets, but we were good for a lot at the concession stands."[10]

By the fall of 1973, fifteen-year-old Alan Trammell had graduated from junior high school and moved on to San Diego's Kearny High School, which was a grades 10–12 school with an enrollment of nearly 1700 students from the Linda Vista, Serra Mesa, and Kearny Mesa communities.[11] His reputation as a middle school athlete proceeded him to the high school, but Alan quickly learned that he would have to pay his dues at the junior varsity level before he could expect to see playing time on the varsity.

"We all knew of this kid and we all wanted his services," remembered Brad Griffith, a teacher and coach at Kearny during that time.[12] "He was a great athlete, but he was always humble, didn't go around projecting himself as the big man on campus." Coaches first showed interest in him for a sport that Alan didn't even play. "I kept trying to get him out for football, but he was too smart," admitted Griffith about his failed attempts to lure the youngster. "He would have been a great football player, a quarterback or receiver or maybe at cornerback," added Hugh McMillan, a contemporary of Griffith's at the school.[13]

The Kearny Komets were a San Diego area prep powerhouse during the early to mid–1970s, fielding championship-level teams in all of the major team sports.[14] The varsity basketball team was on its way to winning the San Diego Region of the California Interscholastic Federation (CIF) 2-A championship in 1974 with a perfect 32–0 mark, while the baseball team was a perennial city league championship contender. Combined with a CIF championship in football, Kearny High School won the highly prestigious Cal-HI Sports–State School of the Year award for the 1973–74 school year.

Keeping sophomores together on the junior varsity during their first year at the grade 10–12 school, however, was part of the philosophy shared by coaches at Kearny during that era. That philosophy even applied to the eagerly anticipated talents of Trammell. "He was probably the best athlete in the school," remembered McMillan who was the junior varsity baseball coach at the time, about his star sophomore. "But he had to earn his stripes, which was a boon to me."[15]

It was on the hardwood, rather than the baseball diamond, though, where Alan first made his mark wearing the maroon and white of the Komets. He was described as an all-around guard, a great floor leader who handled the ball well and could control the game.[16] He was capable of taking over a game offensively or defensively. His offensive skills allowed him to drive with the ball to the basket, or pull up and hit a jump shot. His wisp-thin build and terrific athletic ability permitted him to lead the fast break on offense while subsequently being the first player back on defense. No one was too big, too strong, or too athletic for him. "Baseball was not his first love," said Jesse Martinez, Trammell's Little League Baseball coach and a star athlete himself several years earlier at Kearny. "His first love was basketball."[17]

On the diamond he immediately established himself as the starting shortstop under veteran coach Jack Taylor, an ex-Marine who was described years later by Trammel as being "old school" demanding that his players play the game "the right way" while he employed a "tough love" approach with his players. While he was a standout offensive player at the plate and on the base baths, it was in the field where Alan separated himself from nearly all other players his age in the talent-rich San Diego area. He easily surpassed the play of most high school shortstops, making routine plays look easy, and seemingly impossible plays attainable. Whether snagging a ball hit up the middle behind second base, or fielding a grounder deep in the hole at short and then firing a strike to first base, he could make plays that were beyond the age-level and competition he was facing.

"What I remember was his ability to go back on a ball," recalled McMillan who had moved up a level to become the varsity assistant coach at Kearny in time for Trammell's junior season of baseball. "Not only could he make the play on those shallow balls to the outfield, but he then had the awareness and quickness to double someone off base."[18]

Besides the great physical talents he possessed, characteristics such as toughness, fearlessness, and a no excuses attitude began to emerge in the Komet standout. He was noted for his willingness to get in front of every ball hit towards him, no matter how hard it had been hit or how rough a condition the infield surface might have been in, a characteristic Alan would be known for throughout his professional career. In one game during his high school days, a hard hit ball took a bad bounce off of his face, causing a deep cut and leaving one of his eyes nearly closed. Despite the coach's suggestion that he be removed from the game, Alan wanted to stay in, lamenting the fact that he had let the grounder get away from him.[19]

Another time with Kearny playing a game against San Diego's famed Hoover High School with city playoff implications on the line, a line drive was hit towards Trammell that would have been the game-ending out and given the Komets the victory. Alan needed to jump for the ball, but it was seemingly within reach for the athletic shortstop; a play he had made numerous times. However, Coach Taylor had demanded that all of his players wear a shell-type of helmet in the field for protection, the only school in the area that did so. When Alan leaped for the line drive off of the Hoover's player's bat, the helmet slid down off of his head and obstructed his vision. Trammell missed the ball and Hoover eventually went on to win the game.

"He never complained about anything," recalled McMillan of the play that cost his school the game. "He wouldn't use that as an excuse for not making the play, even though he clearly couldn't see the ball when the helmet slid down his face."[20]

"Alan had a tremendous work ethic. Always asking for more balls to be hit to him, whether it was going into the hole, or turning the double play, or whatever. You couldn't tire him out."[21]

Around the Kearny campus, Trammell was described as "an outstanding kid, well-mannered." He sported shoulder-length hair, fashioned in a "Vinnie Barbarino"-type look, popular for that time. History was among his favorite subjects and he was "well respected by teachers and peers."[22] The school magazine described him as "easy going" and "mild mannered."[23]

By his senior year, the popular Trammell was a dominant player in both basketball and baseball. He had a tremendous season in basketball, leading Kearny to the 1976 CIF San Diego Section title game where they defeated Santana High School in the championship game, 57–44. Trammell was named the championship game's MVP, after he continually broke through the rival Sultan's full-court press. Displaying even then the modesty that he would often be associated with, Trammell told the school paper, the *KHS Galaxy* that "It's not an individual effort, but a team effort that you need in order to be successful."[24]

The school's 30-2 record that season was largely due to the play of their six-foot point guard who was universally acknowledged as the team's catalyst. Whether it was handling the ball in pressure situations, dishing out crisp and accurate passes, or playing great defense, Trammell was looked upon to make the play. If the Komets needed a score, he could do that as well. Some said he might have even been their best rebounder, demonstrating tremendous anticipation, timing, and leaping ability which allowed him to grab errant shots away from larger players.[25]

"He was a bulldog," said Nick Canepa who covered Kearny High School during those years for the *San Diego Evening Tribune*. "I can't say I've covered a high school player with more determination. The kid was the ultimate gym rat. There was a competitive fire inside of him."[26]

"I loved watching the kid play basketball," said McMillan reminiscing nearly forty years later. "I'll never forget the scene after that championship game and that big grin on his face. It was heart-warming."[27]

By the end of his senior season, Alan was sifting through scholarship offers to play basketball at the collegiate level. He had been named first team All-C.I.F. as well as being recognized on the first team All-Western League squad. Realistically, he felt that his size would be a deterrent at the next level, however. "The world is filled with six-foot point guards," he said several years later.[28] He soon would have other options, however; options that might not have existed a year earlier.

Whether it was the momentum from that basketball championship, or the confidence he might have gained, Trammell carried it into spring and had a tremendous final season in baseball, gaining All Western League honors in that sport as well. Typically batting third in a Kearny lineup loaded with college and pro prospects, he hit well over .400. Quick hands and solid mechanics allowed Trammell to hit with an increased authority that seemingly belied the size and strength of the rail-thin, 150-pound senior. At shortstop, he continued to impress all who saw him play, with his consistency and knowledge of the game and situation. He soon had attracted the attention of numerous college scouts who tended to show up at many of Kearny's games. Trammell would eventually draw scholarship offers to play at blue-blood baseball schools like UCLA and Arizona, among others.[29]

It was the offer that didn't come Trammell's way that remains a mystery to this day. Local schools, and in particular San Diego State University, which has a rich baseball tradition, were well aware of the local prep shortstop, but failed to offer a scholarship. Aztec's head coach, Jim Dietz, decided he "didn't like Trammell's game" and failed to recruit him to SDSU, a mistake that he would later say was the worst recruiting mistake he ever made.[30]

While the college coaches were making their evaluations, professional scouts were also starting to take notice. The Major League Scouting Bureau had been founded just two years earlier as a shared resource for any professional organization to subscribe to. Hundreds, if not thousands, of high school and college players with even a hint of pro potential were scouted and rated on a 20–80 scale with a 55 score equating to a player with potential to be a regular in the major leagues. A rating of 50 indicated the prospect had potential to one day play on a big league team, but probably not as a regular.

Initially, Trammell was viewed as a marginal professional prospect, possibly due to his small frame and quiet demeanor. The first reports from the Scouting Bureau in March 1976 rated him with scores ranging between 44 and 48. Once scout, Charlie Metro, filed a score of 42.1 and submitted notes stating: "Bat and power lacking.... Poor knowledge and mechanics of hitting.... Good defensive prospect."[31]

However, later that same week, Pete Coscarart of the Bureau gave the 18-year-old shortstop a much more favorable score of 55 and wrote: "Both feet point out a la Yogi Berra.... Doesn't seem to bother him. Reminds me of Marty Marion.... Has excellent hands w/strong arm. Bat is questionable but has a good swing which should improve with added WT and strength.... Improving."[32]

Marion had been a sure-handed all-star shortstop with the St. Louis Cardinals in the 1940s, with the same type of tall, thin body type that scouts were projecting Trammell to grow into.

As Trammell's strong senior season at Kearny progressed though, scouts were becoming more and more enamored with him. On May 25 Larry Maxie of the Bureau rated him as high as 58.6 and now Trammell was a hot prospect with flocks of pro scouts attending each game and his name ascending quickly up the draft boards of some teams. One of those teams was the Detroit Tigers, who had California scout, Dick Wiencek, and super-scout, Rick Ferrell, following Trammell closely. "He could be a first-draft choice but down the line," wrote Ferrell during that time. "Will develop into a fine def. SS-Ray Oyler type."[33]

While the late first-round potential that Ferrell alluded to showed how highly the long-time scout thought of Trammell's overall ability, the Ray Oyler comparison was telling. Oyler was a poster child for "good field-no hit" infielders in the era just before Mario Mendoza came to represent such players with the advent of the so-called "Mendoza Line." Oyler had been a standout defensive player on Detroit's 1968 World Championship team, but hit a paltry .135 that season as part of a 6-year career that saw him amass a lifetime batting average of only .175. The comparison Ferrell made between Oyler and Trammell clearly demonstrated concern over the young prospect's potential at the plate. "They thought that he wouldn't ever make it in the majors because he couldn't hit," remembered Kearny's athletic director at the time, Tom Barnett. "That's what made him work harder."[34]

Major League Baseball conducted its amateur draft that summer on Tuesday, June 8, 1976. The first pick in the draft was considered a consensus "can't miss" prospect in left-handed pitcher Floyd Bannister of Arizona State who was selected by the Houston Astros. The Detroit Tigers followed and selected another left-handed pitcher, Pat Underwood, with the very next pick. However, when Detroit's turn came around again 24 picks later, they selected Alan Trammell of Kearny High School in San Diego with their second pick (26th overall).

Trammell was one of five shortstops the Detroit organization selected in the 1976 draft. Whether any other organization would have taken him that high is unknown. The following day the *Detroit Free Press* observed the Tigers' selection of the young Californian: "One of the shortstops—Alan Trammell—was the Tigers' second choice. An 18-year-old from Kearny High in San Diego is rated a fierce competitor and according to scouts, 'has good running speed, a good arm, great hands, and fine instincts—all the tools to become a major league regular at shortstop.'"[35]

As his high school graduation drew near later that week, Trammell had to decide between scholarship offers to play either basketball or baseball at the collegiate level, or whether to accept an offer to turn professional with the Tigers. Displaying the nothing to lose attitude, typical of a confident 18-year-old kid, he told his school magazine that "if I make pro (baseball), fine, but if I don't, I don't."[36] By the end of the week he decided to enter professional baseball and signed with Detroit for a relatively modest signing bonus of $35,000. Before reporting to the Tigers' minor league rookie team that June, however, he held fast to a commitment to play in California's high school baseball all-star game. "I graduated from high school on a Friday, played the game on Saturday, and the (rookie league) season began that Tuesday," Trammell later remembered of that whirlwind period in his life.[37]

Although he would spend much of the next quarter century as a player, and then later years as a coach and manager in cities based far from his San Diego roots, Trammell would always call that special place home. "I'm still a Californian at heart," he said years later while playing in Detroit.[38] He always remembered the family, coaches, friends, and others who had helped him along the way. High school friends and former Kearny teammates might have softball or basketball teams and tournaments sponsored by their old classmate. Large numbers of tickets would be provided whenever Detroit played in Anaheim against the Angels, and at least one large group of high school coaches and friends were brought to Detroit to spend a few days with Trammell early in his career. McMillan, his JV coach and then varsity assistant, who saw every game the future major league star would play in high school, summed it up simply: "He never forgot where he came from."[39]

2

Minor League Days

When Alan Trammell reported to Rookie-ball camp in June 1976, he faced not only his indoctrination to professional baseball, but also culture shock. The Detroit organization's entry-level team was based in Bristol, Virginia, where the Bristol Tigers played in the Appalachian League. Bristol sits in the southwestern corner of the state, up against the Tennessee border. In fact, the two states both claimed the small town with the state border running down the main street, splitting the town in half. Alone, some 2300 miles from his family and friends, Trammell was living on his own for the first time, staying in cheap hotels in a town very different socio-economically as well as geographically from the more affluent San Diego area he came from.

Rookie league camp is the Ellis Island of a professional organization's minor league structure. Beginning just days after the completion of that season's amateur draft, it is the port of entry for drafted as well as undrafted prospects discovered by scouts. In 1976 it was not uncommon for 40 or more players to be brought to camp for evaluations and to be assigned to a team in the minor league system. Assessments were made quickly in order to separate those players that would make the Bristol team from those that wouldn't. Some prospects, especially older ones with college experience, might be viewed as more advanced in their development and be sent to a higher level within the Detroit organization. For others the dream would end quickly and they would be released, their abilities being viewed as below pro-caliber.

Sorting through the congregation of players and their varying ages, backgrounds, and abilities was Joe Lewis, the manager of the Bristol club. Lewis, described by a former player as a "rough old codger,"[1] was a veteran manager of the Appalachian League, entering his seventh season overall in the minor leagues. He had a no-nonsense leadership style, but was generally respected by the players and was viewed highly within Detroit's organization as a man that could be trusted with the molding of kids in their first season of pro ball. One of those players was a skinny, 18-year-old shortstop hopeful, who looked to some like he should have been heading to his first day of driver's training.

"I remember this scrawny, acne-faced kid from California," said Larry Corr about the first time he saw Trammell.[2] Corr was a 22-year-old, right-handed pitcher from Memphis, Tennessee, who had been Detroit's 20th round selection in that June's draft. Like many of the players in camp, Corr had played college baseball (Belmont University), and was older and more mature than the kid who was only days removed from his high school graduation.

Most of the camp was made up of players aged in their early twenties. Many had played three or four years of college baseball, proving themselves against that higher level of competition. They were more physically mature; bigger, stronger, faster. They had also had time to hone their skills, working under the tutelage of college coaches for three or four years. Those advantages typically separated the older, college-experienced prospects from those that had been drafted straight out of high school.

"One of the first things the guys learned about [Trammell] was that he had been an all-state or something basketball player in California," said Corr. "How could this little, skinny white kid be that good at basketball?"[3]

It was on the baseball field though, that Trammell quickly showed he fit in. The players worked all day in the heat and humidity of the south-Atlantic summer on the equivalent of a poor high school field, complete with a dusty, grass-starved, dirt infield. The coaching staff worked to break down the egos and techniques of players who had been viewed as ultra-successful at the amateur level only days earlier, reshaping their games to mesh with the professional way. "There was nothing he did that stood out immediately as being extraordinary" said Corr about his initial impressions of the young shortstop. "Other guys stood out more athletically, but he could make all the plays."[4]

Within days the squad had been shaped and was ready to begin a two-month, 70-game Appalachian League schedule where Trammell would first learn the rigors of playing every day in the minor leagues. Performing before tiny crowds each night in ramshackle parks with hard infields, he experienced the physical and mental grind while making the long bus rides between small southern towns sprinkled around Virginia, West Virginia, and Tennessee. They ate fast food out of paper bags and slept on the bus or in cheap hotels. When the Bristol Tigers were on a home stand, it was out to the ball park by late morning, often on little sleep, for midday workouts where they worked on their craft hours before game time.

"Once I signed, I was committed," said Trammell about his determination to do what he had to in order to make it to the major leagues. "I wasn't going to be stopped. Nothing could stop me in my mind. I was going to work and do whatever it took."⁵ That included not using his relatively high draft status as a reason for special treatment or favors, something that his teammates noticed. "He separated right away," remembered Corr. "[He] did it on the field instantly. Nothing was given to him."⁶

Trammell was one of only five 18-year-olds on the Bristol Tiger club that year (the team averaged just over 20 years of age), yet he established himself immediately as the everyday shortstop, displaying the same steady consistency and strong, accurate arm that scouts had noticed only months earlier. At the plate he batted a respectable .271 with an impressive .386 on-base percentage, but had only two extra-base hits in 41 games. It was his poise, however, making clutch plays and knowing what to do in all situations that most impressed those who watched him play.

"He was the best player we had. No doubt," said Corr. "I sure was a better pitcher when Alan was playing shortstop behind me."⁷

His all-around game was recognized league wide that first summer as Trammell was named to the Appalachian League's All Star team. Carl Ackerman, the scout credited with finding and signing Pete Rose, said about Trammell that year: "(He has) good range and a good arm. He'll come on with the bat better later, but he'll play even if he doesn't hit a lick because of that fielding ability."⁸

Within an organization's minor league system, players quickly learn that luck is often a major determinant in whether, or how quickly, a player advances. Injuries at the higher levels often lead to opportunity for those excelling at the lower levels. Although he had already made a positive impression on Detroit's brass, Trammell was likely destined to finish out the summer with Bristol that year. However, an injury further up the Tigers' minor league ladder resulted in Trammell getting the break that propelled his ascension through the system. Barely more than a month into his professional career, he was being promoted to Detroit's Double-A affiliate in Montgomery, Alabama. When the call came, Trammell hopped into Corr's Triumph TR-6 and the two (Corr had also been moved up) made the overnight drive to Montgomery, some eight hours away.⁹

The Montgomery Rebels were in a tight race, battling for the second half, Western Division title of the Double-A Southern League. The Rebels were loaded that year with future major league talent that would soon be making an impact on the parent Detroit team roster. Steve Kemp, Lance Parrish, Jack Morris, Dave Rozema, Tom Brookens, Tim Corcoran, Dave Tobik, and Dave Stegman, were just some of the players that played for the Montgomery team in the bicentennial summer of 1976. The Rebels had started the season out slowly, but by mid-year the team had jelled and was playing well behind the leadership of manager Les Moss. Yet, with only a few short weeks to go in the regular season, and a playoff berth on the line, the Rebels regular shortstop, Glenn Gulliver, was out with an injury.

"We were fighting to make the playoffs and heard some slick fielding shortstop, just out of the draft, was coming up to replace Gully," remembered outfielder Terry Lynch, one of Montgomery's leading hitters that season. "The first time I saw Alan he looked like a kid. Baby faced, tall, thin—physically like a kid. He was very confident though."[10]

Moss immediately inserted Trammell into the lineup as the everyday shortstop. He went 0–4 at the plate in his debut with Montgomery on August 15, but was flawless in the field recording six assists and starting two double-plays in a 6–2 victory over Chattanooga. Trammell quickly gained the trust of his Montgomery teammates, playing well above his modest level of experience. With the young, first-year player commanding the middle of their infield, the Rebels rolled to an overall record of 81–56 and won the second half West Division title. Montgomery then defeated the Chattanooga Lookouts in a one-game playoff for the overall Western Division championship before conquering the Orlando Twins, three games to one, for the 1976 Southern League championship. Trammell held his own as one of only two teenagers (Rozema being the other) to play for a Montgomery team that had a number of 24-year-olds playing regularly and whose average age was 22. Even though he looked like a kid, Trammell had impressed everyone, playing high-stakes, pressure-packed games against *men* several years older than he was.

"You knew just watching him play, that he knew how to play the game," said Lynch years later about that playoff run. "He was always picking the older guys' brains about the game. He wanted to learn."[11]

While Trammell had more than held his own with the glove, he had struggled against the better grade of pitching he faced at the Double-A level. In 21 games with Montgomery, he hit .179 with just two RBI's and no extra-base hits. "He was overmatched at the plate. Physically overmatched that year," said Lynch. "The pitchers knocked the bat right out of his hands."[12]

Despite his late-season struggles at the plate in Double-A, the Detroit organization was elated about the development of their second round selection in that June's draft. Taking a "no rest for the weary" approach, they sent Trammell to St. Petersburg, Florida, immediately after the close of the Southern League playoffs, to participate with their entry in the Florida Instructional League. The invitation was indicative of the fast track the Tigers intended to keep their young shortstop prospect on. The six-week, post-season Instructional League is a post-season spring training of sorts, used by organizations as a highly concentrated crash course to speed the development of their most prized prospects. Generally geared towards players in the lower levels of the minor leagues, some estimate that participation can shave up to a year and a half off of a prospect's minor league stay.

It was during that late September/October 1976, period that Trammell made two contacts that would forever alter the course of his career. The first was an instructor for the Detroit organization that fall, the Tigers' former Gold Glove shortstop, Ed Brinkman, who quickly took a liking to his new protégé. Upon watching Trammell field just a few ground balls on the very first day of camp, Brinkman reportedly proclaimed to no one in particular, "My, my, we've got something here."[13]

The second connection would change Trammell's identify forevermore, as from that autumn forward he would be permanently linked to a shy, spindly-thin, African American infielder by the name of Lou Whitaker. Nicknamed "Sweet Lou," Whitaker had played third base that summer for Detroit's Class-A team in Lakeland, where he had been named the Florida State League's Most Valuable Player and one of Detroit's brightest prospects. Blocking his path to the big league club though, was the presence of third-baseman Aurelio Rodriguez, who at that time was a mainstay in Detroit. Instead, the Tigers' longtime Vice President and General Manager, Jim Campbell, along with his minor league brain trust, made a bold move that changed the course of Detroit baseball history. Campbell made the decision to convert Whitaker to second base, and pair him with the equally-impressive, first-year shortstop, Trammell, in hopes of forming the Tigers' double-play combination of the future.

The Tiger organization paired Trammell with second baseman Lou Whitaker (shown here in a 1984 photograph) in the Florida Instructional League in the fall of 1976. Their identities were forever linked from that point forward as they formed one of the most famous duos in baseball history (National Baseball Hall of Fame Library, Cooperstown, New York).

Louis Rodman Whitaker was nearly a year older than Trammell and was completing his second year of professional baseball. He was born in Brooklyn, New York, but had been raised by a single mother in near-poverty conditions in Martinsville, Virginia. At one point, Whitaker lived in a household of 16, primarily made up of deeply-religious extended family. Family lore contends that Lou's legs grew crooked when he was very young, but the family couldn't afford the type of health care that should be afforded to a child with such difficulties. Instead his uncles twisted his legs as part of a regular ritual and the legs eventually straightened out, perhaps contributing to the rather upright and straight-legged running style he developed.[14]

At age thirteen Whitaker's arm had already drawn praise from a professional scout who happened to see him play. "Son, take care of that arm. People are going to be coming around to see you play pretty soon," the unnamed scout reportedly said.[15] By the time Whitaker was of draft age, scouting reports were spotty and varied. Tigers scout Billy Jurges liked him as much as a pitching prospect as an infielder.[16] Detroit ended up drafting Whitaker in the fifth round of the 1975 draft, only to then watch him hold out for a higher signing bonus than what was being offered. The closer for the Tiger organization came when a $500 spending spree for clothes was thrown in, courtesy of front-office executive, Bill Lajoie. Years later, Lajoie joked that the $497 was "well spent."[17]

Whitaker's first year at Bristol had been nondescript. He hit .237 in 42 games playing both third base and shortstop. In the summer of 1976, however, Whitaker emerged as a top-flight major league prospect, batting .297 in 124 game for the Tigers with 62 RBI's and an eye-popping 48 stolen bases. He was erratic in the field though, committing 30 errors at third base that summer. Nonetheless, his athleticism and rocket arm showed remarkable promise, prompting the organization to shift him to second base as the tag-team partner for Trammell.

It quickly became evident that the Tigers had struck gold with the pairing of the teenage middle infielders. They were the talk of the organization's brass working in St. Petersburg that fall. "Whitaker was such a natural athlete that he took to second base right away," said Brinkman when recalling that Instructional League season.[18] "The very first day, we clicked," remembered Trammell.[19]

Their performance in Florida was such that they earned themselves new suits. Campbell had promised each of them a new sport coat if they performed well. At the close of the Instructional League season, Trammell and Whitaker took him up on his promise, and then some. Recalled Campbell years later, "The next morning we drove to a store and they went right to the rack where they had two suits already picked out. I had promised them a sports coat, remember, but I bought them the suits."[20]

An invitation to the parent club's spring training as non-roster invitees was the next step for the young duo. Trammell and Whitaker took part in spring training drills in Lakeland, Florida, with the rest of the Detroit Tigers throughout the first weeks of March 1977. They accounted themselves well in camp, and were even inserted into a handful of Grapefruit League games, typically mopping up for one of the regulars in the late innings. Although neither was even remotely considered for making the 25-man roster that would play in Detroit that summer, the two had made an indelible impression and were now being mentioned among the organization's most highly-touted prospects.

A summer in Double-A Montgomery was prescribed by a Tiger front office that wanted the pair to continue to develop together. For Whitaker, it was the next step on the climb up the minor league ladder. For Trammell, it was a return to the level he had finished at the previous season, a level that saw him help the Rebels to a Southern League championship, but struggle personally at the plate. Leading the Montgomery team in 1977 was Brinkman, the first-year manager of the Rebels.

The opportunity to play and develop for a season under the tutelage of Ed Brinkman was undoubtedly a boon to the careers of both players, but in particular Trammell. Brinkman was only two years removed from the close of his 14-year playing career in the big leagues. Most of those years had been spent primarily as a fundamentally sound and excellent fielding shortstop for the Washington Senators and Detroit Tigers. It was with the Tigers that he had won a Gold Glove, made an American League All Star team, and had finished ninth in the voting for the 1972 AL MVP award. Astonishingly, Brinkman had batted only .203 that year, but had set a record of 72 consecutive errorless games at shortstop, while being the backbone of a division-winning Detroit club. For Trammell, there couldn't have been a better person to model his game after, or to learn from.

Brinkman made it a project that summer to teach Trammell everything he could about the art and science of playing shortstop in professional baseball. At 35 years of age, he still liked to grab a glove and take infield practice with his young pupil.[21] He worked tirelessly to teach the nuances of the game, drilling his apprentice on the footwork and positioning required to play the position, while honing the quick release and accurate arm that would become trademarks of Trammell's game. Brinkman also tutored Whitaker at second base, and schooled the pair endlessly on the art of turning the double play.

Although he ranks among the most futile hitters in major league baseball history statistically, Brinkman also made significant adjustments to Trammell's approach at the plate, changes that would have a profound influence on the type of hitter the young shortstop would eventually become. In his first year of professional baseball, Trammell had swung a 32-ounce bat, holding it down on the knob of the handle, trying to pull most pitches. Brinkman insisted that he use a longer, heavier bat, and choke up on the handle. Instead of trying to pull everything, he taught Trammell to hit the ball back in the direction it was pitched. The result was that Trammell made contact more consistently and emerged as one of the better hitters in the Southern League in 1977. "They gave him a big bat and told him to hit with it," remembered Whitaker about his sidekick. "He had a 35-ounce bat and they told him to choke up."[22]

"He had much more confidence that year," remembered Terry Lynch, who also returned to Montgomery for that season. "He was a little bigger, a little stronger. He hit with a longer bat and choked up. He started hitting (the ball) where it was at."[23]

Beginning with an opening day 12–0 rout of the Columbus (GA) Astros on April 12, 1977, Trammell and Whitaker were the catalysts for a Montgomery Rebel team that dominated the Southern League that summer. The team raced out to big leads in the Western Division in both half seasons, and won games at a greater pace than the previous season's club that had been chock-full of future major league talent. "Those guys were on base all the time," said Lynch, who typically hit third in Brinkman's lineup each night, and led the club in RBI's.[24]

Defensively, Whitaker struggled in the early going while trying to learn to play second base, and at times the middle infield duo struggled to turn even the most routine double. But once he returned from an early-summer injury that had sidelined him for several games, Whitaker seemed to have figured it out and his defensive play rose to the level of his considerable offensive prowess. Soon Trammell and Whitaker formed the best keystone combination in the Southern League, providing an anchor that the rest of the Rebel team could rely on each night. "It was heaven having those guys behind you," said Larry Corr, also back for his second season on the mound for Montgomery. "They caught everything."[25]

For the 19-year-old Trammell, and the 20-year-old Whitaker, the long five-month season was the truest test yet of their strength, commitment, and endurance. Playing virtually every day in near anonymity (the Rebels averaged less than 1000 fans to their home games at Paterson Field), the 140-game schedule becomes a grind in the central Alabama summer weather where high heat and humidity are the norm each day. The temperature reached at least 90 degrees for thirty straight days at one point that summer. Travel conditions were also trying at times, such as the nine-hour bus ride it took to reach Eastern Division rival, Orlando. "I don't think people realize how tough you have to be to play every day in the minor leagues," added Corr.[26]

Off the field, Trammell and Whitaker roomed together both on the road and at home where they shared an apartment in Montgomery. Despite the notable differences in their backgrounds and personalities, the arrangement worked well both professionally and socially. While Trammell was easy-going and could joke and be one of the guys quite easily, Whitaker was quiet and reserved, almost withdrawn from much of the team. Trammell was a young white kid from San Diego with a largely traditional family background, while Whitaker was a poor African American from southern Virginia, with no father, raised instead by a large extended family and with a large church presence in his life. Trammell's greatest contribution to the team that summer may have been the drawing out of his double-play partner to the rest of the team. "Tram really worked hard with him," remembered Lynch. "[He] got [Whitaker] to open up, not only to each other, but to the rest of the team as well."[27]

"We didn't have anybody else," explained Trammell years later, after they had both become established players with Detroit. "We comforted each other a little. If one of us had a bad night, the other one wouldn't let it get him down. We sort of used each other as crutches, and we became pretty close."[28] Whitaker summarized that first summer with Trammell by saying, "we did everything together."[29]

Outwardly, Trammell carried a "nothing to lose" attitude while toiling in the minor leagues. As one of the younger players on the team at first Bristol, and then Montgomery, the differences between him and some of his older teammates were more subtle than just physical strength and maturity. If he didn't make it in professional baseball, a return to San Diego was likely, back to the family and friends that had always supported him. Many of his older teammates, however, had left school or bypassed college to take their shot at professional ball, and now had wives and small children. For them, failure would result in the immediate and harsh realities of life outside of baseball and a panicked feeling of "what now?"

"Tram was a cocky kid," said Corr about his one-time younger teammate. "He didn't have any worries."[30] The teenager acted the part in other ways as well remembered Lynch, telling a story that illustrated the point. "We lived in the same apartment complex as Whitaker and Trammell," he described more than 35 years later. "I was married and had a young son, Shawn. When we were on a home stand, I'd typically go out by the pool in the afternoon and play with Shawn, often pitching whiffle balls to him and letting him bat. However, it didn't take long in that hot sun, before I'd go back inside and usually take a nap before heading to the ballpark. I'd wake up, and Trammell and Whitaker would still be out there, hours later, playing whiffle ball, knowing that they had a game to play that evening."[31]

At the ballpark, Trammell was having just as much fun that summer. The Rebels were runaway winners in their division, winning both halves of the split-season while their shortstop was having a tremendous season individually, both in the field and at the plate. Defensively, he was better than ever, applying the polish that his manager, Brinkman, had brought to his game. Offensively, the additional year of professional experience had given Trammell both strength and confidence. A player that had been described in the local papers prior to the season as "weak-hitting Trammell"[32] was now hitting the ball with authority, often to the opposite field where his gap shots into right-center or slicing drives into the corner were allowing him to accumulate extra-base hits at an impressive rate. He had a two-run double and a three-run triple in a 13–6 win one night against Jacksonville; four hits, including two triples in a 12–0 rout against Chattanooga; and was the starting shortstop for the Southern League All-Stars when they took on and defeated the Atlanta Braves 6–4 that summer.

By season's end, he had broken the decade-old Southern League record for triples, previously held by none other than the future Hall-of-Famer, Reggie Jackson, who had played for Birmingham (Alabama) in 1967. Trammell's nineteen three-baggers in 1977 remains a Southern League record nearly 40 years later.

"We really hadn't counted on him to provide a lot of offense this year, but you could see him improving in the Florida Instructional League last winter," commented Brinkman late that summer. "He really worked hard and made some adjustments and began to swing the bat a lot better. He hits the ball hard and drives a lot of balls into the alleys between the outfielders."[33]

"He was the glue to our team," explained Lynch years later. "It started with him both offensively and defensively. He was also a great base runner. He could cut the bases as well as anyone." But it wasn't all physical with Trammell. He had a calming influence on the rest of the team, and knew what to do in every situation, something that wasn't lost to Lynch. "Fundamentally, in every phase of the game—he was way ahead of his years. He never made mental mistakes, even at that young age. Plus he was just so much stronger physically that season."[34]

Trammell's play was recognized league-wide where he was the unanimous selection as the Southern League's Most Valuable Player in 1977. He finished third in the league in batting with a .291 average in 134 games, with nine doubles, three home runs, and 50 RBI's, to go along with his record-setting total of 19 triples. He finished second in the league in runs scored with 78, trailing only Whitaker who also had a tremendous season, batting .280 with 81 runs scored, and 38 stolen bases.

"I think Alan is a definite big league prospect," stated Brinkman. "It's hard for me to compare him with other shortstops I have seen, because they've all been major league shortstops for many years. But he's only nineteen years old and he has no limitations. All he needs is experience, to play every day, and to correct a few minor mistakes. After all, this is really his first full season in professional ball and I'd say he's handling it rather well."[35]

At the close of the regular season, the playoffs seemed almost anticlimactic. Montgomery had dominated the Southern League all summer, finishing with an overall record of 86–51, and then had to wait for nearly a week while rain played havoc with the Eastern Division playoff which eventually saw the Jacksonville Suns defeat the Savannah Braves two games to one. The first game of the championship series between the Rebels and Suns was finally played on Monday, September 5, in Montgomery. The key moment of the game occurred in the top of the ninth with Montgomery leading 2–0 behind outstanding pitching from starting pitcher Gary Christenson. However, a leadoff walk brought up Jacksonville's slugger, Pete Koegel, who smashed a shot towards shortstop. Trammell played the hard-hit ball, bad hop and all, and turned it into a rally-extinguishing double-play. The significance of the clutch play was illustrated moments later when the next Suns batter homered, making the score 2–1, which ended up being the final score.

The two teams moved south to Jacksonville, Florida, the next night, with the Rebels having an opportunity to wrap up the league championship in the best of three series. A sparse gathering of only 844 fans turned out to watch a contest that stretched on for over four hours. After the Suns scored twice in the eighth inning to tie the game 2–2, neither team scored again until the top of the fourteenth inning when future Tiger outfielder Ricky Peters led off the inning with a single for Montgomery. Trammell then laid down a sacrifice bunt to move him to second base. A two-out double by Whitaker brought Peters home with the game-winning and championship-clinching run. Trammell, in what turned out to be the last game he would ever play in the minor leagues, finished a disappointing 0–4 at the plate, with a walk, a sacrifice bunt, and an error; but he left a champion.

Amid the sweat-filled hugs and the spray of beer in the tiny visiting clubhouse in Jacksonville, Brinkman told Trammell and Whitaker that they were flying to Detroit the next day. The two were going to the big leagues. The parent Tigers were taking advantage of the expanded September roster limit to take a look at their prized, young middle infielders. For Trammell it completed a tremendous journey. Only fourteen months after graduating from high school and signing a professional contract, he was on his way to the Major Leagues. He was just nineteen years old.

"It was obvious he wasn't going to be in the minor leagues very long," recalled Lynch about the skinny kid he played with long ago. "I knew he was going to get to the Major Leagues."[36] Their teammate, Corr, agreed. "It was obvious he was going someplace. The organization liked [Trammell and Whitaker]. Each level was a big step, but he was destined and everyone knew it. He earned it."[37] "They were in the right place at the right time," added Montgomery pitcher Sheldon Burnside who would also briefly play in Detroit.[38]

The next day, the pair arrived at Detroit's Tiger Stadium, where the hometowns Tigers were playing an afternoon game against the Baltimore Orioles. Their flight had gotten them into town too late to make the beginning of the game, so after arriving at Detroit's Metro Airport, the two immediately caught a ride to the stadium they would call home for most of the next two decades. Trammell's first exposure to venerable Tiger Stadium made a less than spectacular impression.

"You would come around the corner of the freeway and as you got closer, you could see all the paint was chipped off on the outside," he remembered shortly after his playing career had ended. "Basically, if you didn't see the light towers, it kind of looked like an old warehouse. When I first got there, I was just overwhelmed by the stadium, about how close the people were to the field. I had grown up in San Diego, where the stadium was new and had a big parking lot all around it. When I first saw Tiger Stadium, I wondered where all the people parked."[39]

They quickly dressed in the clubhouse where Trammell pulled on jersey number 42 and Whitaker wore number 46. They made the short walk down the dark, dingy tunnel leading to the home team dugout of the Detroit Tigers. "That runway was always kind of musty," recalled Trammell. "I called it the dungeon down there. You couldn't do much because the walls were all concrete."[40]

Only hours removed from the emotional high of winning the Southern League championship, what he saw that afternoon had to be disheartening. Less than 2,000 fans speckled the stands of the 54,000-seat stadium, watching a getaway contest between the Tigers and Orioles. The interior of the stadium was in disrepair, long overdue for the major makeover that would finally take place that off-season. Trammell was catching a glimpse of the final days of a ball park that hadn't seen any significant change in years, other than changing of names from "Briggs" to "Tiger" Stadium in 1961. The interior was a deep, dark, canoe-green, with wooden seats matching the paint color of the façade and stadium supports all around the ballpark. The smell of years' worth of stale beer and cigar smoke permeated the air. It was like taking a step back in time, playing in a ballpark and for a franchise that had struggled to be competitive in the game as it existed in 1977.

"I remember standing out there during batting practice—back when we had the old green seats all over," said Trammell of that first September in Tiger Stadium. "And looking up there at the upper deck, and when somebody would hit a ball up there, you could see the seats splinter, especially in right field, when no one was out there."[41]

On the field, the Birds' ace right-hander, Jim Palmer, was handling Detroit's lineup with ease, on his way to a four-hit, 4–0 shutout victory. The loss was the fourth in five games for the Tigers, and the start of a six-game losing streak that was turning September into a dismal month for the team. It was the fourth consecutive year that a Tigers team would be playing meaningless games during the season's final month. The loss to Baltimore left Detroit nineteen games behind the American League's Eastern Division leading New York Yankees. With three weeks of the schedule yet to be played, and the team mired in fourth place, the Tigers were already planning for the next season.

The organization wanted to evaluate three prized prospects at the major league level, while looking ahead to 1978. Besides Trammell and Whitaker, Detroit had called up a highly-touted, 20-year-old catching prospect in Lance Parrish, who in addition to having a howitzer for an arm behind the plate, had hit .276 with 25 home runs and 91 RBI's at Triple-A Evansville. "We've got three, maybe four, outstanding kids that we think are ready to help," said the Tigers' veteran manager, Ralph Houk.[42]

After the game against the Orioles, the team flew to Boston to open a four-game weekend series with the Red Sox. It was there, on Friday, September 9, 1977, that Trammell and Whitaker made their major league debuts, playing in storied Fenway Park. Houk started both of his rookie infielders in the second game of a twi-night double-header. Trammell's first official entry in the scorebook came when he made a putout on Red Sox icon, Carl Yastrzemski, who hit a pop foul to the rookie shortstop in the bottom of the first inning.

By the time he batted with one out in the top of the third inning, Detroit trailed 5–0. In the initial at bat of his major league career, Trammell—batting ninth in Houk's lineup—grounded a single up the middle and into center field off of veteran right-handed pitcher, Reggie Cleveland. After advancing on a walk, Trammell scored the first run of his career when Whitaker crashed a ball off of the famed left-field "Green Monster," allowing him to score from second base. Trammell struck out in the fourth inning against Bosox reliever, Jim Willoughby, before singling again to center field in the sixth inning, this time off of another veteran, Rick Wise. Trammell's two-for-three debut paled only slightly in comparison to his keystone partner, Whitaker's, three-for-five performance.

Over the next few days, the Trammell-Whitaker combo at shortstop and second base continued to astound all who watched them play. After four games they had already demonstrated their considerable defensive skills, while at the plate, Trammell was hitting .444 and Whitaker .353. Their ability to assimilate themselves smoothly into the game at the major league level, especially at such early ages and with only minimal time spent in the minor leagues, impressed even those who might have felt the Detroit organization had rushed them up to the parent club.

"I was amazed at those two when they showed up, how daring they were in their play," remembered Roland Hemond, the Chicago White Sox general manager at the time. "They wouldn't even cheat on double-plays. They would come running across the bag, like they knew they belonged. There was no question whatsoever that they were ready, even though they had jumped from Double-A."[43]

"They're doing exactly what everyone said they could do," said Houk who was winding up his fifteenth year as a big league manager, and fourth with the Tigers. "They've looked like major leaguers these last few games. They know what they're doing. Neither one of them has made a bad play yet."[44]

Trammell and Whitaker immediately increased the talent level at positions that had been a wreck in recent years for Detroit. Shortstop had historically been a weak spot for the Tiger franchise with a recent exception being the four years that Brinkman had so ably handled the position from 1971 to 1974. The incumbent at the position, Tom Veryzer, had failed to impress during his three years as the starter, and was suffering through his worst season thus far. Second base had been nothing more than a revolving door in the four years since long-time stalwart, Dick McAuliffe, had left Detroit. Gary Sutherland, Pedro Garcia, and most recently, Tito Fuentes, had each failed to take hold of that position as a long-term solution.

As the team gained confidence in the abilities and demeanor of its two new middle-infielders, what was intended to be a September "looksee" turned instead into full-fledged auditions for the shortstop and second base jobs in 1978. "I'd really like to play them as much as I can," stated Houk shortly after the two had come up from the minors that September. "We'll be facing mostly contenders the rest of the way, so nobody can accuse me of playing favorites by using my rookies. Besides, with the way those kids are playing, I'm not doing anybody any favors by putting them in the game."[45]

The contenders Houk made reference to were New York, Baltimore, and Boston, who all fielded heavyweight ball clubs that season. They would all play Houk's young Detroit team in multiple series that September, and each possessed talent, experience, and motivation that far exceeded anything a Tiger squad, playing out the string, would be able to counter with. 1977 was a watershed year in baseball history, the first full-fledged season where high-priced free agent signees had altered the makeup of the season-long pennant races. Organizations like the Yankees, Red Sox, and California Angels had aggressively pursued and signed notable impact players like Reggie Jackson, Catfish Hunter, and Don Gullet (New York); Bill Campbell (Boston); and Joe Rudi, Don Baylor, and Bobby Grich (California), to multi-million dollar contracts.

Meanwhile, the fiscally conservative Tigers chose to watch the off-season spending frenzy with disdain, and instead were content to try to improve through the farm system and the traditional, as well as less expensive method of player development, where patience was preached by a franchise that had been among the worst in baseball over the previous three seasons. In contrast to the free-spending Yankees and Red Sox who won 100 and 97 games respectively that year, Detroit finished out 1977 with a 74–88 record with sixteen players on their roster making the minimum salary of $19,000.

The brutal schedule over the season's final month took its toll on what had otherwise been a season of improvement for the Tigers. After finishing an average of 25 games under .500 the previous three years, Detroit certainly would have viewed a break-even record as highly successful in 1977. That goal was certainly within reach early in September as the club moved to within three games of .500. But an 11–21 record for the month removed any chance of reaching that mark and the Tigers tumbled to a fourth place finish, fourteen games below .500.

The rough final month also took a toll on the team's highly-prized prospects. After getting hits in three of his first four appearances, Trammell suffered through an 0-17 stretch, and in fact, hit safely in only two of his final fifteen games. He finished his September trial in Detroit with a .186 batting average in nineteen games. Defensively, Trammell handled 49 chances with only two errors, impressing everyone who watched. Whitaker finished at .250 and Parrish batted just .196 in their late-season debuts. Despite the rather modest numbers they posted, the Detroit organization glowed about the talent that appeared ready to join the big league club.

The keystone positions were especially in need of help and appeared wide-open heading into 1978. While the veteran Milt May had put together a solid season as the starting catcher, allowing Detroit to take its time while breaking in Parrish, the options were less numbered at shortstop and second base. Veryzer had finished poorly in 1977 and was being booed lustily by the Tiger Stadium crowds. Fuentes had hit well at second base, finishing over .300 in his single season with the Tigers, but his showboat style and erratic defensive game made the long-time National League veteran only a temporary fix at that troublesome spot in the lineup. That left an opportunity for two of the most highly-anticipated young players Detroit's minor league system had produced in years. Could a pair of kids that had never played a season above the Double-A level other than their September cameos, really be considered for the crucial middle infield spots so soon? Houk saw enough in the season's closing weeks to believe that they could. "They've got a helluva shot. I wouldn't want to make any decisions now. I'd have to wait and see how they do in the Instructional League again this fall. But I'm really pleased with the way they've played."[46]

3

Rookie Sensation

As the Detroit Tigers gathered for spring training in late February of 1978, two major storylines readied to play out at their Lakeland, Florida spring base. The first concerned the health of their ace pitcher, Mark "The Bird" Fidrych, who was coming off of an injury-plagued 1977 season. Fidrych had been the talk of the baseball world in 1976, winning the Rookie of the Year Award while bringing a freshness and spontaneity to the game that hadn't existed in the major leagues for years. While his loping jaunts to and from the mound, the combing and sprucing of the mound, and his frequent gestures and pep talks to both himself and the ball—electrified fans all across the American League, Fidrych meant more to the team than just being a colorful character who helped sell (a lot of) tickets. He was the new face of the franchise, something that had been sorely needed following the nondescript last-place teams Detroit had fielded in 1974 and 1975, while also being a legitimate top-of-the-rotation starting pitcher, having gone 19–9 with a 2.34 ERA and 24 complete games in his rookie season. After a 1977 season that had gone badly for him, beginning with knee surgery in the spring and then bouts of tendinitis in his pitching shoulder that limited him to only nine regular season games, the Tigers eagerly welcomed back their greatest asset.

The other major storyline in Lakeland revolved around the middle of the Detroit infield. Who would be manager Ralph Houk's keystone combination on a team that had aspirations of returning to the plus side of .500 and perhaps even being a dark horse in the American League's Eastern Division race? With a core of young players that included the likes of Fidrych and fellow starting pitcher Dave Rozema, outfielders Ron LeFlore and Steve Kemp, first baseman Jason Thompson, as well as the veteran designated hitter, Rusty Staub, the Tigers were entering the 1978 season with a proven nucleus that offered promise for the first time in several seasons. The shortstop-second base positions were unsettled, however, with no proven starters and were wide-open entering camp.

The sexy choices for the positions were the tandem of Alan Trammell and Lou Whitaker, the young phenoms that had played so well during their September trial the previous season, and who arrived in Lakeland that spring with as much advance hype as any Tiger prospects in recent memory. Few doubted that they were the future middle infield combination for the Tigers. Many more doubted whether a pair of 20-year-old kids could really hold up over the rigors of a 162-game schedule against competition as steep as the American League promised to present that summer. A full year at Triple-A Evansville in 1978 would be the expected path for the young prospects.

"We both want to stay up in the big leagues this year," said Trammell, displaying an early sense of confidence and belonging as spring training commenced. "The way I look at it, if I do my thing, the job will be mine. If I don't, I don't deserve it."[1]

Competition for the positions centered on shortstop Mark Wagner and second baseman Steve Dillard. Wagner was a 24-year-old candidate drafted in 1972, who had spent six seasons working his way up through various stops in the Detroit minor league system before finally spending parts of the previous two seasons with the big league club. Like Trammell, he was considered a fine fielding shortstop but his ability at the plate was in question, having batted only .227 at that point in his brief major league career. Dillard had been picked up over the winter in a minor trade with Boston, once it became apparent that Detroit's regular second baseman in 1977, Tito Fuentes, was not being brought back. The 27-year-old Dillard had spent two full seasons as a utility infielder the Red Sox, playing 123 games in 1976 and 1977 with over 300 at bats for strong Boston teams. Detroit's incumbent utility infielder, Chuck Scrivener, was also in the mix, but was considered a long-shot for an everyday claim on either position.

Conspicuously absent from the competition was Tom Veryzer, who had manned the shortstop position for the Tigers over the past three seasons. Veryzer had been Detroit's first round pick in the 1971 amateur draft, taken eleventh overall—projected by longtime Detroit scout Wayne Blackburn to be "the best hitting shortstop since Honus Wagner," a tag that would cause anguish for the front office for decades to come.[2] In drafting Veryzer, the Tigers bypassed a local schoolboy legend at Detroit Catholic Central High School, Frank Tanana, who was taken two picks later by the California Angels. Tanana quickly ascended to major league fame as a flame-throwing left-handed pitcher for the Angels. By age 23 he had already accumulated 66 career victories, led the league in strikeouts one season, and was coming off of a 1977 campaign in which he had gone 15–9 with seven shutouts and an American League leading 2.54 earned run average.

Meanwhile, Veryzer, despite putting up less than sterling offensive numbers, had been rushed through the Tigers' minor league system until he showed enough in a half-season stint at Triple-A Evansville in 1974 to justify a permanent promotion to the parent club in August. By the end of that campaign the Tigers were in a free fall in the standings and a full-fledged youth movement was underway in Detroit. The team traded Ed Brinkman, making room for Veryzer as the everyday shortstop. After finishing a respectable rookie season in 1975 in which he hit .252 with 48 RBI's, making the Topps All-Rookie team, Veryzer's game seemed to deteriorate. His batting average dropped to .234 in 1976 and his run production similarly declined by nearly half. In 1977 things got even worse; his average dropped below .200 in early May and he never recovered. He finished batting .197 with a paltry two home runs and 28 RBI's in 125 games. His fielding, while respectable for the shortstop position, was not enough to justify his being an everyday player. He averaged nearly twenty errors per season over his three years as Detroit's starting shortstop, with mediocre range. By mid-1977 it was becoming apparent to the Tiger front office that Veryzer wasn't the long-term answer. With Wagner playing more and more, and Trammell establishing himself as one of the brightest prospects in the organization in years, Veryzer was dealt to the Cleveland Indians in December 1977 in a straight swap for washed-up outfielder, Charlie Spikes.

While there is little doubt that the Detroit brass desperately wanted Trammell and Whitaker to be the keystone combination in 1978, at least outwardly they were determined to make it an open competition with the two kids having to win their respective jobs. As the team prepared to open spring exhibition play, Houk said "I'm going into the situation completely open-minded. I've found that in situations like this there is usually no doubt left in your mind when the time comes to make a decision."[3] He alternated Trammell-Whitaker with Wagner-Dillard almost religiously, playing those combinations on an every-other-day basis. The two kids looked good in the Grapefruit Season opener on March 10 in Lakeland as Trammell went 1–3 at the plate, scoring a run, while his sidekick Whitaker had two hits and two RBI's in the 6–0 Detroit victory over Boston. Two days later they repeated the strong performance with Trammell (2–4) and Whitaker (2–5) again making solid contributions to the offense in a 9–5 drubbing of Minnesota.

Offensively questions still lingered for the two, especially regarding Trammell's readiness to play in the major leagues that spring. The .186 average he had posted in his late-season cameo the previous September, along with his slight frame, left many doubting that a just-turned 20-year-old kid, not even two years removed from high school, would be able to contribute enough offensively to hold a spot on Detroit's 25-man roster.

"I know I looked overmatched at times last year," he said partway into March when asked about his ability at the plate for that summer. "I had the same feeling in 1976, the first year I played A-ball at Montgomery. But the next year I really improved. I've always improved, everywhere I've been."[4]

In the field there was little doubt that Trammell would contribute, and likely even improve upon the spotty play that had plagued the shortstop position in Detroit since Brinkman's departure. The same steady ability to field ground balls and the quick and accurate release he had shown in the minor leagues followed Trammell to the Tigers. In one exhibition game that spring against Boston, he put on full display his ability to make all of the plays required at shortstop. Early in the game he backhanded a ground ball hit deep into the hole between short and third and threw out George Scott. Shortly afterwards, he ranged far to his left to field a ground ball behind the bag and throw out Fred Lynn. Later he charged a ball off of the bat of the hard-hitting Scott, and made a difficult play seem routine as he flipped a throw to first to get the runner. "Physically, he wasn't very strong, but he had good, good hands and a very strong arm," said Tigers coach Dick Tracewski about his first impressions working with Trammell that spring.[5]

The *Detroit News* in a March 22 assessment of the battle for roster spots said about Trammell: "If he beats out Mark Wagner, he will be Detroit's best fielding shortstop in years, hit about .225 and get better. Ought to be kept up and learn while playing every day."[6]

That assessment was consistent with what other players, media, and the sunshine-soaked fans of Lakeland were saying as spring training passed into its final days. Houk, however, was not going to be rushed into a decision and had every intention of letting things fully play out. But even he was more assertive than ever that the Tigers had struck gold with their double-play combination of the future. "I think Whitaker and Trammell will eventually be our shortstop-second base combination, even if they don't make it this year. They have the ability. It all depends on how quickly they mature."[7]

One thing Detroit's management was not going to do was break up the duo. After hand-picking the two and pairing them up a little more than a year earlier, General Manager Jim Campbell and the rest of the Tiger organization's brain trust had already determined that Trammell and Whitaker would be joined at the hip in 1978. Either they both would make the big league club and stay in Detroit, or they both would be sent to Triple-A Evansville for an additional year of experience.[8] That philosophy was fine with Trammell who said at the time, "we would really prefer to stay together."[9]

Helping the young duo's cause that spring was the play of the team around them. Detroit was having its best spring training in years, winning seven-straight Grapefruit games at one point, and showed signs of being a much improved team in 1978. The pitching had been upgraded, Fidrych was healthy and throwing well, and another wave of talented, young players was on the verge of joining the Tigers' club. All spring, Trammell and Whitaker seemed to be major contributors to the improved play of the team, whether with their bats, running the bases, or making plays in the field. It came as no surprise then, when on March 28, General Manager Jim Campbell and Manager Ralph Houk announced that the two young infielders had made the team and would be traveling to Detroit to open the regular season.

Trammell seemed to take the news in stride, stating that he and Whitaker were "happy" and "we figure we can learn all we need up here." He also said that the news hadn't really sunk in yet and probably wouldn't hit him until the team got back to Detroit.[10] He ended the exhibition season batting .262 in 47 at bats and scored seven runs. Whitaker was one of the real stars of the spring, batting .340 with fourteen RBI's as Detroit finished with an 18–9 mark, best in the Grapefruit (Florida) League, and second only to the San Francisco Giants who amassed an 18–8 record in the Arizona Cactus League.

Optimism was high as 52, 528 fans turned out for the Tigers' home opener in Detroit against the Toronto Blue Jays. Tiger followers were eager to get their first view of a promising young team, believed to have moved beyond the dreadful rebuilding years of the past half-decade, and now housed in a refurbished Tiger Stadium with its shiny new blue and orange seats. Many watched with curiosity, eager to get their first real look at the highly-touted rookie double-play combination that would be in Ralph Houk's opening day lineup.

For Trammell and Whitaker, only months removed from playing before sparse turnouts in Montgomery, Alabama, Opening Day represented their first time playing in the Detroit spotlight. Their debuts the previous September had been spent in the less threatening shadows of a non-contending team playing out the string in September. Nerves got the better of Trammell early on in the season opener, as he first misplayed a ball hit off of the bat of the Blue Jays' Tom Hutton in the top half of the second inning—allowing two runs to score—and then took a called third strike to end Detroit's half of the inning. "I thought I was going to get it," he said after the game. "But I took my eye off it and then didn't get my glove down far enough. I should have had it, that's all."[11]

The mistake was short-lived. His second trip to the plate Trammell walked behind a Whitaker double, and then rode home on third baseman Phil Mankowski's three-run homer which gave the Tigers a lead they wouldn't relinquish. Jason Thompson later added a roof-landing blast of his own and Fidrych, getting stronger on the mound as the game went along, finished with a 5-hit complete game performance in Detroit's 6–2 victory. Trammell finished 1–3 at the plate with a run scored in his 1978 debut, singling off of journeyman right-hander, Jesse Jefferson, in the sixth inning.

The Opening Day victory served as a springboard for the Tigers who won eight of their first ten games, and fifteen of their first twenty, putting them in first place, three games ahead of the New York Yankees. The young Tigers seemed intent on proving that their spring training record was not a mirage, and for the first time in years, appeared to have the horses to compete on a daily basis. "The best young team in baseball," stated Houk without reservation to anyone who would listen, a sentiment that was being echoed by knowledgeable baseball observers all over the league.[12]

In Ron LeFlore, Jason Thompson, and Steve Kemp, Detroit had three of the best young offensive players in the game. The muscular LeFlore was a fleet-footed centerfielder in his fourth full season with the Tigers and had developed into one of the most electric players in the American League. He would hit .297 that year and lead the league in both stolen bases and runs scored. Kemp was a second-year outfielder that had been the number one overall pick in the 1976 amateur draft and then was rushed to Detroit after only a single season of minor league seasoning. The Tiger front office felt so strongly about Kemp that they traded away their longtime strong man and hometown legend, Willie Horton, in order to open up left field for him. Kemp impressed everyone in his rookie season by hitting eighteen home runs with 88 RBI's in 1977. Thompson was a left-handed slugging first baseman and appeared on the verge of superstardom. He was a dead-pull hitter with spectacular power, seemingly tailor-made to hit in Tiger Stadium. He had crashed 31 home runs and drove in 105 runs the year before, only his second in the major leagues, and was off to a fast start again in 1978. Rusty Staub, the team's celebrated designated-hitter, said at the time of Thompson, "if there was such a thing as stock in a player, I'd invest in Thompson."[13]

On the mound the Tigers had greatly improved their starting rotation, adding veteran right-handers Jack Billingham from Cincinnati and Jim Slaton from Milwaukee in off-season trades. Together with Fidrych and second-year player, Dave Rozema, Detroit ventured into 1978 with a legitimate quartet of big league starting pitchers, something that had been lacking in recent seasons. The solid starting pitching combined with an explosive offensive attack made the Tigers a dangerous team in the American League's Eastern Division.

The big question marks in the lineup leading into the season, shortstop and second base, were playing out much better than anticipated. The team had kept four middle-infielders on the roster: Trammell, Whitaker, Wagner, and Dillard. All four had performed well in the early season. Houk was carefully easing his rookie keystone combination into the campaign, as Trammell and Whitaker played mostly whenever a right-handed starter opposed Detroit. That allowed the only left-handed batter of the four, Whitaker, to avoid left-handed starting pitchers. However, the organization had no intention of keeping the talented rookies out of the lineup too long, especially after they both got off to solid starts both in the field and at the plate. It appeared to be only a matter of time before Trammell and Whitaker took over the positions full time.

"They'd have to do a backbend to be sent down," said Houk in an early season interview. "I've started them off slow because I don't want to put pressure on them. Once they get their feet on the ground, they'll be in there every day."[14]

Both were hitting over .300 late into May as the Tigers continued to hold on to first place. Among the early season highlights for Trammell was a three-game stretch early in the month in which he had six hits, including the first two extra-base hits of his big league career. He doubled on May 6 in Oakland and then the next day, an afternoon game in the Oakland-Alameda County Stadium, he led off the third inning with his first career home run—a blast off of A's right-hander, Dave Keough.

As spring turned to summer, their days sharing the middle-infield positions with Wagner and Dillard were drawing to a close. Whitaker was among the league leaders in batting and provided an additional element of speed in Detroit's attack as he settled into the number two slot in Houk's batting order. Trammell, although starting to lose the battle to stay above the .300-mark, was still contributing offensively—usually from the number nine slot in the batting order—while continuing to play a solid, if not spectacular, game at shortstop.

It was more than just the stats in the box scores, however, that impressed anyone who saw the young tandem. They played well beyond their years, showing remarkable poise and an innate sense for the game. The young infielders made all of the plays in the field, ran the bases aggressively, and handled themselves well in tough situations. Fidrych, like Rozema and Billingham, was a sinkerball pitcher and commented early on about the improved infield defense that Trammell and Whitaker provided the team. "One of the good things about this team is that if the ball is hit on the ground with a man on first, you know you're going to get the double play. I couldn't be sure about that before."[15]

They could also make plays in clutch situations, such as the mid–June night in Toronto when the Blue Jays were threatening in the bottom of the ninth inning with runners on first and second and only one out. Toronto's slugging first baseman, John Mayberry, then sliced a pop-fly into shallow left field that appeared as if it would fall in for a game-winning hit. Trammell, who had been shifted up the middle behind second base for the pull-hitting Mayberry, raced out to his right and into left field where he caught the ball on his backhand while fully extended. He then whirled and doubled off the runner at second base for an inning-ending and game-saving double-play. The athletic play in the field paid off when the Tigers rallied to win the game in thirteen innings, breaking a losing skid for Detroit.

Unfortunately, the team couldn't maintain its torrid early-season pace as spring teases turned into summer realities. A late May double-header split in Tiger Stadium against the Red Sox before 52,368 pennant-starved fans left the team in a first place tie with Boston, with the Yankees lurking only a game behind. Houk had cautioned over-zealous media and fans about the team's fast start: "Great teams invariably come in first, "good" ones finish second, and "good young" ones end up third."[16] His young Tigers weren't ready to compete in a division loaded with experienced heavyweights. The club went on the road following that double-header split with Boston and lost seven of eight games against the Orioles and Red Sox. In a week's time they fell six games back of the division lead and effectively out of the race. By the end of a disastrous month of June, the team was below .500 and 15½ games behind the division-leading Red Sox.

The team's slide coincided with a slump Trammell was experiencing at the plate. After hitting over .300 for most of the first two month of his rookie season, his average had dipped to near .250 in the early days of July. Yet, whenever doubts crept in to people's minds as to whether the young kid from San Diego would be able to hold up hitting-wise, Trammell answered with a resounding "yes." For every 0–10 or 1–14 stretch that inevitably set in that summer, he quickly rebounded with a cluster of hits. In mid–June Trammell had three hits in a game at Kansas City after being held hitless the previous three days. Less than a week later in Toronto, he hit his second career home run off of the Blue Jays' Don Kirkwood, setting off a hot streak that saw him go 6–16 and raise his average again into the mid-.270s. In Texas on July 7, Trammell exploded for five hits, scored two runs, and had two RBI's to lead Detroit to a 12–7 win in the first of a three-game series just ahead of the All Star break.

With Houk now playing Trammell and Whitaker nearly every day, the team regained its momentum and climbed back above the .500 mark, winning regularly for the most part against American League West competition. The young double-play duo was the more consistent headline makers of

Early in his career, some doubted whether Trammell would ever be anything more than the good-glove, weak-bat type of shortstop that mostly existed when he came to the major leagues. Trammell primarily batted ninth in the lineup under manager Ralph Houk in Detroit, and twice led the American League in sacrifice bunts (National Baseball Hall of Fame Library, Cooperstown, New York).

Detroit's rookie class, but they were far from being the only first-year contributors on the Tiger roster. Catcher Lance Parrish and pitcher Jack Morris were also in their first full seasons, making up what was arguably the rookie group with the most long-term impact of any in the Detroit Tigers' 115-plus year history. Parrish was splitting time behind the plate in a platoon with May, while Morris was being used as a spot-starter and long-reliever. The four rookies were contributing greatly to the improved product on the field in Detroit and had immeasurably upgraded the talent level of an already improved Tigers' roster.

While some may have been surprised by their first-year success on the field, the confident Trammell was not one of them. A quick learner at each of the brief stops he had made thus far in his professional career, Trammell was quick to point to the experience he had gained the previous September after being called up. "It helped a lot to play at the end of last season. My first game was in Fenway Park before a sellout crowd of 35,000. I saw Jim Palmer, Ron Guidry, and Mike Torrez—all of them—in those first few days and what else could be tougher?"[17]

As Trammell's rookie season wound down to its final days, the accolades rolled in for him and his sidekick, Whitaker. While the team had upgraded itself greatly in a number of areas, it was the 20-year-old Trammell and 21-year-old Whitaker who were being given much of the credit for Detroit's one year improvement from fourteen games under .500 in 1977, to ultimately, ten games over .500 a year later.

"How about Alan Trammell for the most valuable player on this club?" asked Tigers television broadcaster George Kell late in the year about the rookie shortstop who was already being recognized as the "glue" of the team.[18]

"Those two kids seem to know what's going on all the time," added Mr. Tiger, Al Kaline, choosing not to credit one over the other. "They know just what they have to do on every play."[19]

In a season-ending wrap-up of 1978, *The Detroit Free Press* analyzed the good and bad from an up-and-down 86–76 Tiger team that finished in fifth place, 13½ games behind the division-winning (and eventual World Series champion) New York Yankees. As was the case from almost any assessment of Detroit that season, the focus quickly turned to the rookie middle-infielders who had turned a troublesome area into strength: "There simply is no way to accurately measure how much Lou Whitaker and Alan Trammell have meant to the Tigers this year. The two young rookies who anchored the middle of the infield like a couple of seasoned pros have been the talk of the American League. And everyone who has seen them play agrees on one thing: They're both going to get better."[20]

Trammell finished his rookie season in 1978 batting .268 in 448 official at-bats with fourteen doubles, six triples, and two home runs. He had 34 RBI's, scored 49 runs, and also stole three bases. He played 139 games at shortstop and committed only fourteen errors in 674 chances (.979 fielding percentage) and with Whitaker turned a league-leading 95 double-plays. For his efforts he was paid a salary of $21,000 for his rookie season in the major leagues. Beyond the sheer numbers however, Trammell had performed above and beyond expectations, solidifying a position that had been unsettled since Brinkman's departure four years earlier.

Statistically at least, Whitaker had been even better in his rookie campaign. He batted .285, while mostly hitting in the second slot behind LeFlore, with three home runs and 58 RBI's. In the field he played with a smooth and gliding sense of "cool," making difficult plays seem routine. Despite his quiet, almost sleepy persona, Whitaker had caught on as a crowd favorite at Tiger Stadium; his every move was greeted with a loud and long "Louuuu …!"

That November Whitaker was named the 1978 American League Rookie of the Year, garnering 21 of the 28 votes cast. Trammell came in a distant fourth, tied with Kansas City pitcher Rich Gale, and behind two other first-year infielders, Milwaukee's Paul Molitor and California's Carney Lansford.

Together, the two young Tigers appeared to be future stars and cornerstones for the franchise to build around for years to come. Trammell and Whitaker formed a middle-infield combination, both offensively and defensively, the Detroit organization hadn't dreamed of in decades. With the plethora of talented young players already in Tiger uniforms, and with more making their way up through the minor league system, the future again looked bright for a team more than a decade removed from World Series glory.

4

Sparky

For the first time since turning professional, Alan Trammell found himself with little to prove as the 1979 season commenced. His rookie season had gone surprisingly well, surpassing all expectations the Detroit organization could have had for a 20-year-old rookie shortstop with less than two years of minor league experience under his belt. Now firmly established as the Tigers' regular shortstop, Trammell looked to improve on his solid first season and for Detroit to continue their climb.

Trammell's personal life was also firmly established by this time. He had married his high school sweetheart, Barbara Leverett, just before heading to Lakeland a year earlier. They had married on Trammell's 20th birthday, February 21, and now a year into their marriage, the young couple could look forward to another summer in their home away from home in Redford, Michigan, a northwest suburb of Detroit. "You have to get away from baseball when you go home," Trammell said about his private life. "We just don't talk about it," added his wife, Barbara, talking about the on-field results at the ballpark. "I don't even know whether he wins or loses."[1]

Leading the Tigers from the dugout in 1979 would be Les Moss, who had taken over as field manager for the retired Ralph Houk. Houk, nicknamed "The Major," had completed a five-year stint with Detroit the previous October. The even-tempered, sixteen-year major league manager had been brought in by General Manager Jim Campbell to oversee the rebuilding project that faced the Tiger organization beginning in 1974. Tired of the travel and with a winning record in 1978 signifying a milestone in the rebuilding project, Houk announced his retirement shortly before the previous season had ended.

Moss was a safe choice within the organization to take over the major league job. Like Houk, he had been a long-time backup catcher in the major leagues. He had coached for, and even managed on an interim basis, the Chicago White Sox before coming over to the Detroit organization in 1975. Working his way up through the Tigers' minor league system, Moss had managed Class AA Montgomery to back-to-back championships in his first two seasons, before being promoted to Triple-A Evansville for the 1977 and 1978 seasons. Most of the home-grown players on the Detroit roster had played for Moss at one level or another, including Trammell during his month-long run at the end of the 1976 Southern League season with Montgomery. Campbell and the rest of the Detroit front office was banking on that familiarity between Moss and a developing core of young players to help turn the Tigers into legitimate contenders in the ultra-competitive American League East.

Complicating Moss' ability to guide Detroit to a fast start were the absences of a couple of high-profile contributors the team was relying on in 1979. Rusty Staub, the reigning AL Designated Hitter of the Year, was holding out in a contract dispute, having missed all of spring training and the first month of the regular season. Losing Staub's experienced presence in the Tiger lineup put more pressure on Jason Thompson and Steve Kemp in the middle of Moss' batting order. The other big void stemmed from what was turning into all-too-familiar arm ailments plaguing the team's star pitcher, Mark "The Bird" Fidrych. Fidrych had gotten off to a sensational start the previous season, winning his first two starts in dominant fashion and with the same flair he had displayed during his storybook 1976 campaign. But he was forced out of his next start after four innings, complaining of pain in his shoulder area. Despite initial diagnoses that deflected alarm about Fidrych's fragile wing, he never pitched again the rest of the season. Several rehabilitation periods and comebacks were attempted, but none proved effective. With a new campaign ready to begin, he once again was unable to answer the bell. Fidrych—for all intents and purposes—had already pitched his last effective game in a Tiger uniform.

Unlike the previous season, Detroit struggled to get its head above water through the first two months of 1979, scuffling along around the break-even mark. Trammell batted at nearly a .500 clip through the first three weeks of the schedule, but then saw his batting average slowly decline until he was down near the .250 mark heading into June.

He had four three-hit games in the early weeks, including a 3–4, 5 RBI-game against the Orioles on May 27. On June 9 in Anaheim against the Angels, where Trammell always played before a large number of family members and friends, he struck out all three times against Nolan Ryan in a 9–1 loss. However, the next day with his team trailing 3–2 in the top of the third inning, Trammell dropped a bunt single down the third base line to lead off the third inning, which keyed a four-run rally for the Tigers. Later in the game he hit his first home run of the season off of left-handed reliever Dave LaRoche, as Detroit held on for a 10–7 win. "It definitely felt good, with my family here and a lot of friends here from the San Diego area," said a jovial Trammell after the game. "They're all excited because they know someone famous."²

That Sunday afternoon game against California was noteworthy for more than just a Detroit victory. In the Anaheim Stadium press room that day was the deposed former Cincinnati Reds' manager, Sparky Anderson, who crossed paths with Tigers' GM, Jim Campbell, who had made the west coast swing with the club. The chance meeting spurred a series of discussions over the next 24 hours between the two, during which Anderson was eventually offered the Detroit Tigers managerial position. When Anderson accepted a five-and-a-half year deal for greater than $110,000 per year, the normally-conservative Campbell had pulled off the coup of the year in baseball.

Moss was fired after only 53 games with his team holding a winning record at 27–26. "I just wasn't terribly pleased with the progress we were making," explained Campbell of the uncharacteristically bold move he had made. "It was only semi-satisfactory. We were up and down. We just weren't consistent. It's hard to put my finger on it, but our overall pattern was not what I had hoped it would be. We would win a couple, then lose a couple. We were kind of treading water. I just didn't feel that ... there was something missing—I don't know exactly what."³

By replacing Moss with Sparky Anderson, the Tiger organization couldn't have put a more polar opposite personality in charge of its baseball club. The 54-year-old Moss represented "old-school" baseball; tobacco chewing, wary of the media, he spoke in low-key, short-answer bites that gave little to the press. The white-haired 45-year-old George "Sparky" Anderson was one of the most recognizable figures in the game, the extraordinarily successful ex-skipper of the Cincinnati Reds "Big Red Machine" that won four pennants and two World Championships in his eight seasons as manager. He brought bravado and a loud personality to a club that was suffering through an identity crisis in the void created by Fidrych's career-threatening injuries. Anderson immediately became the face of the Detroit franchise.

"I've promised (Detroit owner) John Fetzer and I've promised Jim Campbell that before I leave Detroit we will have a world's championship here," the new manager said boldly in his introductory news conference after landing in Detroit. "No club in baseball has more ability for its age than this ball club. The Tigers have the finest young talent in baseball today."⁴

"I said last year that in two or three years at the most, the Detroit club would be a team everybody in baseball would have to contend with. And

I still believe that." When questioned about the potential of Detroit's team in comparison to that of the Cincinnati club that had been filled with All-Stars at nearly every position, Anderson didn't flinch. "When you look at young Lance Parrish and you look at Steve Kemp and you look at Jason Thompson and you look at Alan Trammell and you look at Lou Whitaker—they could be there someday, because they have the ability."[5]

"We've got five guys from catcher to third base who can catch that ball

Trammell (shown throwing to first base in his 1978 rookie season) was an elite fielder at shortstop and as fundamentally sound as any player of his era at the position (National Baseball Hall of Fame Library, Cooperstown, New York).

as well as anybody in baseball. And we've got Ron LeFlore and Alan Trammell and Lou Whitaker who can all run."[6]

Trammell, like most of the players on the club, was shocked and relatively tight-lipped about the abrupt change in leadership. The 21-year-old shortstop was getting an early taste of the realities of professional sports, and the unfairness that sometimes goes along with it. "I feel sorry for Les," he said about the replacement of managers. "On this team, we're finding out anything can happen."[7]

With Anderson serving at the helm, the rest of the schedule played out as an extended spring training with the new manager carefully mixing and matching lineups, bringing players up from Triple-A Evansville, and evaluating 41 different players who played in Detroit at some point that season. Anderson's young shortstop was one player who immediately caught his eye. Trammell stole home on the front-end of a double-steal on June 12, the first such feat by a Tiger player in six years. Then he homered and drove in three runs on June 17, providing the bulk of the offense in Anderson's first victory with Detroit, 8–4 over the Angels. Batting .255 at the time of Anderson's hire, Trammell raised his average into the .270s by the end of June, where it would hover for the remainder of the season.

While Ed Brinkman is credited with developing the tools Trammell needed to play shortstop in the major leagues, it was Anderson who would be the driving influence that would shape and mold the rest of his career. Anderson's credibility was immediate, forged through nearly a decade of winning in Cincinnati, where he had advanced the development of players like Joe Morgan, Ken Griffey, George Foster, Cesar Geronimo, and Dan Driessen, turning them all into polished professionals. However, it was the development of the Reds' Venezuelan shortstop, Dave Concepcion, that most grabbed Trammell's attention. Concepcion had come up to the majors as a 21-year-old rookie when Anderson took over the Reds in 1970, and then developed into one of the finest all-around players in baseball. Paired with Morgan, the two had formed one of the greatest shortstop-second base combinations in baseball history.

Anderson knew the finer technical points of the game, but more importantly he drilled into his young club the importance of being professional, on and off the field. He talked about preparation and what it took to win at that level. He instilled the mindset to battle for 27 outs, understanding that unlike most other team sports, a clock didn't serve as either an ally or a second opponent. In baseball the players control the pace of the game, and until all 27 outs are used against you, victory is still possible. Those that didn't buy into Anderson's message were quick to find out about the "my way or the highway" mantra that the new manager ruled by.

Trammell finished the 1979 season batting .276, while displaying more punch than he had as a rookie—ending the year with six home runs and 50 RBI's. The fourteen three-hit games he put together demonstrated the potential he had to one day be an offensive force. Late in the season, Anderson experimented with Trammell by moving him into the number two slot in the batting order, the first time in Trammell's big league career that he had batted with any regularity outside of the ninth position. He was also being utilized more aggressively on the base paths, as Anderson brought his National League style of play. Trammell stole seventeen bases (sixteen of them after Anderson took over), including thirteen in the last two months of the season.

In the field, he started 138 games at shortstop and despite an increased error total, Trammell continued to prove that he was the long-term answer at the position. Combined with Whitaker who batted .286 and enjoyed another solid year both offensively and defensively, the Tigers were becoming comfortable with one of the best double-play combinations in baseball. "I'm not saying Whitaker is better than Paul Molitor of Milwaukee, and I'm not saying Trammell is better than Davey Concepcion at Cincinnati," stated Anderson ahead of the 1980 season. "But as a pair, I think right now they're better than anybody else in the major leagues."[8]

Detroit finished the season in fifth place, eighteen games behind the division-winning and eventual pennant winning Baltimore Orioles. Their 85–76 record was one game worse than they had finished in 1978, proving that even with Sparky Anderson, the Tigers still had a long climb before they would compete in the AL East. "I'm not a fool," said Anderson early on in Detroit. "I know we're in with New York, Boston, Baltimore, and Milwaukee. I don't want the fans to think that now that Sparky Anderson is here, everything will be all right."[9]

Anderson boasted that his team was ready to win 90 games in 1980, a figure that probably wouldn't win the American League East, but might keep them in the chase late into the season. The year began impressively enough with a 5–1 win on opening night in Kansas City, behind a dominant, three-hit, complete game effort by 24-year-old Jack Morris, and a home run and triple by the team's rookie centerfielder, Kirk Gibson. However, Detroit proceeded to lose its next seven games, dropping to last place in the division.

Trammell started the season on the sidelines, courtesy of a pulled muscle in his left thigh that caused him to miss the entire opening series. He returned to the lineup in Boston, vaulting off the injured list to get hits in five of his first six starts, including four contests with multiple hits. He batted .364 for the month of April and maintained a lofty mark well into May, finishing that month at a still torrid average of .336. He went 9–15 with five runs scored during the week of May 12, earning himself the American League's Player of the Week award. Anderson rewarded Trammell's hot start by promoting him to the second slot in the batting order, beginning at the start of the Tigers' first west coast swing. June wasn't any different for Detroit's blossoming young shortstop, as he hit safely in 16 of 25 games, including ten multi-hit games, and finished that month among the AL leaders in batting with a .327 average. He also scored a run in sixteen of the games he played in June and ranked among the league leaders in that category as well.

In the field, Trammell was performing better than ever, having elevated his game to the point that he was being compared with the best defensive shortstops in the league, including Baltimore's Mark Belanger, Milwaukee's Robin Yount, Boston's Rick Burleson, and New York's Bucky Dent. Talent, confidence—and now in his third full season—experience, were combining to make him a superior defender. He committed only thirteen errors all season, exactly half of his 1979 total, while continuing to make plays that were of a spectacular nature. The .980 fielding percentage he posted that season would be among the highest of his entire career.

Trammell's strong first half generated all-star buzz that got louder as the mid-season classic in Los Angeles drew nearer. When Baltimore manager Earl Weaver called with the news that Trammell and his buddy and fellow Californian, Lance Parrish, had both made the American League squad as reserves, a life-long dream had been realized. "When I go home I start thinking about it and I just break out in a big smile," said Trammell barely suppressing another smile. "It's a dream come true."[10]

"I wanted to make it," he added despite finishing seventh in the balloting by fans. "I thought I deserved it."[11] With the game being played at Dodger Stadium in Los Angeles, Trammell had a large contingent of family and friends on hand. Despite his impressive credentials, the third-year player played a deferential role in the actual game. Playing behind the leading vote getter at the position, New York shortstop Bucky Dent (he of the matinee looks, but only a .249 batting average at the time), as well as his replacement, Milwaukee's Robin Yount, Trammell saw little action. He entered the game in the bottom of the eighth inning at shortstop, but did not make a plate appearance.

With Trammell now serving as a significant cog in Detroit's offensive attack, the team got hot in the summer months and worked themselves up in the standings. The Tigers were a sizzling 19–6 in June, finally reaching the .500 mark on June 21. From there they won nine of their next twelve and found themselves tied for second place, 7½ games behind the front-running New York Yankees, a week into July. "We kept saying if we could only get to .500 it would be like a new season," said Trammell about Detroit's ascension in the standings. "But the big thing is that once we got to .500 we didn't even blink or look back. We just kept going."[12]

The Tigers' strength in 1980 lay in its ability to score runs, which it did in bunches, and when combined with even adequate pitching, Detroit had the capability to go on winning streaks. A retooling of the Tigers' attack had already taken place under their new manager. Gone were Staub, Thompson, and LeFlore, each considered quintessential to the rebuilding effort of the Detroit franchise only a year earlier. They had been replaced by Anderson in an attempt to diversify the attack, which had too often proved susceptible to left-handed pitching. The mainstays of the lineup were now Kemp, Whitaker, Trammell, and Lance Parrish who had blossomed into one of the top offensive catchers in all of baseball. That core was being complemented by a strong group of role players which included switch-hitting outfielder Ricky Peters, veteran right-handed hitter Al Cowens, journeymen John Wockenfuss and Champ Summers, as well as a new cleanup hitter and established RBI-man that Anderson knew well from his National League days, former Pirate Richie Hebner.

It was the pitching, however, that prevented Detroit from becoming a legitimate factor in the divisional race. The Tigers had neither the quantity or quality of arms to rely on; too many times the team faced either an early deficit, or conversely, couldn't hold on to a lead. With Fidrych's career all but over, Morris was the assumed leader of the starting rotation after having won seventeen games in 1979. However, at age 24, he wasn't ready for that burden and showed an exasperating lack of consistency in 1980, finishing with an overall record of 16–15 and an ERA well above four. Following behind Morris were Milt Wilcox, Dan Schatzeder, Dave Rozema, and Dan Petry (in only his second season) who all showed promise at times, but lacked steadiness from game-to-game. When John Hiller retired mid-way through the season, severing the last active tie to the organization's last World Series team from 1968, Aurelio Lopez remained as the only proven member of an already shallow bullpen.

The high point came on August 3 when Detroit completed a four-game sweep of the Seattle Mariners at home and reached its season high of 12 games over .500. But, the Tigers still hadn't been able to inch any closer to the top of the standings. The pitching collapsed soon after, as the team surrendered an average of seven runs per game over a two-week stretch and lost 12 of 15 games. The cold spell dropped the team to fifth place in the division and effectively ended whatever remote shot they may have had at making a late charge in the race. Despite leading the Major

Leagues with 830 runs scored, the Tigers finished a disappointing 84–78, tied with Boston for fourth place in the American League East standings.

For Trammell the waning weeks of the season became a challenge to finish out what had otherwise been an outstanding season personally. He entered August with his average still a very robust .319. But after slumping badly through much of that month, his average finally dropped below the .300-mark on August 29. By mid–September, Trammell had watched his average dip all the way to .289, the toll of playing 146 games through a long summer schedule finally catching up with the 22-year-old. But then he heated up again, getting hits in 13 of his next 23 at bats covering a six game stretch, lifting his chin back above that magical .300-bar that separates the great hitters from the good hitters. The rest of the season turned into a race to keep him above that bar with Trammell's average fluctuating on both sides of that line.

He started the final game of the year in New York batting .299. After walking in the top of the first against Yankee left-hander Tim Lollar, Trammell dropped a perfect bunt single down the third base line in the third inning. In the top of the sixth inning, Trammell flied out to left field; his season's batting average stood at an even .300. Following a well-worn precedent of the game, Anderson lifted his star shortstop for a pinch-hitter the next time Trammell's turn came around in the eighth inning. "I think when you've played as hard as Alan has all year, you deserve something," he said about getting Trammell out of the game and preserving his first .300 season in the major leagues.[13]

Trammell's third full season in Detroit had clearly been his best. Besides the milestone

George "Sparky" Anderson came to Detroit in 1979 and was Trammell's manager for all but the first and last full seasons of Trammell's career. Anderson mentored Trammell throughout his career, and guided the Tigers to a World Championship in 1984 (National Baseball Hall of Fame Library, Cooperstown, New York).

breakthrough in batting average, he had career highs in runs scored (107), doubles (21), home runs (9), RBI's (65), walks (69), sacrifice bunts (13), and sacrifice flies (7). He also stole twelve bases, had an outstanding .376 on-base percentage, and raised his slugging percentage over the .400-mark, to .404. For the first time in his short career, Trammell was being singled out separately from his side-kick, Whitaker, who had fallen off notably in 1980. Whitaker batted just .233, the lowest mark of any regular player in the American League that season. It was Trammell who was being recognized in some corners as the better all-around player, a reversal from the perception that many had held up until then.

Trammell's efforts were not forgotten when the post-season awards were announced. In November he was named by the Detroit chapter of the Baseball Writers Association of America as the Tiger of the Year, netting 36 of a possible 38 votes. He also finished 20th in the American League's Most Valuable Player Award voting, the first time he had garnered consideration for that prestigious honor. But perhaps most notably and deservedly, Trammell was recognized with the 1980 AL Gold Glove at shortstop for superior individual fielding performance.

His sterling all-around performance triggered a seismic shift in the Detroit organization's willingness to consider long-term contracts for its core of young players. With little fanfare, word leaked in late August that the Tigers had signed Trammell to an unprecedented 7-year contract totaling $2.8-million. Saying only that his star shortstop's contract was "a very fine one," Detroit GM Jim Campbell broke new ground by locking up one of the keys to the fiscally conservative franchise's rebuilding efforts, well ahead of Trammell's eligibility for free agency.[14]

For Trammell the contract not only gave him guaranteed money and a financial windfall by 1980 standards, but also eliminated the need for yearly negotiations, a process that he found unsettling. He had taken the team to binding salary arbitration the prior winter, and like his alter ego Whitaker, had won his case and with it a salary of $130,000 for the season. Wanting to avoid that painful course again, he and Campbell had entered into a month-long series of discussions, without an agent serving as the middle-man, and had reached the monumental agreement.

"I hope this is a breakthrough," said Trammell about the Detroit front office's stunning commitment. "I can't speak for the other guys, but I'm thrilled at staying in Detroit and I hope they feel the same way."[15]

"I know we're making a lot of mistakes, but I think we can win. I love this place. I love the ball park, the people, the city … the whole thing. I know no city is perfect, but Detroit is a good place and it has been very good to me." Mentioning the likes of former Tiger icons such as Bill Freehan,

Jim Northrup, and Mickey Stanley—all of whom had built successful post-baseball careers in the greater-Detroit area, Trammell added, "I also look at how the old ball players have done in Detroit. They've been treated well."[16]

Nineteen eighty-one began with high aspirations in Detroit, fueled even more by the Tigers winning 8 of their first 10 games, even though five of the wins were against a Toronto Blue Jays club that had lost 95 games the year before. Those high aspirations proved to be fleeting, however, as the team followed the 7–1 start with ten consecutive losses, repeating the maddening pattern of streakiness that had plagued the Tigers for several seasons. The early disappointment over the team's record ran parallel to the struggles at the plate of its All-Star shortstop. Trammell batted less than .250 for most of the first two months of the schedule, failing to find the stroke that had made him such a model of consistency the year before.

As the weather warmed though, the Tigers did, too, and they inched their way back towards the break-even mark. But, Detroit's inspired play was overshadowed by a foreboding that permeated all of baseball as the threat of a player's strike loomed in early June. At stake was the future of free agency as it then existed, a right the players had won in court half a decade earlier. The owners were now demanding some form of compensation for clubs losing a player that signed with another team. The Players Association of course resisted, claiming that such a practice would curtail the aggressiveness of teams actively bidding for eligible players on the open market. When negotiations broke down between the two parties, the players walked out on June 12, launching the first in-season strike in major league baseball history.

The timing couldn't have been worse for a Detroit club that had won ten of its last twelve games leading up to the walk-out, and had reached a season best mark of 31–26. The work stoppage which many predicted would last only days, held strong for nearly two months, resulting in the cancelation of 713 games league-wide (approximately 38 percent of the regular season schedule). Most of the players eventually found their way back to their off-season homes forfeiting more and more of their seasons' salary with each passing day. For Trammell, who was in line to make $250,000 in the first year of his new seven-year agreement with the Tigers, each day on strike resulted in a personal loss of nearly $1,500.

On July 31 a compromise was finally reached with free agent signees defined as "premium" triggering compensation to their former teams via a pool of players provided from all teams, rather than the compensatory player being taken directly from the team that signed the free agent. On the field, the pre-strike standings were deemed a completed half-season with the division leaders winning a playoff berth. The balance of the scheduled games would be played out with each team starting fresh at 0–0, and the division winners for the second half season would also be thrown into an enlarged and modified playoff structure.

For Trammell and his teammates, it was a chance to start again with a clean slate. Although they had finished strong in the first half, they had landed in an all too familiar place: fourth place. They resumed their season beginning on August 10 and lost three of their first four games, before then winning three straight in Tiger Stadium against the first-half winners, the New York Yankees. The final game of that series was a season-changer for Detroit. Trailing 4–1 entering the bottom of the ninth inning, the Tigers, who hadn't done much all day against Yankee starter Dave Righetti or his replacement, Rudy May, managed to scratch out a run on a couple of walks and a single. New York manager, Gene Michael, then brought in his relief ace, Ron Davis, the hard-throwing right-hander with the three-quarters motion who liked to intimidate batters with a stare masked behind dark-tinted glasses. With two men on base and only one out, he faced Detroit outfielder, Kirk Gibson, who had just entered the game in the eighth inning.

Gibson had been the organization's first round draft pick in 1978, an amazing blend of raw power and speed who had been an All-American in both football and baseball at Michigan State University. His potential had been likened to Mickey Mantle by the over-enthusiastic Anderson, and he had graced the cover of Sports Illustrated a year earlier—before he had even played his first full season in the major leagues. Gibson had been plagued by injuries, however, in his one-and-a-half years in Detroit, slowing the development of an athlete that had only picked up the game again in college just three years earlier.

Gibson crushed a Davis fastball that afternoon, the ball carrying into the upper-deck bleachers in far-right-center field, giving the Tigers a 5–4 win over the Yankees. The titanic blast sent what had otherwise been a sleepy Sunday afternoon crowd at Tiger Stadium into delirium over the unexpected comeback victory. More importantly, it ignited a spark for a team that would go on to win nine consecutive games and eighteen of twenty-three overall, while opening a three-game lead in the division a week into September. Benefitting from the quirky two-month schedule that turned baseball's customary marathon of a regular season into a ten-week sprint, Sparky Anderson's young team found themselves for the first time in the throes of a full-fledged pennant race.

The rest of the season evolved into a series of stops and starts as the Tigers' penchant for streakiness continued. A three-game winning streak was followed by a five-game losing streak, which in turn was followed by a four-game winning streak. They entered the last ten games of the campaign holding a game-and-a-half lead over both the Brewers and Red Sox. In a reverse from its 1980 persona, the post-strike Detroit club largely relied on a vastly improved pitching staff, more than a sputtering offensive attack, to win games. Thanks to Morris, who tied for the league lead in wins that season, along with a much more effective bullpen, the team ERA fell from 4.25 twelve months earlier, to 3.53 in 1981. However, a Tiger lineup that had led the major leagues in runs scored the year before—fell all the way to ninth in the American League, with Gibson and Kemp as the only consistent threats in what had otherwise turned into a docile lineup.

The malaise that seemed to hover over the Detroit hitters late that summer afflicted the struggling Trammell as well. He had lifted his average to near the .300 mark shortly after play had resumed in August, before he slumped for the remainder of the year. Batting .281 entering September, Trammell hit only .208 the rest of the way, finishing with a disappointing .258 average overall. Anderson, in a desperate attempt to shake up the lineup, shifted Trammell to the leadoff spot for the final two weeks, but with little impact.

They entered the final series in Milwaukee, having fallen behind the first-place Brewers by just a half-game. Whichever club could win two of the three games in the series would clinch the second-half division title and qualify for post-season play. Milwaukee pounced on a shaky Dan Petry in the Friday night game, jumping out in front early on the 22-year-old pitcher, before putting the game away in the middle innings as the Brewers coasted to an easy 8–2 win that brought them to within one victory of taking the prize.

On Saturday, October 3, the Tigers and Brewers engaged in a tensely fought pitcher's duel between staff aces Morris and Milwaukee's veteran right-hander, Pete Vuckovich. Detroit broke a scoreless tie by scratching out a run in the sixth inning when Gibson scored on an error. Morris held the Tigers' 1–0 lead until the bottom of the eighth inning, when a walk and then two botched bunts by Detroit infielders loaded the bases with no outs. A ground-out and a sacrifice fly gave the Brewers a 2–1 lead, before the year's AL MVP and Cy Young Award winning relief pitcher extraordinaire, Rollie Fingers, set Detroit down meekly in the top of the ninth, giving Milwaukee the second-half title.

"This is a terrible way to end it," mused Trammell in a solemn visitor's clubhouse afterwards. "Those bunt plays...."[17]

"We had a good year," he reasoned moments later about Detroit's overall mark of 60–49, which would have placed them fourth in the combined AL East standings. "But we had to fight and claw for everything we got. Every game was close, which is why I thought we might pull this one out."[18]

By the time the 1982 season rolled around, the Tigers were expected to be hardened from their near-miss that last weekend in Milwaukee and ready to move up in the American League East standings. Trammell was now firmly established as one of the best shortstops in all of baseball. He had picked up his second consecutive Gold Glove Award at the position, and was set to enter his fifth full season with the Tigers. He had already shown that he could be a potent two-way player, having hit .300 over the course of a full 1980 season. He was displaying improved power while developing the ability to steal a base on occasion. His scaled back offensive numbers in 1981 were largely written off due to the uneven schedule and interruption caused by the 50-day strike. A return to 1980 form was the expectation as the team landed in Kansas City to start a new season.

An embarrassing incident in a Kansas City bar, however, two nights before the season-opener, set the tone for a mostly forgettable year for Trammell. After dinner he went out with five teammates to a nightclub in Kansas City's Alameda Plaza district, where seemingly innocent horseplay resulted in Trammell being rushed to St. Luke's Hospital.

"We were standing by the railing—watching the people dance," explained Trammell. (Dave Rozema) was standing next to me, and all of a sudden he put his hand on the back of my head and went to pull it forward and down."[19] When Trammell tried to dodge the maneuver, he banged his head on a drinking glass, resulting in a three-inch gash just above his left eyebrow and in close proximity to his left eye. "I think I probably ducked my head down after he started pushing on it."[20]

The cut resulted in 40 stitches, twenty on the surface and twenty below the skin. It also infuriated the Detroit manager counting down the hours until the season opener. "I guess he was more disappointed than anything else," said Trammell of a closed door session between Anderson, Rozema, and himself. "I guess we've got to put a stop to it."[21]

The incident was the second of the spring involving Rozema, who seemed to be in the thick of most of the mischievous stories during that period. He had been victimized himself earlier that spring when he went to sit down in a bar, only to have a teammate pull the chair out from under him. When Rozema hit the floor it shattered a flask he had put in his back pocket, resulting in cuts that required a dozen stiches on his buttocks.

Although the cuts suffered in the Kansas City nightclub had no lingering effects, Trammell got off to the slowest start of his career. He struggled at the plate from the very beginning, barely staying above the .200 mark for most of the first half of the season. One of the few highlights from the early months came when he hit the first grand slam home run of his career. It came in the second inning of a May 16 game in Tiger Stadium off of Minnesota left-hander, Brad Havens. The slam cut into an early 5–0 Detroit deficit and was the game-changing moment in what eventually turned into a 7–6 Tiger victory.

The win against Minnesota became the type of occurrence that was happening with regularity in Detroit that spring. They put together seven- and eight-game winning streaks in the season's first two months, eventually building their record to 35–18 by June 9. A double-header sweep that day against Cleveland pushed them into a virtual tie with Boston for the best record in the majors, seven games ahead of the rest of the teams in the division.

Anderson's young team was maturing, with many of the "kids" that had come up through the system in the late 1970s now developing into experienced big league players. Despite his difficulties at the plate, Trammell—now 24—was playing as dependably as ever in the field, going the first 35 games of the season without an error. Whitaker was off to a solid start at the plate, after having suffered through two off-years with the bat. Parrish had developed into one of the premiere two-way catchers in the game and would hit 32-home runs in 1982, settling into his regular spot as the cleanup hitter in the Tiger lineup. Morris and Petry had formed a formidable pairing as the 1–2 kingpins at the top of Detroit's pitching rotation, logging over 500 innings that season between them.

Off-season shakeups had changed the makeup of Detroit's roster, giving it more of a National League feel. Kemp had been traded in the off-season to the Chicago White Sox in a straight-up swap for outfielder Chet Lemon. The trade of Kemp had a two-fold purpose: First, it shed the Detroit organization of a player that was becoming increasingly difficult to control financially. Kemp had developed a pattern in his short career of being difficult to sign each season, having taken the club to salary arbitration twice already. With free agency looming in the not-too-distant future for the five-year player, the Tiger front office jettisoned him for the better all-around player in Lemon, who eventually became Detroit's every day centerfielder.

The trade of Kemp also helped free the Tigers from the vulnerability they had developed over recent seasons of having a very set and rigid lineup of predominantly left-handed hitters, something Anderson had tried to change since inheriting the club in 1979. In addition to the right-handed hitting Lemon, Detroit had added Larry Herndon, a tall, rangy right-handed hitter who came over from the San Francisco Giants to play leftfield, and a jack-of-all-trades National League veteran, Enos Cabell, that split time playing first and third base. The three new arrivals provided Anderson with the type of two-way players he coveted, players that could win a game with their bat, glove, or with their legs—qualities that had been in short supply otherwise on the Tigers' roster.

The good times that spring didn't last however. As had become customary in Detroit during those early years under Sparky Anderson, the team had a penchant for streaks, both winning and losing. Three days after the June 9 doubleheader sweep of Cleveland, the Tigers lost the first of what would turn into a ten-game losing streak, kicking off a three-week stretch that would see them drop fifteen of seventeen games, all within the division. The slide continued into the next month until after losing the first game of a doubleheader at Texas on July 10, Detroit had fallen all the way back to the .500 mark.

It was another stunning reversal for a team that couldn't seem to shake their Jekyll-Hyde persona. The Tigers could never regain the momentum they had established while racing out to the best record in baseball at the one-third mark in 1982, and spent the remainder of the schedule finishing out a disappointing 83–79 campaign, ending up twelve games behind the World Series-bound Milwaukee Brewers.

For Trammell, the season proved to be a mixed bag. After struggling horribly at the plate over the season's first half, resting at .205 at the All Star break, he rediscovered his offensive prowess over the final two and a half months. Banished to the ninth position in the batting order for most of the year, Trammell quietly hit .310 over the second half of the schedule, raising his final overall batting average to .258. Later in his career, he would look back at that second half of 1982 as a turning point of sorts. "Things were looking down, and I wasn't handling it very well," he said about his struggles at the plate that year. "I just couldn't get out of the bad groove. I overcomplicated things, trying to get two or three hits a night to get my average back up."[22]

Instead he broke down his goal into bite-sized chunks, and set as goals to raise his average ten points at a time. "That was the biggest point in my career, right there. I could have been buried if I hadn't come out of it. The team stuck with me, and I fought out of it, and it made me a better ballplayer."[23]

While his final mark was mediocre overall, the second half surge had re-established his personal momentum at the plate. There were other signs of progress that year as well. He set a career-high with 34 doubles and tied his career high to that point in home runs with nine, which included a second grand slam on July 30 against Jim Clancy in Toronto. Trammell knocked in 57 runs, a very respectable total from the number nine slot, stole 19 bases, and played in what would be his career high in games played at 157.

Now five full seasons into a major league career, Trammell had established himself as a Gold Glove-caliber shortstop defensively, and a productive, and at times very potent, offensive player at the plate and on the base paths. Questions remained, however, as to whether Trammell was truly the

.300 caliber hitter of 1980, or the .258 hitter of the previous two seasons. He would be 25 years old by the time the 1983 season started, and it was time to turn his game up another notch. It was also time to win for he and a band of teammates that outside of an artificially-induced chase for a second-half divisional title in 1981, had never seriously competed on a season-long basis in baseball's toughest division at that time. Sparky Anderson had promised a pennant within five years. Time was starting to run short on that promise. For Anderson, Trammell, and the rest of the Detroit Tigers, the time to deliver was drawing near.

5

Breakthrough

The Detroit Tigers entered the 1983 season ready to win. It was time for a roster chock full of talent to end the teases that had accompanied campaigns for the past half-decade and begin to win with the consistency required to compete in baseball's toughest division. Sparky Anderson had three-and-a-half years to tinker with the roster and mold the young talent he had inherited. In addition, the timing appeared to be right for a team to make a move in an American League that was going through a bit of transition. The New York Yankees and Boston Red Sox, while still formidable, were no longer the ogres that had dominated the AL East in the late 1970s. The Milwaukee Brewers had outlasted the Baltimore Orioles the previous season for the division title and an eventual pennant, mostly by bludgeoning their opponents with a terrifying offensive attack. But Milwaukee's mediocre pitching staff, and questions about their veteran everyday players being able to repeat the career years they had in 1982, left many doubting their reign would be long-lasting, and created a sense of vulnerability towards them.

The 1983 season's first two months did nothing to indicate the Tigers were going to be any more competitive at year's end than they had been in the years just past. They came out of the gates firing both barrels when they scored six runs in the very first inning of the season opener in Minnesota's Metrodome, eventually routing the Twins, 11–3. Ten days later, Milt Wilcox reached for baseball immortality when he retired the first 26 Chicago White Sox in order, before serving up a pinch-hit single to Jerry Hairston, breaking up his bid for a perfect game. But despite the early heroics, Detroit had mostly alternated short winning and losing streaks and found themselves in sixth place, one game below .500 as the calendar flipped to June.

For Alan Trammell the season had progressed in much the same nondescript way. He was playing as well as ever defensively, but even though he had started strong with three hits in the opening game against the Twins, he entered June batting just .252 with only one home run and sixteen RBI's.

5. Breakthrough

It was at this time, however, that the team and Trammell both went on torrid hot streaks. By June 10 Detroit had built up their record to 30–25, while their shortstop had increased his batting average to .272. A week later the team was eight games over .500, trailing only the Orioles by one-and-a-half games in the AL East, while Trammell had nudged his average a few points higher to .278.

The positive vibes were quickly halted though, when on June 17 in a game against the Cleveland Indians, Trammell felt pain in his right forearm after making a slightly off-balance throw to first base. "I didn't set myself properly," he said a couple of days later when asked about the injury. "I didn't drive with my legs the way you're supposed to. I knew I pulled something, but I didn't hear a pop."[1]

The immediate diagnosis was a strained tendon in his right arm, which was expected to keep him out of action for only a couple of days. However, as the days passed and a key early-season series in Baltimore loomed against the first place Orioles, Trammell was still unable to shake the pain that persisted in his throwing arm. "All I know is I can't throw more than forty feet yet," he said, frustration mounting in his voice.[2] The Detroit organization was not without concern as it impacted both their short-term prospects in what was developing into a very nice season for the ball club, but also towards the long-term investment they had tied up in the 25-year-old shortstop. The heartbreak over the career-ending arm miseries suffered by Mark Fidrych was still fresh in the minds of the Tiger front office. Trammell would be out of action for some time.

The injury to Trammell deprived Detroit of the glue to its infield, while also taking away a key cog in its offensive attack. While he alternately rested and rehabbed his right arm, Trammell watched from the dugout as the Tigers continued their winning ways, going 18–10 for the month of June. For the first time in his career, Trammell's name would be absent from the lineup card for an extended period, yet that didn't diminish his value to a team that was coming together.

He was extremely popular among his teammates, often finding himself in the midst of the banter and humor associated with a collection of rambunctious young men, most still in their twenties. He blended easily in all circles of the team, whether it was with the high-strung and sometimes moody Jack Morris or Kirk Gibson, the more carefree and prankster types like Dave Rozema, or the supremely talented, but quieter types like Lou Whitaker or Lance Parrish. He was the team authority on all matters related to the sports page. He religiously read *Baseball America*, *The Sporting News*, and *Sports Illustrated*, and was a knowledgeable reservoir of statistics from baseball's past and present, and for most other sports as well. He flashed his Southern California roots as an unabashed Los Angeles Lakers' fan, his basketball yearnings still running strong.[3]

"Trammell is a sports junkie," Parrish would say about a teammate he spent nine full seasons in the major leagues with. "And not just baseball, any sport. Baseball, football, basketball, hockey—he follows them all. I think he knows every college basketball team in existence, their nicknames, their colors, who coaches them, who plays for them, when they won this, when they won that. It's unbelievable."[4]

Trammell's affinity for being the life of the clubhouse got him in trouble that season when the Tiger players' judicial system took notice. The team had instituted a Kangaroo Court, a practice that has been part of baseball clubhouse culture for decades. The players set their own rules and then hold occasional mock court sessions, where fines are levied for both on-field and off-field violations. Typically, the mock hearings are used as an opportunity to dole out good-natured ribbing to a teammate. Fines could be doled out for infringements ranging anywhere from an on-field transgression such as missing a sign or failing to score a runner from third base with less than two outs, to more subjective grievances like sporting a bad haircut or playing unpopular music in the clubhouse. Oftentimes late in the season, the money collected in fines is pooled and the players hold a big party.

With his teammates serving as jury and the honorable John Wockenfuss presiding over court, Trammell was found guilty as charged. "Alan Trammell, he got fined for too much talking," said the veteran first baseman, Enos Cabell. "We'd hold our meetings and he'd never shut up. We'd fine him for contempt of court, but he kept on talking."

"He's always talking," said Morris about Trammell. "He's like a kid on the sandlots. He loves the game. He's a gamer in the true sense of the word. He wants to go out there and get dirty and have some fun. He's pleasant to be around because he jokes a lot and keeps you loose. He's also the butt of a lot of jokes, but he can take it. You need guys who can take it. He's definitely one of them."[5]

The ability to take it made Trammell a natural target for one of the club's longer-running gags. While his teammates marveled at the soft and sure hands he displayed while playing shortstop, it was a different story around post-game clubhouse spreads, the hotel coffee shop, or any of the other eating establishments scattered around the American League circuit. He tended to spill things, whether on the table, himself, or an innocent bystander. It was a trait that didn't go unnoticed in the no-holds barred culture of a professional sports team's clubhouse sanctuary.

"He's the world's worst eater," teased the veteran Cabell. "You better sit on his left side or else he'll spill on you."⁶ Catcher-third baseman Marty Castillo added, "If it's not a baseball, Alan drops it. I usually put plastic on the floor around Trammell's locker when he eats. I don't see how he gets nourishment. Nothing reaches his stomach."⁷ The good humored Tom Brookens stated that his partner on the left side of the infield should "Scotchgard all his pants."⁸

Trammell accepted the ribbing by admitting, "I've got no explanation for it. On the baseball field I've got good hands, but at the dinner table I tend to spill things."⁹

His ailing arm caused him to be out of the lineup for more than three weeks, the longest such stretch he had endured since turning professional seven years earlier. His status was listed as "day-to-day" during that time, as team physicians struggled to pinpoint a precise remedy or timeframe for his return. In past seasons, an injury to Detroit's regular shortstop might have triggered an extended losing streak—the type that could doom an entire campaign. But in 1983 the Tigers treaded water for the 23 days that Trammell was unable to play in the field, going 8–9 during that stretch, keeping their season alive.

Finally, he regained enough of his arm strength and was cleared to play, though the pain still persisted. His first appearance was a ninth-inning pinch-hitting assignment on July 10 against Oakland at Tiger Stadium. Trailing 3–0, he led off the bottom of the inning against right-hander Chris Codiroli, who had two-hit Detroit up to that point. Trammell drew a walk before coming around to score on singles by Whitaker and Larry Herndon. Moments later he watched as Parrish blasted a game-ending, walk-off grand slam home run off of A's reliever (and future Tiger's pitching coach), Jeff Jones. "I didn't have to swing, but at least I got something started," Trammell said about his first appearance at the plate in more than three weeks; one that had ignited the five-run rally.¹⁰

He returned to the lineup at shortstop the next evening, getting two hits and scoring a run in a 12–6 drubbing of the California Angels. More importantly, the arm held up allowing him to make the necessary plays in the field, where he recorded six assists and was part of two double-plays. "It hurt," he said afterwards. "I can't pretend it didn't. But the pain never lasted more than 30 seconds, so that was a good sign. I'm going to play with some aches for a while and hope the arm gets stronger. But I had to get back in there. This is too much fun to miss."¹¹

The fun Trammell was referring to was the roll that he and his teammates were on as they closed in on the 100-game mark of the schedule. They had put together a blistering 18–8 mark in June and were now tearing through July as well. In the weeks following the All Star break, Trammell ignited the team even more as they won 16 of 22 games to close out the month, feasting on weaker AL West competition. Trammell picked up where he left off at the plate prior to the injury, batting .406 during that streak while scoring 17 runs.

Trammell's personal hot streak could be attributed at least in part to an adjustment in his batting stance that had been suggested earlier in the season by Tiger batting coach, Gates Brown. Brown believed that Trammell had a tendency to pull off the ball, which caused him to move his head before making contact. To counter that habit, he had his pupil further close up what was already a pronounced closed stance. Trammell's front (left) foot was now much nearer to the plate, his left shoulder tucked under his chin, hands back. The new stance conquered his propensity for opening up his shoulder too early in the swing, oftentimes taking his head with it. He was now able to better track pitches on the outward part of the plate, while his lightning quick hands allowed him to turn with authority on inside pitches.

"Just the slightest movement of the head messes you up when the ball's coming in at 90 miles an hour," explained Trammell of his newfound success with the changed stance. "The better you see the ball, the better you're going to hit it. I can still pull the inside pitch, but I can hit the outside pitch to right."[12]

He made his debut with the new stance in a July 24 game in Anaheim against the Angels. He went 5–5 that day with a walk. Four of the five hits were to right field. The five-hit day pushed his batting average above .300, where he would remain for all but one day the rest of the season.

Detroit began August 17 games over .500, the best win-loss differential they had attained at that point of the season in more than a decade, and trailed first-place Baltimore by only one game. They were in the process of bridging the chasm that exists between a young team with talent and potential, and a team in its prime and ready to win. Morris was enjoying a spectacular year in which he would win twenty games, including ten-straight victories during one stretch, while leading the league in strikeouts and innings pitched. His sidekick, Dan Petry, would win nineteen games himself, giving the Tigers one of the best top-of-their-rotation combinations in the game. Herndon and Cabell were both on their way to .300 seasons at the plate. Herndon was enjoying his second consecutive big year for Detroit where he had averaged over .290 with 20-plus homers and 90 RBIs. Gibson was playing through his first full injury-free season after three seasons where varying afflictions had plagued his development to that point. Outfielder Glenn Wilson, catcher/first baseman/DH John Wockenfuss, first baseman/outfielder Rick Leach, and outfielder John Grubb all played important roles, and made key contributions throughout the season.

Detroit's strength, however, was the tremendous up-the-middle personnel Sparky Anderson was able to write into his lineup most days. Parrish, by now, had established himself as the best catcher in the American League, if not all of baseball. Defensively, he had smoothed out the rough edges that characterized his first few years in the majors, and his rifle-arm was an intimidating deterrent to would-be base stealers around the league. Offensively, he was on his way to a 27 home run, 114 RBI campaign that confirmed him as one of the top cleanup hitters in the game. Centerfielder Chet Lemon had blossomed into one of the premier ball-hawks to ever play in spacious Tiger Stadium, where the center field fence sat some 440 feet from home plate. His ability to run down balls hit into the gaps or over his head prevented countless numbers of extra-base hits against Tiger pitchers. While his offensive game was inconsistent at times, Lemon did provide a source of power (24 home runs) in the lower portion of the batting order, with many of his homers being of the clutch variety.

Trammell displays the athleticism that made him a standout high school basketball player as he completes a double-play against the White Sox in Chicago's Comiskey Park during the 1983 season. Whitaker watches in the background as Chicago's Rudy Law is too late to break up the double-play attempt (National Baseball Hall of Fame Library, Cooperstown, New York).

The middle of the diamond belonged to the now well-established combination of Trammell and Whitaker. They were in their sixth season together in the majors, seventh overall, and were already being touted as one of the great double-play combos in recent generations. Individually, they both possessed consistency, range, and the ability to make the difficult play seem easy. Collectively, they played off each other, anticipating the other's movements, knowing just where to deliver the ball in order to turn over the exchange at second base. Time and again the double-play ball bailed Detroit pitchers out of a tough situation.

While the two had always been linked as a defensive pairing, Trammell and Whitaker were now exploding as an offensive duo. After winning the league's Rookie of the Year award in 1978, Whitaker had enjoyed a solid second season before tailing off badly in 1980. Pitchers had learned to pitch away from the left-handed hitting Whitaker, who continually slapped weak fly balls into the teeth of defensive alignments that were playing him shallow and to left field. Gradually adjusting his approach at the plate, he improved his batting average from .233 in 1980 to .263 in 1981, and back to .286 in 1982. Working closely with his pal, Gates Brown, Whitaker learned to pull the ball with authority, as his fifteen home runs in 1982 attested.

An eighteen-game hitting streak in June lifted Whitaker well above the .300 mark at the plate. When Trammell continued his amazing hot streak into August, Anderson elevated him from the number nine position he had hit in for most of the season, to the number two slot right behind his sidekick, Whitaker. Detroit now had multi-dimensional players in the first two spots in the batting order. Both were hitting over .320, could draw walks, hit with occasional power, and were excellent base runners. From August 1983 through the next three seasons—they formed one of the most lethal top-of-the-order combinations in the game.

"The advantage to hitting second is that Lou's on base so much," said Trammell. "And it seems when a guy's on base, it's contagious. You just want to do it too. You can't help but get a few hits."[13]

"They never thought we'd do much as hitters," explained Whitaker. "I don't think anybody expected anything out of us except defense.[14] "We wanted to prove these people wrong," added Trammell. "I don't think we're going to hit .240 anymore."[15]

Trammell explained how his maturation at the plate lended itself to being the all-around player he always thought he was capable of being; one that could contribute to a win in many different facets of the game. "I don't want to settle for that," he said about being labeled as an all-glove, no-bat shortstop. "I figure one time during a game, offensively or defensively, I can do something that helps win the game."[16]

5. Breakthrough

By the middle of August, the American League East had evolved into a five-team dogfight with Detroit, Baltimore, New York, Toronto, and Milwaukee all vying to take control of the division. Each game had added meaning, but head-to-head contests against the other contenders took on particular importance. One such game took place on August 12 in Detroit when the Tigers were taking on the Yankees. The two teams were separated by only a half-game at the time, just barely trailing the first place Brewers. The Yankees had taken two of three games in New York just the week before, beating Detroit quite badly in a couple of the contests. Now back in Tiger Stadium, the two teams had opened a four-game series, with the Yankees taking a hard-fought series opener, 6–5 in ten innings.

The second game saw New York jump out to a quick 1–0 lead on a Dave Winfield home run in the first inning. That slim lead was still on the board when Trammell drilled a Matt Keough pitch in the third inning for a three-run home run, giving the Tigers the lead. That lead held until the sixth inning when Winfield hit his second round-tripper of the game, putting the Yankees back in front 4–3. The two teams were tied 5–5 heading into the eighth inning, when New York's Willie Randolph reached base on a rare error committed by Trammell. Two batters later, Tiger killer Dave Winfield (he also hit the tenth-inning game-winning home run the night before) made Detroit pay for the miscue, by doubling in Randolph with the lead run. The 6–5 New York lead held into the bottom of the ninth inning. A leadoff walk gave momentary hope to the 44,565 fans in attendance, but that was quickly dashed when Whitaker hit into a double-play.

With two outs and nobody on base, Detroit was in danger of dropping the first two games of the home series to a dreaded-rival. It was the type of sequence that could send a contending team into a tailspin that might be difficult to recover from. In stepped Trammell against Yankee relief pitcher Dale Murray, who had made 76 relief appearances for Sparky Anderson when he played for the Cincinnati Reds. Trammell was just trying to reach base, with Gibson on-deck, and Parrish hitting behind him. Instead, he hit a drive that carried to the left field wall. Winfield, all six-foot, six-inches of him, braced at the base of the nine-foot fence and then sprang as high as he could, reaching for the ball. The ball carried just over the screen and into the first rows of seats in left field for a game-tying home run. When Herndon singled in Parrish an inning later, the Tigers had pulled off an improbable 7–6 victory.

The game was Trammell's first two-homer performance of his career. More importantly, his ninth-inning heroics served as a potential season-changing moment. It symbolized the type of effort that Anderson had preached since arriving; play all 27 outs and then let the chips fall where they may.

"I had ended the game last night, and you ask any ballplayer, you never want to make the last out of a game," said a charged-up Trammell afterwards. "This time, I just wanted to hit the ball hard and get on base. I wasn't trying to get the ball out of the ballpark, not at all."

"But he gave me a sinker down here and that's my zone," explained the Detroit shortstop, gesturing to indicate a thigh-level pitch. "That's where I can get a little lift."[17]

Two weeks later he pulled off a similar feat, when he crashed a tenth inning home run against the Blue Jays in the first game of a weekend series in Detroit, giving the Tigers a 4–3 victory. The home run was his 11th of the season, marking his career high with still more than a month to play. "I have no way to explain it," said Trammell about his home run surge. "I guess when you're seeing the ball well and hitting the ball hard, those things just happen."[18]

Actually the increase in power was quite explainable. Trammell had lifted weights seriously for the first time the previous winter, following a rigorous four-month program.[19] Combined with the physical maturation that was naturally taking place in a player approaching his 26th birthday, his playing weight had increased to 185 pounds, up considerably from his early days in a Tiger uniform where he might have been hard-pressed to match his listed weight of 165 pounds. The Detroit shortstop was no longer the meek, slap-happy, singles-hitter he had been in his first couple of seasons. He was now a threat that could punish opponents for a poorly thrown pitch.

"He's probably just gotten stronger," said rival shortstop Robin Yount of the Milwaukee Brewers, who had gone through a similar transformation after reaching the big leagues himself as an 18-year-old. "That really helped me out—I got older and stronger."[20]

"They're both getting stronger," said Anderson. "Trammell and Whitaker, with their bodies, they should play till they're 37, 38."[21]

"You've got to know your limitations," explained Trammell about his home run prowess. "I know I'm not going to hit thirty home runs a season. But I can hit double figures, ten or 15, and that's good enough."[22]

After struggling through a difficult schedule in August, the Tigers were still 17 games over .500 and only four games behind the hard-charging Orioles as the final month began. They went 10–5 over the first half of September, but still lost ground to Baltimore who was winning at a .650 clip over the second half of the season. As the days grew short, the Tigers showed a steely resolve to battle to the finish, establishing themselves as one of the better teams in either league.

"They're not sure what's going to happen in these final weeks of the season and they're trying to figure out how to handle the pressure," stated the ten-year veteran, Cabell, who had been through pennant races previously with Baltimore and Houston. "They've started watching the scoreboard. You can see them all taking peeks up there. That's OK. It's scoreboard season. It's working all right for us because you can see them bearing down even more if a certain team is winning up on the board. They don't want to fall out of the race."[23]

While Parrish, Herndon, Lemon, Morris, and Petry were all enjoying banner years for Detroit, it was obvious to Cabell that the catalysts for the team, both offensively and defensively, were the two guys surrounding second base and hitting one-two in the batting order. "Those two guys are leading this team," he said. "Whitaker carried the club through the first half of the season, and now Trammell is doing it. Alan is doing things nobody thought possible from him. They're the main men."[24]

With two weeks left on the schedule, the Tigers entered a stretch where they would play Baltimore seven times in a ten-day span. The Orioles had pulled away from the rest of the pack and now led second-place Detroit by seven full games. The Tigers were in a last-gasp effort mode, needing to win at least six, if not all seven, of the head-to-head meetings in order to have any chance of overtaking Baltimore. Detroit made it clear that they would not roll over for the Orioles as they sent 16 batters to the plate in the bottom of the first inning, scoring 11 runs on 11 hits—on their way to a 14–1 romp in the first game of that stretch.

"It was contagious," said Trammell who had two hits and scored a pair of runs in the first-inning bludgeoning. "Everyone wanted to be a part of it. But I know the Orioles are going to forget about it and we better too. It won't be remembered if we lose the next three."[25]

Any illusions the Tiger Stadium faithful might have formed regarding a miraculous late-season collapse by Baltimore were quickly dispelled the next evening. Eddie Murray, the Orioles hard-hitting first baseman and cleanup batter, set the tone early in the first game of a doubleheader by launching a towering drive off of the third deck in right field. It would be the first of three home runs the Orioles would hit off of Morris in a 6–0 thrashing of the Tigers. Mike Boddicker struck out 12 while going the distance for the shutout.

The second game was even more sobering as Detroit carried a 3–1 lead into the ninth inning, only to have Baltimore explode for six runs in the top of the inning. The big blow was a grand slam home run by John Lowenstein. The 7–3 loss in game two, and doubleheader sweep on the night, effectively ended any post-season hopes the Tigers might have harbored.

The dynastic Orioles were on the verge of their seventh title since the inception of divisional play some fifteen years earlier. While the players had changed over the span of that time (pitcher Jim Palmer was the only Baltimore player on all seven of those division-winning teams), their style of play had remained largely the same. Solid starting pitching and teams built with solid role players around a small core of superstars typified Oriole clubs. Mike Boddicker, Scott McGregor, Storm Davis, Dennis Martinez, and Mike Flanagan held up the tradition of strong Oriole rotations. Eddie Murray and second-year shortstop, Cal Ripken, Jr., were the outstanding constants in a lineup that manager Joe Altobelli surrounded with exceptionally strong platoon players.

Even though the race officially ended just days later, Detroit was determined to finish strong, and won six of ten to end the season, including three straight in Baltimore. When the dust settled in the hotly-contested American League East that year, Baltimore was on top at 98–64, with Detroit finishing second with a 92–70 mark, one game ahead of New York, three games ahead of Toronto, and five games ahead of Milwaukee. Several of the Orioles left little doubt as to the club they had feared the most in September's stretch-run.

"Detroit," said Baltimore lefty, Mike Flanagan. "Because they beat us this year (5–8 record head-to-head against the Tigers), and because we're predominantly a right-hand hitting club and they're predominantly right-handed pitchers."[26]

"Detroit most of the way," stated Oriole outfielder/DH, Ken Singleton. "That's who had us worried. With those two good starters, Petry and Morris, they were going to avoid any losing streaks."[27]

The Tigers' 92 wins were third most in the major leagues that season and the franchise's highest total since their World Championship season of 1968. Each player walked away with a little more than $3,000 for finishing second in the division, along with a sharpened commitment towards their future. "This leaves us a little hungry," said their manager, Sparky Anderson, after the final game. "Overall, it was a satisfying year, but there are things we have to improve."[28]

One area that wouldn't need a lot of improvement was the keystone combination of Trammell and Whitaker. Trammell enjoyed his best season yet, being recognized for his third Gold Glove award after missing out in 1982. At the plate he batted a robust .319, fourth best in the American League, but the highest average by any right-handed hitter in the circuit that season. He set career highs in home runs (14) and RBI's (66), while accumulating impressive totals of 31 doubles and 83 runs scored. He led the AL in sacrifice bunts with 15, the second time in three years he had done so. Trammell also stole a career-high 30 bases (out of 40 attempts), as Anderson complemented his shortstop's outstanding .385 on-base percentage with an aggressive running game. Whitaker had an equally outstanding season, batting .320 with 12 homers while hitting in the leadoff position, and scored 94 runs. He also won a Gold Glove at second base, the first of three-straight years he would claim the award. Together they formed the backbone of a Detroit team just entering its prime, providing defensive excellence in the middle of the diamond, while also making up the premier one-two combination at the top of any lineup in the major leagues. The impact that Trammell and Whitaker had on the fortunes of the Tigers was appreciated by the Baseball Writers Association of America when the American League MVP voting was announced that fall. Whitaker finished eighth in the voting, while his sidekick Trammell finished just seven spots behind in 15th place.

The duo was a hot commodity off the field as well, illustrated by their cameo appearance in the December 1 broadcast of the CBS hit-television show, Magnum, P.I. The primary character of the series, Thomas Magnum, played by actor Tom Selleck, is a Hawaiian-based private detective typically adorned in Hawaiian shirts and a Detroit Tigers' cap, honoring the fictional character's home town. In the episode titled "A Sense of Debt," Magnum is back in Detroit, sitting at a bar stool, lamenting to the bartender that he has been in the city for ten days, but without any time to attend one of his beloved Tigers' games. Standing at the bar next to him is a pair of youthful men in sports coats and open-collared shirts, feigning interest in the troubles of the beleaguered series star. As the two finish their drinks, they tell Magnum that they have "been to every game" and hand over "their business cards" which are a pair of tickets to the final game of the home stand. When Magnum realizes that they have given him prime box seats, he excitedly starts to question them but is puzzled by the young men's comments upon leaving that they "will be between first and third" the next afternoon. As he turns back to the bartender, Magnum is directed to a couple of framed autographed photos behind the bar of the star Tiger middle-infielders—the same faces that had just exited the scene.

The 90-second guest spot for Trammell and Whitaker on the top-five rated show on television at that time was indicative of the momentum that the Detroit Tiger brand was generating as 1983 was drawing to a close. Aided by Selleck's affinity for wearing Detroit's classic ball cap with the Old English "D," Tiger merchandise had climbed in sales to the point that it ranked among the most popular in all of baseball. Sparky Anderson, as he always had been, was a lightning-rod for media attention and publicity, as well. Working as a radio color commentator during the post-season, he had repeatedly been asked by baseball pundits from all across the country about his exciting young team. Detroit's on-field performance that season and the plethora of young talent that was coming into its own, generated buzz and made them a sexy pick for even bigger things in 1984. Having proven that they could compete well into September with the eventual World Series Champion Baltimore Orioles, and with a galvanized determination to control their own destiny in the future, Alan Trammell, Lou Whitaker, and the rest of the Detroit Tigers were about to make their dream a reality.

6

"Bless You Boys"

A quiet confidence permeated the Detroit Tigers organization leading into the 1984 season. A 92-win campaign the previous summer had served witness to breakthroughs for many of the players individually, but more importantly, collectively. They had learned how to win in the ultra-competitive American League East, easily the toughest grouping in baseball. With the experience they had gained, and the confidence they now effused, the organization was ready to take the next step and claim the division as theirs.

The off-season had been eventful, more so perhaps than any off-season the organization had experienced in decades. In a realignment of the front office, Jim Campbell had been promoted to chief executive office for the Tigers, with long-time scout and front office executive, Bill Lajoie, becoming the new general manager. Lajoie quickly enamored himself with Detroit fans when he aggressively pursued and signed free agent Darrell Evans to a three-year, $2.25 million contract. Evans represented another breakthrough of sorts for the organization, as the Tigers' first foray into the world of high-stakes free agency signings. By inking the 36-year-old National League slugger, Detroit had added an experienced left-handed bat that would give some much needed power to the corner-infield positions. The hope was that Evans would provide the Tigers with the final ingredient needed to shape a very formidable lineup.

Perhaps the most shocking news, though, came in early October when it was announced that the franchise was being sold by long-time owner John Fetzer. The 81-year-old Fetzer had owned the Tigers for more than a quarter century, and with his long-trusted baseball executive, Jim Campbell, they had set the tone for what had been a very well-run, but conservative franchise over that period. Feeling that the time and suitor was right, a series of clandestine meetings took place during the summer of 1983 to discuss the sale of the ballclub. The new owner would be 47-year-old Domino's pizza mogul, Tom Monaghan, who had built a fortune with his fast food franchises worldwide. And while Fetzer had rarely set foot in the domain of on-field personnel, and deferred all baseball-related matters to Campbell, Monaghan immediately showed that he would be a much more visible owner in Detroit. In the press conference announcing his acquisition of the Tigers, the obviously elated new owner was asked if there was anybody in the world he would want to trade places with. "Yes," he replied quickly. "I would gladly trade places with Alan Trammell."[1]

What the Tigers' wannabe shortstop/new owner didn't know, however, was that some 2,300 miles away, Detroit's regular shortstop was suffering the scare of his professional-baseball life; a scare that could jeopardize what was shaping up as a potentially memorable season for the ball club.

A seemingly innocent Halloween costume had been the cause of many anxious moments during the late fall and early winter months of 1983 and 1984. Trammell had borrowed a Frankenstein costume to wear to a party he was attending with his wife Barbara, who was dressing as the monster's bride. The Frankenstein guise came complete with army boots that had blocks attached to the bottoms, increasing Trammell's overall height to nearly seven feet. During a dress-rehearsal he stepped outside his house to pose for pictures, but soon lost his balance and fell awkwardly into the surrounding shrubs. The seemingly innocent mishap didn't seem troublesome at the time, but Trammell soon noticed that his left knee was starting to bother him. "I felt the knee stretch, but I didn't really think I had hurt it bad," he later said about the incident.[2]

As he pushed himself through off-season workouts at San Diego's Jack Murphy Stadium, however, he became alarmed that the knee was still bothering him weeks later. "My knee was catching on me," Trammell finally reported to Padres trainer Dick Dent.[3] After an examination it was discovered that there was cartilage damage, a potentially very serious injury by 1983 orthopedic standards. Trammell underwent arthroscopic surgery late in November, a little more than ninety days from the opening of spring training in Lakeland. He faced a winter of uncertainty, including seven weeks with the knee in a brace and rehabilitation to follow. "I was scared," he admitted later. "Being in a brace was playing mind games with me. I'd never had an injury like that before."[4]

News of the injury was kept under wraps from the media and only slowly leaked out with sketchy detail to the general public. Nervous optimism held in check fears over what could have been a devastating blow to Detroit's fortunes for the upcoming season. "I didn't want to announce I had gotten hurt doing something stupid," Trammell said. Fortunately, the cartilage didn't have to be removed and was instead repaired, allowing for a more speedy recovery. As soon as doctors cleared him to do so, Trammell attacked his rehabilitation with vigor, focusing on the use of weights and bicycling, before finally graduating to jogging and then running. "I had to work my butt off," he said about that period.⁵

By the time spring training opened the knee was nearly healed; a catastrophe avoided. Trammell joined a clubhouse full of determined teammates in readying for a season that they believed would belong to them. Standing in their way, however, would be powerhouse teams within their division in New York, Milwaukee, Boston, and Toronto, let alone the near consensus pick to repeat as world champions, the Baltimore Orioles. Only *Baseball Digest*, amongst major baseball publications, picked Detroit as the Eastern Division favorite in 1984 with most others picking them second or third. Even long-time Tiger radio broadcaster, Paul Carey, entering his 12th season with the club, picked them to finish in third place. Those prognostications were probable catalysts for Jack Morris' alleged tone-setting statement where he told his teammates to "F**K Baltimore." That brash display of bravado, displayed by one of the Tigers' leaders at the time, now resides in Tiger lore.

Despite a spring training record of just 11–17, the Tigers were ready to hit on all cylinders when they opened the season in Minnesota's Hubert H. Humphrey Metrodome for the second straight year. The opening game served as a microcosm for the season to come, as Detroit rolled to an easy 8–1 victory over the hapless Twins. Trammell and Whitaker combined for four hits and scored five runs, picking up where they had left off the previous season. Evans, who had struggled through a miserable March in Florida, hit a three-run homer that broke the game open in the seventh inning. Morris was dominant in seven innings of work on the mound, and then the bullpen tandem of Aurelio Lopez (eighth inning) and Willie Hernandez (ninth inning) closed out the game with perfect innings of relief.

Hernandez had been picked up only ten days earlier as the central piece in a somewhat surprising trade with the Philadelphia Phillies. To get him and backup first baseman Dave Bergman, the Tigers traded two home-grown favorites in long-time catcher/DH John Wockenfuss and outfielder Glenn Wilson. The trade appeared to give Detroit a quality left-handed reliever and added depth to an otherwise suspect bullpen. Hernandez had good, but not great, numbers the previous season with Philadelphia, which included seven saves and a 3.28 ERA. What the Tigers couldn't have envisioned, is that the 29-year-old rubber-armed pitcher with the good fastball and sharp-breaking screwball was about to come into his own and become the most dominant relief specialist in the majors that season.

More than two weeks into the season, the Tigers were still undefeated, not letting an unusually wet and frigid April filled with numerous postponements, dampen their hot start. It was the beginning of a 200-day journey filled with moments that would define an entire era of baseball in Detroit:

- April 7—Morris throws the first no-hitter by a Detroit pitcher in 26 years, winning 4–0 over defending AL West champion, Chicago, in Old Comiskey Park. The game is the inaugural *Saturday Game of the Week* on NBC for 1984 and puts the Tigers on the front-burner nationally.
- April 10—Detroit is 5–0 heading into their home opener before 51,238 giddy Tiger fans. Evans belts a three-run homer into Tiger Stadium's right field upper deck on his very first swing in his new home park, part of a four-run first inning that turns into an eventual 5–1 decision over the Texas Rangers.
- April 13—Detroit explodes for eight runs in the first inning at Fenway Park and then holds on to beat the Red Sox in their home opener, 13–9. It is the third home opener that the Tigers have spoiled as the visiting team, winning in Minnesota, Chicago, and Boston.
- April 18—The Tigers blow a 3–0 lead at home to Kansas City, but win the game in the tenth inning when 6-time Gold Glove second baseman, Frank White, commits an error on a routine ground ball with two outs.

With a perfect 9–0 start, Detroit had already built an eight-game lead over defending champion Baltimore who was off to a disastrous start to their season. The other AL East rivals were struggling in vain to keep up with the torrid pace of the front-running Tigers.

Trammell showed no ill-effects from his knee surgery and was off to a tremendous start at the plate, batting .412 with two home runs and five stolen bases over the nine-game winning streak to start the season. More importantly, he had been one of the key contributors towards Detroit's pattern of scoring runs early in games; he had scored twelve runs already and had gotten on base in every game. Positioned in the number-two slot in the batting order from game one, Trammell was off to his best start ever.

When the Tigers finally lost their first game of the year, 5–2 at home to the Royals on April 19, the club responded by winning nine of its next ten games to close out the month. Detroit had already built up a six game lead on the second-place team in the division, the Toronto Blue Jays, and was threatening to bury the rest of their competitors by Memorial Day. With an 18–2 record, the Tigers were off to a start of historic proportions. All of baseball was taking notice.

On May 1, Trammell banged out two hits, drew a walk, and scored two

By the mid-'80s, Trammell had established himself as one of the most versatile and productive offensive players in the American League, regularly batting over .300 with extra-base power. His combination of high-batting and on-base average, power, and base running ability—along with his outstanding ability as a fielder, differentiated him from most other shortstops of his era (National Baseball Hall of Fame Library, Cooperstown, New York).

runs in an 11–2 trouncing of the Boston Red Sox. It was the eighteenth consecutive game that he had gotten a hit, the longest such streak in his career. He had hits in 20 of the first 21 games of the season, collecting multiple hits in a game ten times. He scored a run in 14 of those games, while crossing the plate multiple times in seven of the contests. Trammell already had seven doubles and ten RBI's, proving that he also packed a punch as the quintessential spark in the high-flying Detroit attack. Combined with his consistently stellar defensive play, the Detroit shortstop had developed into one of the game's best two-way players.

"I don't know if Trammell is the best player in all of baseball, but I've never seen a shortstop that can do as many things as well as he does," said Sparky Anderson near the end of April. "I've never seen a more complete player."[6] Trammell's fast start resulted in his being named the American League's Player of the Month for April, having batted a league-leading .403 with a .495 on-base percentage. He was the first Tiger to have received such an honor since Ron LeFlore was named Player of the Month for May in 1976.

After they dropped consecutive games for the first time all season, during the first week of May, the Tigers reeled off seven consecutive victories as part of a streak that would see the Tigers put 16 of 17 games in the win column. It was during this latest hot streak that Trammell put his most indelible mark on any single game of the regular season. On May 8 in Kansas City, the Tigers were playing the middle game of a three-game series with the always-tough Royals. Morris was engaged in a scoreless pitching duel with KC left-hander, Bud Black, who had always been tough on Detroit batters. Batting in the bottom of the fourth inning of a scoreless game, the Royals strung together one-out singles from Hal McRae and Frank White, and then Morris walked Steve Balboni to load the bases. First-baseman Don Slaught then banged what looked like a sure base hit; a hard ground ball to the right of shortstop that barely slowed down coming off of the artificial turf of Royals Stadium. Trammell, however, got a good jump on the hard-hit ball, crossing over to his right and snagging the ball while lunging to the ground. While on his backside, he snapped a throw to Whitaker at the bag at second to force Balboni. Whitaker then fired the ball to Tiger rookie Barbaro Garbey at first base to complete a spectacular double-play to end the inning.

Trammell's heroics were far from finished though. After Kansas City scratched out single runs in the fifth and sixth innings, they led Detroit 2–0 heading into the seventh. Three straight singles scored a run for the Tigers, but with two outs and the bases loaded, they still trailed 2–1 with Trammell coming to the plate. Royals manager, Dick Howser, wasn't about to let his lead slip away at such a key juncture, and called on his ace reliever, Dan Quisenberry, to enter the contest to face Trammell.

Quisenberry was arguably the league's top relief specialist during that era, having led the American League in saves in three of the previous four seasons, including a whopping 45 in 1983. Quisenberry was a right-handed hurler that threw with a submarine-style delivery, seemingly falling sideways off of the mound towards third base; an extremely difficult matchup for a right-handed hitter like Trammell. His specialty was a sinking fastball that hitters often pounded into the turf, allowing KC's excellent defensive infielders to make plays behind him. Quisenberry also had an outstanding changeup that could be devastating at times.

After starting Trammell off with a breaking ball for strike one, Quisenberry's second pitch was a sinker that caught too much of the plate. Quisenberry later stated that he was shocked at "how loud the hit sounded" when Trammell's bat made contact.[7] The ball soared towards left field, carrying in the night air through an inward wind that had dissipated seemingly at that very instant. Seconds later the ball disappeared over the left field fence and into Detroit's bullpen for a game-changing grand slam home run, the first blow of its type that Quisenberry had ever allowed.

Morris, buoyed by Trammell's home run, retired the Royals in order over the last three innings to preserve the 5–2 win. But after the game, it was the play of the Tigers' star shortstop that everyone wanted to talk about. "A Hall of Fame double play" said one Royals player about the rally-killing play that Trammell and his keystone partner, Whitaker, made in the fourth inning.[8] Others were more inclined to bring up the game-winning blast that came just three innings later. "He hit it into North Dakota," said a stunned Quisenberry after the game. "That's a lot longer ground ball than I'm used to."[9] For his part, Trammell said he had only been trying to make solid contact and put the ball in play. "I was amazed," he said modestly of the dramatic blast off of Quisenberry. "I wasn't looking to hit the ball out of the park. You don't expect a game-winner like that off of a premier relief pitcher."[10]

"I never thought I would see a shortstop as great as Dave Concepcion," said Anderson of Cincinnati's star shortstop during the "Big Red Machine's" heyday of the 1970s. "Now I've seen one better. I think Alan Trammell may be the best player in baseball, and he's also a great person."[11]

While Anderson had a reputation for exaggerating the exploits of some players to the media, a one-man hype machine of sorts, he wasn't alone in the praise being doled out this time for one of his most prominent players. "The old timers will give me a lot of static for this," said Howser about the player that had almost single-handedly defeated his team that night with spectacular plays both at the plate and in the field. "But there are three shortstops in this league who are probably as good as any who've ever played the game—Yount, Trammell, and Ripken. And as great as Ripken was last year, this could be Trammell's year. If he doesn't get hurt, he has got a chance to be one of the greatest ever to play the position."[12]

As the month of May unfolded, the Tigers continued winning at a dizzying pace—feasting primarily on a steady diet of AL West competition. By the time they had swept the California Angels on the first leg of a west coast swing, Detroit's record had reached the astounding mark of 35 wins against only 5 losses. Theirs was the best start in baseball history. Perhaps even more incredible, they had won their first seventeen road games on the schedule, tying the major league record for consecutive road victories. They were making a mockery of the race in baseball's toughest division, leading second-place Toronto by eight and a half games before the month of June had even started. The entire country was then taking notice.

The 1984 Detroit Tigers were an almost perfect confluence of talent and experience, power and speed, pitching and defense, motivation and leadership. Anderson's club rolled through the American League that year with the deepest roster in baseball. Morris and Dan Petry again headed up the starting rotation as two of the premier right-handers in either league, winning 19 and 18 games respectively. 34-year-old Milt Wilcox harnessed a level of consistency that summer that had been missing previously. Pitching much of the campaign with a sore right shoulder, he finessed his way to 17 wins against just eight losses. Flame-throwing Juan Berenguer and soft-tossing Dave Rozema combined for 18 wins as the fourth and fifth starters in a quality rotation.

The core of the everyday lineup was highlighted once again by two-way standouts and up-the-middle defenders that were the envy of managers across the league. "I challenge you to name anyone better than Parrish, Trammell, Whitaker, and Chet Lemon," bragged Anderson about his catcher, shortstop, second baseman, and centerfielder. "Three of them are Gold Glovers, and it's a crime Lemon isn't."[13] Manning the left side of the infield that summer were third basemen Tom Brookens and Howard Johnson. First base was manned by Evans, Bergman, and rookie Barbaro Garbey, a 27-year-old Cuban that Anderson compared to the Reds' Tony Perez with his slashing hitting style and ability to drive in runs. The corner outfielders were primarily Larry Herndon, who by mid-season was splitting time in a highly-effective platoon with Ruppert Jones in left field, and Kirk Gibson who played right field.

Gibson was one of the most improved players in baseball that season, having rebounded from a disappointing 1983 campaign in which he hit only

.227 and sulked for much of the season. He came to spring training in 1984 a new player with a determined attitude. He figured out how to channel his abundant intensity and fury towards opponents, and was willing to do whatever was necessary to win games. Whether he was slashing a triple into the gap, stealing a base, terrorizing middle-infielders with a viciously hard slide, or slamming one of the 27 home runs he blasted that summer, Gibson had transformed himself into one of the most dynamic players in the league. Elevated to the third spot in the batting order behind Whitaker and Trammell, the Tigers had impact players in the top three spots in their lineup. Each of them possessed speed and power, and gave Detroit the capability to score runs in bunches.

The re-emergence of Gibson was one of the keys to the Tigers' formula for success that summer. They specialized in jumping out to leads, typically setup by Whitaker and Trammell getting on base before Gibson, Parrish, Evans and a plethora of dangerous hitters knocked runners in behind them. The starting pitching was generally strong, and at times dominant, especially at the top of the rotation with Morris and Petry. However, Anderson generally looked to get just six or seven steady innings out of his starters, especially at the back half of the rotation with Wilcox, Rozema, Berenguer, and journeyman Glen Abbott. He then turned the game over to baseball's best bullpen that year. Hernandez put together one of the greatest seasons in history by a relief pitcher, winning nine games and saving 32 others (out of 33 chances), while being seemingly untouchable to opposing hitters. Lopez saved fourteen games as the right-handed compliment to Hernandez, and put together his own remarkable season with a 10–1 win-loss record. Doug Bair, Bill Scherrer, and Sid Monge made solid contributions as well in Anderson's deep and effective bullpen, combining for nine wins and four saves.

Despite being pulled back down to Earth in a sobering three-game series sweep at the hands of the lowly Seattle Mariners, Detroit wrapped up their nine-game western swing by taking two of three games in Oakland, and entered June as one of the hottest stories in the country. They transcended the sports page, and became the target of attention as a national news story. *The CBS Morning News* and *ABC's Good Morning America* did feature stories on the team in late May. *Time Magazine* was ready to release a cover story on the team. Locally, the team captured the imagination of Tigers fans that turned out in droves at Tiger Stadium that summer, as Detroit's all-time attendance mark was well on its way to being broken. The local television broadcasts of Tiger games played to a soaring viewership and dominated the ratings against network competition on other channels. The flagship station for local Tiger broadcasts, WDIV in Detroit, captured the mood of the city and entire state that summer when it videotaped sound bites of celebrities, both local and national, spewing out the catchphrase, "Bless You Boys." A different clip was played on WDIV's newscasts after each successive win, and as the victories mounted it became the slogan of the summer. By season's end, the A-list of congratulators citing the catchy slogan even included President Reagan.

As usual, Anderson was the focus of media attention that had grown by early June to the point that Detroit's ball club had the feel of a traveling group of rock stars. One player though, seemed to be drawing the most attention, both from media as well as from peers. As the calendar flipped to June, Alan Trammell showed no sign of slowing down from what had been the fastest start in his professional career. He was leading the American League in batting at .354. He also held the league lead in doubles (15) and runs scored (41), was tied for the league lead in hits (67), while running third in on-base percentage (.433) and fourth in slugging percentage (.566). He graced the cover of the May 28 edition of *Sports Illustrated* and at the one-third mark of the American League schedule, and with his team dominating the circuit like no other club had done in recent memory, Trammell's name was being whispered as the early leader for the AL's MVP award.

"That's very premature," Trammell cautioned, trying to deflect talk at such a relatively early stage of the season. "Anytime you start popping off like that or get too high, you get burned."[14]

Much of the talk stemmed from the American League's previous two MVP selections—both shortstops on pennant-winning clubs. In 1982, Robin Yount of Milwaukee had led the league in hits and doubles while scoring over 100 runs and playing steadily at the busiest position in the field. A year later, Cal Ripken, Jr., of Baltimore played every inning of every Oriole game at shortstop, led the league in hits, runs scored, and doubles, while batting .318 with 27 home runs. Both had been irreplaceable cogs for pennant-winning clubs during their MVP campaigns, which naturally caused comparison with Trammell who was off to such a dazzling start in 1984 while the Tigers were running away from the pack in the standings. "I don't think that baseball has ever seen three shortstops that every year will be in the top ten in the MVP balloting," said Anderson, obviously beating the drum for his own candidate.[15]

In the field, Trammell was playing as spectacularly as ever—on his way to another Gold Glove, his fourth in five years. What was being most noticed about his defensive game at shortstop, was the amazing consistency he provided day after day. While he might not have been the best athlete to ever play the position, or possess the strongest arm, he was among the most reliable. He was very cerebral in studying hitters, pitching patterns, and game situations. When the ball was hit to him, he rarely made a mechanical error or failed to know where to go with the play. "If I patterned myself on any shortstops, they would be Eddie Brinkman and Mark Belanger. They both got in front of every ball, and they tried to throw accurately."[16]

In his former manager at Montgomery, Brinkman, and the long-time Orioles shortstop of the late 1960s and 1970s, Belanger, Trammell selected outstanding role models to pattern his game after. Both were fundamentally sound at the position, fielding whenever possible with two hands and throwing with an over-the-top motion that rarely lent itself to tailing, off-line throws. Similarly, Trammell came to be known for his quick release and accurate overhand throws. When combining his great physical skills with the knowledge and experience gained through seven full seasons in the major leagues, many thought Trammell was truly reaching the pinnacle of his career defensively.

"He's been with the same pitching staff for five, six years," explained Milwaukee manager, Rene Lachemann. "He knows how they're pitching. That way he can move a step or two. That improves his range."[17] Oakland manager Steve Boros, a former major league infielder himself, said about the Detroit shortstop: "He has the best fielding mechanics I've seen in 20 years."[18] Not to be outdone was Trammell's own manager who claimed "Alan is the most improved player over a five-year span that I have ever seen in baseball. I have never seen a player get stronger and stronger, better and better, and improve his mind the way Alan has done since I arrived in Detroit in 1979."[19]

As spring turned to summer, the Tigers leveled out a bit in their play and returned to the pack somewhat, with the hard-charging Blue Jays and Orioles, primarily, becoming worrisome. With the schedule returning to mostly AL East competition in June, some of the most memorable moments of the season took place:

- June 1—More than 47,000 fans pack Tiger Stadium for the highly-anticipated first meeting of the season between the Tigers and Orioles. Detroit jumps all over Baltimore starter Scott McGregor, scoring six runs in the second inning on their way to a 14–2 rout. Trammell's two-run homer in the second knocks McGregor out of the game.
- June 4—The ABC Monday Night Baseball opener is a classic as Detroit comes back from a 3–0 deficit against Toronto ace, Dave Steib. Howard Johnson ties the game with a three-run homer off of the foul pole in the seventh inning, and then Dave Bergman battles Blue Jays' reliever, Roy Lee Howell, in a thirteen pitch at-

- bat in the tenth inning, fouling off seven full-count pitches before drilling a three-run homer to win the game, 6–3.
- June 7—Newly signed outfielder, Ruppert Jones, hits a three-run homer in the sixth inning, breaking open a tight game and giving Detroit a 5–3 win and a split in the four-game series with Toronto.
- June 10—Playing in stifling 100 degree heat and high humidity in Baltimore's Memorial Stadium, the Tigers sweep a doubleheader before almost 52,000 Oriole fans, winning 10–4 and 8–0. Trammell has five hits, scores three runs, and drives in four runs on the day which knocks Baltimore to eleven games back. After the game he says, "They've got a little more to think about."[20]
- July 5—Trailing 4–1 with two outs in the ninth inning in Arlington, Texas—the Tigers explode for six runs and win 7–4 against the Rangers. Trammell ties the game with a single and then rides home on Gibson's game-winning three-run homer.

Despite the heroics, the Tigers limped into the All Star break having gone a very pedestrian 22–22 since their unbelievable 35–5 start. Though their lead was holding steady at seven games ahead of Toronto and 11 ½ games over Baltimore, Detroit hadn't played especially well in over a month. More troubling than their mediocre record during that stretch, was a series of ailments bothering several of the pitchers on the staff, as well as a troublesome shoulder injury that was affecting Trammell's ability to play in the field.

He first noticed discomfort while playing catch in front of the dugout before the June 30 game against Minnesota. What was described as pain in a spot on his shoulder, turned into a more serious problem when he altered his throwing motion to favor the shoulder.[21] The Tigers tried resting their star shortstop for a series against Chicago in early July (he served instead as the designated hitter), but when Trammell returned to the field, the pain persisted. On July 8, the last game before the All Star break against Texas, he was again forced out of the game, this time after making a relay throw which resulted in numbness in his throwing arm.

The next day, Anderson, who was in San Francisco serving as a coach for the American League squad in the All Star Game, announced that Trammell would miss the game because of the injury. The shoulder and arm ailments denied Trammell from making his second All Star Game appearance, as well as a chance to bask in recognition for his magnificent first half of the 1984 season. Even though he had placed second to the Orioles' Cal Ripken in fan voting for the starting position at shortstop, Trammell had garnered more than a million votes and was an obvious choice to be named as a reserve by AL manager, Joe Altobelli. However, instead of being showcased as one of the premier players in the American League that season, he watched in uniform as the National League took a rather non-descript 3–1 victory. The game ended up being an ugly display with a combined 21 strikeouts, many of them occurring during the evening twilight, with hitters for both squads struggling to pick up pitches in the bright glare of the setting California sun.

While his teammates resumed pursuit of the Detroit franchise's first division title in 12 years, Trammell went through a battery of tests lasting nearly ten hours at Detroit's Henry Ford Hospital on Friday, July 13. Fearing major damage that would require season-ending surgery, the Tiger organization was relieved when tests showed that Trammell was suffering from tendonitis in his right shoulder, an inflamed ulnar nerve (running down the back of his arm), and soreness in his right hand. "I feel fortunate," said Trammell after the results were made known. For the first time in his professional career he was placed on the disabled list and shut down completely for the remainder of July to let the arm rest.[22]

Despite playing without arguably the most indispensable cog in their lineup, the Tigers actually played eight games over .500 while Trammell was on the disabled list and increased their lead from seven to twelve games. Feeling a need to increase their potency against left-handed pitching however, Detroit decided to activate Trammell on July 31, where he would be utilized as a designated hitter while continuing to let his arm and shoulder recover. Trammell would serve as the primary DH in Sparky Anderson's lineup for most of the next three weeks.

Trammell's stint on the disabled list effectively ended any chance he might have had as a serious threat to win the league's MVP award. He had already suffered through an extended cold spell at the plate in June, one that saw his average drop from the mid-.350 range to down near .300. Once activated, he stumbled even more—going two for eighteen in his first five games back in the lineup. Meanwhile, Gibson and Hernandez' stock was ascending in AL MVP discussions, and they appeared to be the top considerations for a Detroit club that was likely to see votes split among several candidates.

As July turned to August and then finally to September, the Tigers continued to maintain their sizable lead in the AL East. The defending champion Orioles were a non-factor from mid-season on, with Detroit easily keeping them at arm's length more than ten games back. Toronto was the lone stubborn antagonist over the season's second half, intermittently cutting the deficit down to single-figures, only to watch the Tigers build it back up to a seemingly insurmountable eleven or twelve games again. The most promising summer in sixteen years for the Detroit organization and its fans continued to roll towards its rightful conclusion, and with it, generated even more unforgettable moments:

- July 13—With two outs in a 3-3 game at Minnesota in the bottom of the ninth inning, Gibson throws out a runner at the plate that would have been the winning run. Two innings later, Whitaker hits a two-run homer to win the game, 5-3.
- July 14—For the second straight night the Tigers and Twins went into extra-innings where the two teams remained tied in the twelfth. This time it was Gibson trying to score from second on a base hit, and he bowls over Minnesota catcher, Dave Engle, to break the tie. Detroit wins 6-5 in twelve innings.
- August 5-8—Detroit plays three straight days of double-headers during a period when their pitching was both ailing and ineffective. After being buried in the first game of a twi-nighter in Boston, 12-7 on August 7, and facing the prospect of blowing the night-cap—having given up a 4-1 lead—they rally to tie the game in the ninth inning 5-5, and then win it in the eleventh on Parrish's two-run homer. Detroit ends up splitting four games against the red-hot Red Sox with Lopez doing yeoman's work out of the bullpen, pitching six innings over the two days and getting both of the Tiger wins.
- September 5—After losing six of their previous seven games, Detroit scratches out a 1-0 win against Baltimore in the final game of a three-game series at home. Berenguer and Hernandez make an unearned Tiger run in the first inning hold up for the badly needed victory.
- September 7—Leading by 8½ games, Detroit travels to Toronto to face a Blue Jay team determined to ambush the Tigers and get themselves back into a race to the finish. Toronto leads 4-0 in the eighth inning of the first game of the series when Gibson hits a three-run homer to put Detroit back in the game. They score another run to tie the game before Bergman hits a three-run shot in the tenth for the crucial opening-game victory.
- September 9—The Tigers cap a three-game sweep against Toronto and effectively end the AL East race with 10-4 and 7-2 victories over the final two days of the series, extending their division lead to 11½ games with only three weeks left to play. Johnny Grubb hits three home runs in the series.

- September 18—After systematically paring down the "magic number" over the previous week, the end finally comes when Detroit shuts out Milwaukee 3-0 in Tiger Stadium. Rookie Randy O'Neal pitches seven scoreless innings as the starting pitcher with Hernandez cleaning up for the shutout. Trammell goes 2 for 5 at the plate and scores a run as the Tigers clinch the AL East.

Despite falling back to the pack a bit following their record-breaking start, the injury to Trammell, and the late-summer scare from Toronto, the Tigers finished what they started in style. They won nine out of 12 games to stomp out any possibilities of a late-season collapse, clinching baseball's toughest division with nearly two weeks left in the regular season. "It's the right way to cap the season," exclaimed Trammell in a joyous clubhouse after the clinching victory over Milwaukee. "We had to do it ourselves."[23]

When the 1984 season ended in New York 12 days later, Detroit had completed one of the great regular season rides in major league baseball history. They posted a final record of 104-58, the winningest in Tiger history, and among the better records in modern baseball history. The final margin of 15 games they held over second-place Toronto exemplified the dominance the Tigers displayed in running away with what had been expected to be a fiercely competitive division that season.

Detroit's supremacy was apparent by almost any common measure. They had a winning record in head-to-head competition against ten of the other 13 teams in the American League that year, and no team managed more than a 7-6 mark against them. They compiled winning records during each month of the schedule, displaying an unrelenting consistency that made it nearly impossible for anybody to catch them after their amazing start. The Tigers strung together two nine-game winning streaks, a pair of seven-game winning streaks, as well as several lesser streaks, while never losing more than four games in succession. They led the major leagues in runs scored that season with 829, and home runs with 187, yet demonstrated their offensive diversity by also stealing over 100 bases. They could bludgeon teams with their offensive firepower or manufacture runs with speed on the base paths and timely hitting. Their pitching staff had the lowest ERA in the American League by a considerable margin (3.49), while allowing the fewest earned runs and total runs. Their bullpen tied for the most saves (51) of any team in baseball with the St. Louis Cardinals. Less measurable, but no less recognized, was their tremendous team defense, especially from home plate and through the middle of the diamond and into centerfield.

The 1984 Detroit Tigers joined legendary teams such as the 1927 New

York Yankees and 1955 Brooklyn Dodgers as the only clubs up to that time in baseball history—to hold first place from wire-to-wire. However, the regular season marks would ring hollow if the Tigers could not duplicate that same success in the post season. They would enter the post season as prohibitive favorites to win the World Series. But baseball history was littered with teams that had dominant regular seasons, only to succumb to lesser teams in the post season. Just fifteen years earlier, the Baltimore Orioles had won 109 games in 1969, rolling over American League competition before losing in the World Series to a seemingly inferior opponent in the upstart New York Mets. Sparky Anderson's Big Red Machine Cincinnati Reds had felt post-season heartbreak three different times in the early 1970s, before finally winning back-to-back world championships in 1975 and 1976. For Trammell and the rest of the Tigers, validation of the 35–5 start, the gaudy win total, and the huge margin of victory over the rest of the American League East competition, would only come through post-season success, including a World Series title.

7

MVP

Alan Trammell entered his first ever post season with an ailing right shoulder and pain in the left knee he had injured the previous off-season. He sat out the final three games of the regular season, with the exception of a token pinch-running appearance in New York against the Yankees, hoping to be as healthy as possible for the American League Championship Series. The injury to his throwing arm was the more alarming ailment of the two, as his shoulder packed in ice after every game demonstrated. It wouldn't prevent him from playing in the post season, but did put into question one of Detroit's greatest strengths: the dazzling defensive play of their star shortstop. Since returning to the lineup at shortstop on August 17, Trammell had protected his weakened shoulder, relying on a quick release on throws to first base, rather than cutting loose at full velocity. "I need six to eight weeks to completely heal," he said at the time. "I feel good, but I'm guiding the easy throws. I have to watch the easy ones. They're dying on me."[1]

Offensively, Trammell had finished on an upswing, raising his final batting average to a team-leading mark of .314, which placed him fifth overall in the American League. He also ranked among the league leaders in doubles (8th with 34) and on-base percentage (8th at .382). Trammell's 14 home runs, 69 RBI's, and 85 runs scored were all highly productive for the number two hitter in any lineup of that era, and were consistent with the numbers he had posted a year earlier.

On paper the American League's playoff series appeared to be a mismatch. The Kansas City Royals, winners of the Western Division, had finished with only 84 wins on the season, 20 fewer than the Tigers. In fact, their record would have placed them sixth in the loaded American League East. Conversely, the Royals were the only team in the much weaker AL West to finish over the .500 mark, despite being outscored on the season by 13 runs. While the Tigers had steamrolled their competition, starting with the nine-game winning streak to start the season, Kansas City had struggled for most of the year. They dropped below .500 on April 26, never to reach the mark again until the last days of August. Their low point came on July 18 when they found themselves eleven games below .500 and mired in sixth place in their division, eight games out of first place.

From that point forward, however, Kansas City won games at a .620 clip over the final 70 games; a better record than Detroit had over that same period. Included in that hot streak was a four-game sweep of the Tigers in Detroit during the first week of August, which left both sides feeling that the outcome of the American League Championship Series was not necessarily the forgone conclusion that many pundits made it out to be.

Kansas City stalwarts George Brett and Hal McRae had suffered through injury-riddled campaigns that year, but remained among the most dangerous hitters in the American League when healthy. Frank White, Willie Wilson, John Wathan, Larry Gura, and U.L. Washington had a wealth of post-season experience, most having battled the Yankees in three post-season series back in the late 1970s, before finally making the World Series in 1980. Bud Black, Charlie Liebrandt, Brett Saberhagen, and Mark Gubicza provided the Royals with solid starting pitching, and Dan Quisenberry was again the ace of the bullpen, leading the league in saves for the fourth time in five years.

As the two teams prepared to play Game One in Kansas City's Kauffman Stadium, Royals manager Dick Howser reminded anybody who would listen that his ball club didn't have to beat the Tigers over 162 games, or string together long winning streaks to advance. They only had to beat Detroit three games out of five to advance to the World Series. "We win series," he said. "We don't have a club that can win fifteen in a row. But we can win ten out of fifteen. We have that kind of pitching."[2]

Any fears Tiger fans may have harbored of a Royals upset were quickly eased in Game 1 which was played before a national television audience on ABC. Detroit rolled to an easy 8–1 victory behind the overpowering pitching of Jack Morris and Willie Hernandez. The tone of the game had been set early when the Tigers jumped on Kansas City left-hander Bud Black for two runs in the top of the first inning. Trammell was the catalyst as he tripled off the left field wall to score Lou Whitaker who had led off the game with a single. Trammell then scored on a sacrifice fly off of the bat of Lance Parrish. After Larry Herndon homered to make it 3–0 in the fourth, Trammell hit a solo shot of his own an inning later, adding a single and two walks to finish with a perfect night.

"We played a good ball game all around," he said afterwards in his typically understated fashion. His stat-line in the crucial first game of the best-of-five series, showed him going three for three with two runs scored, three

RBI's, and two walks. "I'm glad national TV could see that, because that's how we play. We use everybody."[3]

Both clubhouses agreed that the first inning rally was the key to the game. "The first inning when they scored twice," explained Howser from the home side when asked if there had been a turning point. "Black got two strikes on Whitaker and Trammell, and couldn't put them away."[4] Morris cruised for most of his seven-inning stint, setting the Royals down in order in five of those innings and working out of his only real jam in the KC third inning, when he got Brett to fly out to end the inning and leave the bases loaded. But even he admitted that the quick start by the Tigers which saw them jump out to an early lead followed a script that was all too familiar to American League competition in 1984. "That's all I had to see. That's the way we've won a lot of games this year."[5]

Trammell, who was only a two-base hit shy of hitting for the cycle in the first post season game of his major league career, looked quite at ease on the big stage. "After getting a hit in my first at-bat in the playoffs, I felt good at the plate all night." If anything, he felt that the win would allow the Tigers to relax and play to their abilities, considering the enormous expectations that Detroit fans and the rest of baseball world had for their team. "We had pressure on us. If we don't win, people will come up with names for us, supreme chokers."[6]

Game Two of the 1984 ALCS would prove to be the classic game of the series and produce its most memorable moment. Once again the Tigers jumped on the Royals with two first inning runs, knocking around Saberhagen, with back-to-back doubles by Gibson and Parrish. Gibson homered in the third inning to extend the lead to 3–0, before Kansas City chipped into the lead with a single run in the bottom of the fourth. The score remained 3–1 into the bottom of the seventh inning when with two outs and a runner on first base, KC catcher Don Slaught hit a grounder to Trammell. Rather than flipping the ball to Whitaker for the inning-ending force, or simply throwing to first base to get the slow-footed Slaught, Trammell instead raced toward the bag at second trying to make the force-out himself. The Royals' veteran second-baseman Frank White had gotten a good jump on the pitch however, and beat Trammell to the bag to keep the inning alive. When pinch-hitter Dane Iorg followed with a looping single to right field that scored White, Trammell's uncharacteristic gaffe had allowed the home team to seize momentum while cutting the Detroit lead to one run.

Kansas City tied the game an inning later when McRae doubled off of Hernandez. Saberhagen, meanwhile, had shut down the Tiger bats since allowing the three early runs, continuing a mastery he seemed to have over the Eastern Division champions, having defeated them three times during the regular season.

The game remained tied as both managers turned the pivotal game over to their respective bullpens. Sparky Anderson brought in Aurelio Lopez in the ninth, while Howser put the game in the hands of his ace reliever, Quisenberry. The second game of a five-game series often proves to be the determining point that decides which team will ultimately advance. A Detroit win would leave them needing only one more victory to advance to the World Series, while a KC triumph would even the series and turn it into a best-of-three crapshoot, where anything could happen. Under those heightened stakes, the game moved into extra innings tied 3–3.

In the top of the 11th, the Tigers put two men on base with only one out. Johnny Grubb, serving as the designated hitter that evening, settled in at the plate to face Quisenberry. With the count 1–2 and Quisenberry seemingly in command on the mound, Grubb scalded a drive to deep right-center field that landed just out of the reach of the league's fastest player, Royals centerfielder Willie Wilson. Grubb's double scored Darrell Evans and Ruppert Jones and swung the likely outcome of the series dramatically in Detroit's favor. Lopez worked out of trouble in all three innings he pitched and shutout Kansas City to preserve the eleven-inning, 5–3 victory.

With the win, Trammell and his teammates were on the cusp of going to the World Series, and would be heading home to try to close out the Royals. Despite suffering the four-game sweep in Detroit back in August at the hands of Kansas City, Trammell was confident that the Tigers would be able to finish off the series once they got back to the friendly confines of Tiger Stadium. "Yes, I'm confident. Very confident," he said resolutely after the Game Two victory. "If we can't win one of three games at home, we don't deserve to go any further."[7]

Any doubts as to whether the American League's best team in 1984 would represent the junior circuit in the World Series were put to rest two nights later in a tense, but mostly uneventful, 1–0 Tiger win before 52,168 chilly fans. The teams managed only three hits apiece and the game's only run crossed the plate when Royals shortstop Onix Concepcion fielded a ground ball in the second inning off the bat of Detroit third baseman Marty Castillo, stepped on second base to force Darrell Evans, but then threw high to first base, drawing KC first baseman Steve Balboni off the bag. What should have been the third out on an inning-ending double-play, instead allowed the slow-footed Castillo to reach first base safely while Chet Lemon scored from third base. That second-inning run held up as Milt Wilcox pitched one of the finest games of his career, working a season-high eight innings while striking out eight batters and allowing only two hits. Hernandez worked the pennant-clinching ninth inning, making a loser of Royals pitcher Charlie Liebrandt, who had also pitched masterfully, not allowing a Detroit hit after the second inning.

The Tigers' short work in the ALCS left them waiting impatiently through the entire first weekend of October to see who their opponent would be from the National League in the Fall Classic. It had appeared that the Chicago Cubs would also make quick dispatch of their opponent, the San Diego Padres, creating the dream matchup that many baseball purists had been pining for since mid-summer. While it had been 16 years since Detroit's 1968 World Championship, and 12 years since Tiger followers had celebrated a post-season appearance of any kind, Cubs fans had suffered even worse. There had been a 39-year drought since Chicago's last post-season appearance of any kind; their last was the 1945 World Series they lost to the Tigers in seven games. When the Cubs took the first two games of the National League's playoff series in relatively easy fashion at Wrigley Field, a dream matchup of sorts appeared eminent. Most neutral fans and media looked forward to a World Series between two traditional baseball franchises, the Tigers and Cubs, that would be played out before championship-starved fans filling two of the truly classic ballparks in the game.

The NLCS shifted markedly, however, when the series moved to San Diego for the final three games. After the Padres cruised to an easy 7–1 win in Game Three, the next two contests saw dramatic events play out that landed in favor of the home team. Game Four was a back-and-forth affair with both teams rallying from deficits to regain the lead before they headed into the bottom of the ninth inning tied 5–5. Then with Lee Smith, one of the dominant relief pitchers of the era, on the mound for the Cubs, San Diego first baseman Steve Garvey walloped a drive over the right-center field wall for a two-run home run to win the game 7–5, and even the series at two games apiece.

The deciding fifth game was even more disappointing for Chicago fans as they saw their team carry a 3–0 lead into the bottom of the sixth inning with their staff ace, Rick Sutcliffe—who went 16–1 in the regular season for the Cubs after coming over in a June trade from Cleveland—on the mound. The Padres erupted however for six runs over the next two innings, with most coming in frustrating fashion. A walk, an error on an easy ground ball, and a Tony Gwynn double that fell just out of the reach of Chicago's star second baseman, Ryne Sandberg, were the key moments in a disastrous four-run seventh inning meltdown for the Cubs. The 6–3 San Diego victory wrapped up the National League pennant for the Padres, and ended any notions that may have existed of a Tigers-Cubs World Series.

Members of the Detroit organization spent the weekend expecting to open the World Series at home against the Cubs. As apparent pennant-clinching victories slipped away from Chicago on both Saturday and Sunday, Tigers players, coaches, and staff members started to instead pack for a Sunday evening flight to San Diego where they would open against the Padres on Tuesday night.

Like the rest of his teammates, Trammell would have relished the reduced travel burden that would have come traveling between Detroit and Chicago, especially on the tail end of a season that was now well into its seventh month. The opportunity presented, however, would allow him to play in his hometown in front of the family and friends that he grew up with, as well as to stay in his own house, located only three miles from the stadium and away from the hoopla surrounding the rest of the team. Since finishing off Kansas City nearly 48 hours prior, Trammell had killed time by cleaning out the garage of his suburban Detroit home, and wearily handling the media crush that accompanied a team only one step away from their seemingly destined claim to a world championship. "It's not a lot of fun any time you have to talk about yourself all the time," he said. "You like to talk to an extent, but not continually. At the same time, it's been about what we expected."[8]

Despite winning 92 games that year, the San Diego Padres did not carry the aura befitting a World Series opponent, when matched up with a Detroit team that had overpowered the rest of the American League that season. The franchise had been in existence for just 16 years and enjoyed nowhere near the cache of other traditional National League powers of the era such as Los Angeles, Philadelphia, or St. Louis. In fact, San Diego had managed to finish above .500 only once prior to the 1984 season, and had finished in last place with over 90 losses in more than half of the seasons of their brief major league existence.

The Padres' general manager "Trader" Jack McKeon had been building a competitive team over the previous two seasons and then added key pieces in former Yankee stalwarts, Craig Nettles and Rich "Goose" Gossage prior to the 1984 campaign. The moves pushed them over the top in the National League's Western Division as they took control in mid–July and then cruised to a final twelve-game margin over the second-place Atlanta Braves. The Padres were a curious mix of youth and experience, more likely to beat their opponents with speed and base running than to overwhelm them at the plate. They scored 143 fewer runs than Detroit that season and hit only 109 home runs, a total that would have placed them 13th (out of 14 teams) in the American League. The San Diego offense was more likely to be fueled by the 152 bases they stole, or a timely base hit.

The Padre lineup was keyed by the first two batters in their lineup,

7. MVP

Alan Wiggins and Tony Gwynn. Wiggins was a mediocre second baseman, and batted only .258, but was adept at drawing walks which proved beneficial as he was one of the real base thieves in the game, having swiped 70 bases that year. Gwynn was in only his third season in the majors, and his first playing as a regular, but was a budding star. He hit .351 in 1984, and took the first of the eight NL batting championships he would win in an eventual Hall-of-Fame career.

The middle of the order was filled by two old war horses in the 40-year-old Nettles and former Dodgers first baseman Steve Garvey, 35. Neither was the player they had been half a decade earlier, but each was still a dangerous run producer who could hit the occasional long ball. Catcher Terry Kennedy, left fielder Carmelo Martinez, and shortstop Garry Templeton filled out the rest of manager Dick Williams' regular lineup. Missing would be one of San Diego's better young players in 20-home run centerfielder, Kevin McReynolds. McReynolds broke his hand during the NLCS and was unable to play in the World Series. His spot would be taken in the Padre outfield by the former American Leaguer, Bobby Brown.

The series opened in San Diego's cavernous Jack Murphy Stadium on Tuesday, October 9, a ball park named after a local sports writer, and best known perhaps for its extremely hard, and irregular, infield. The Tigers started their half of the first inning with a familiar and successful formula. After going a combined 2–17 at the plate over the final two games of the Kansas City series, Whitaker and Trammell came out smoking against Padre's left-handed starter, Mark Thurmond. Whitaker led off the game by battling back from an 0–2 count, fouling off five pitches, before he doubled over the head of the centerfielder, Brown. Trammell pushed Thurmond's pitch count even further, working the count to full, before he stroked a solid base hit to left field, scoring Whitaker easily and giving the Tigers the early lead. An over-anxious Trammell, however, was then thrown out at second base after being picked off by Thurmond. The out short-circuited a possible big inning by Detroit who managed only one run despite getting four hits.

By the fifth inning, a constant parade of Tiger base runners seemed to take its toll on the San Diego starting pitcher. Although they trailed in the game 2–1, Detroit had already accumulated three walks and six hits before Larry Herndon deposited an outside pitch into the right-centerfield seats with Parrish on base, allowing the Tigers to regain the lead, 3–2. From there, Morris picked up where he left off against Kansas City one week earlier, recovering from a shaky first inning in which he gave up two runs, to shutout the Padres the rest of the way.

The key play of the game came in the bottom of the seventh inning when San Diego designated hitter Kurt Bevacqua sliced a ball just inside the right-field line and into the Detroit bullpen in the corner. But a perfectly executed relay from Gibson to Whitaker to Castillo at third base, cut down the over-zealous Bevacqua who was trying to stretch his hit into a leadoff triple, and took the wind out of the 57,908 raucous pro–San Diego fans. When Gwynn was thrown out attempting to steal two batters later, the final threat by the Padres had been extinguished. Morris set down the final six batters with ease and Detroit escaped the first game of the World Series with a narrow 3–2 victory.

For Trammell the game had been extra special. Not only had he played well in his first career World Series game, but he had done it in his hometown. He got hits his first two times at the plate, including driving in the game's first run, and had hit the ball hard in three other plate appearances. He also added a stolen base in the third inning. His ailing shoulder had been tested in the field when a second-inning groundball hit deep into the hole by Carmelo Martinez, was fielded cleanly by Trammell and then rifled across the diamond to easily record the putout at first base.

"That was a special feeling, going back home to play against the team I had always rooted for as a kid," he recalled years later of that first World Series game played in the venue he had snuck into as a kid. "I had never played at Jack Murphy Stadium before, and to be on that field for my first World Series … isn't that what you dream of when you're a kid that loves baseball?"[9]

As good as Game One had started for the Tigers, Game Two started even better. Whitaker, Trammell, and Gibson all singled on the first pitch delivered to them from Padres starter Ed Whitson. By the time seven Detroit batters had come to the plate, the Tigers held a 3–0 lead and had driven Whitson from the game.

The rest of the game did not go as smoothly though, as San Diego chipped into the lead with single runs in the first and fourth innings before Bevacqua capitalized on a hanging slider from Petry and launched a three-run homer in the fifth to give the Padres a 5–3 lead. And while the Padre bats were coming alive, the Tigers were being stymied after the first inning by San Diego long-relievers, Andy Hawkins and Craig Lefferts, who held the Tigers scoreless the rest of the way. The Padre relievers combined for eight strikeouts over the game's final 8 1/3 innings. Hawkins allowed only a single hit in his five-plus innings, and a Trammell single was the only tally off of Lefferts over his three innings. The Padres defeated Detroit by the final margin of 5–3, evening the series at one game each, with the two teams shifting to Detroit for games three, four, and five.

Once the teams arrived in Detroit, discussion centered around whether there would be a return trip to the west coast. The Tigers were determined to end the series in front of their home fans and not risk having to return to San Diego to close out the series. The Padres were equally determined to win at least one game in Motown and bring it back to Jack Murphy Stadium. 51,970 stoked fans in Tiger Stadium had waited 16 years since their team's last World Series appearance at the corner of Michigan and Trumbull. What they saw the evening of October 12 was far short of a Fall Classic contest. In a sloppily played game that dragged on more than three hours, Detroit ground out a 5–2 victory to go up in the series, two games to one.

Three Padre pitchers issued a World Series record-tying eleven walks, but Detroit batters were almost equally as magnanimous, leaving fourteen runners on base. The home team exploded for four runs in the second inning to take a commanding lead. With one out, Castillo crashed a two-run homer into the upper deck in left field off of left-hander, Tim Lollar, to start the scoring. Lollar then walked Whitaker, who then came around from first, when Trammell rocketed a line drive just inside the foul line and into the left field corner for a run-scoring double. Three batters later, Trammell came around to score when Herndon walked with the bases loaded; the third base on balls issued by Padre pitching that inning.

The rest of the game was a constant display of runners on the base paths, but missed scoring opportunities; neither team could deliver the big blow via a game-changing hit. The two teams exchanged runs in the third inning, but other than a single tally in the seventh inning, San Diego could draw no closer. Hernandez pitched one-hit ball over the final two and one-third innings to close out the victory for Wilcox, who hadn't been as sharp as he had been in his masterful 1–0 pennant clinching win over Kansas City.

Saturday, October 13, 1984, would prove to be the pivotal day of the series as well as the singular day that the national spotlight would shine brightest on Alan Trammell. Playing on the biggest stage of his career, on a team having a once in a decade season, Trammell would command the day and form the indelible image of him as a ballplayer to a national audience. It was a gray, fall day with darkened skies that belied the 1:30 p.m. start time set to accommodate NBC's television broadcast. With the hysteria of the first World Series home game over, and the short-turnaround from the previous night's game that had ended at almost midnight, there was a more sedate feel within Tigers Stadium for the start of Game 4.

The day got off to a dubious start for Trammell, who realized only after he had arrived at the ballpark, that he had the keys to the family van in his pocket. The van, now minus keys, had been the intended transportation to the game that day for a household full of guests at the Trammell residence. "I took the keys to the van. I took them with me," he explained sheepishly afterwards. "We've got a million people in the house from all over, and my wife is steaming. She called the ballpark at about 12:15, mad as hell, and said "where are the keys?" "I don't know if she got to the game or not."[10]

Morris returned to the mound for the Tigers and easily shut down San Diego in the top of the first inning before Whitaker reached base for the Tigers on an errant Wiggins' throw that pulled Garvey off the bag at first base. That brought up Trammell, who worked the count to two balls and no strikes, as Padres right-hander Eric Show seemed more focused on holding Whitaker close to the bag ahead of a suspected hit-and-run attempt. Instead, on the next pitch, Trammell got the barrel of the bat out in front of a belt-high pitch and drove it high and deep down the left field line before it eventually landed some half-dozen rows back in the lower deck, about twenty feet fair.

Trammell's two-run homer not only gave Detroit a 2–0 lead, but put San Diego on their heels yet again, in what most deemed a must-win situation. "I can't believe this," said Garvey, the Padres' first baseman and a veteran of four previous World Series with Los Angeles. "Every time we go out there we've got to start running uphill." "It takes away our running and some of our offense."[11]

In the Tigers' half of the third inning, Trammell came to the plate with Whitaker on base once again. And for the second time in the game, Trammell connected off of Show. This time the ball carried even further into the gray sky before it finally landed in the first rows of the upper deck in straight-away left field. The NBC Network's cameras barely had time to hone in on Trammell as he circled the bases at a rapid pace, head down with a business-like demeanor. It was decorum representative of baseball from the 1950s, rather than the "all eyes on me" mindset that many players of the day would have taken with a two home run performance in a World Series game. "When I hit a homerun I'm in a daze," Trammell explained after the game. "I don't like to jump up and down. That's not me. I just smiled coming back to the dugout."[12]

Upon reaching a jubilant Tigers' dugout, the Detroit shortstop was able to let loose with his emotions in response to the congratulatory flesh-pounding he took from teammates beginning to sense a series turning irrefutably in their favor. Before he could even sit down and collect his thoughts however, Trammell was being pushed up the dugout steps by pitching coach Roger Craig to take the briefest of curtain calls and acknowledge the roaring adulation of the 52,000-plus in attendance that day. "That's embarrassing," said Trammell about the in-game bow he was coerced into taking. "I just feel I'm a regular guy. I appreciate that, but I'm not used to it."[13]

The crowd roared again in both appreciation and anticipation when Trammell batted in the fifth inning. Whitaker had led off the inning with a double into left field, before Trammell dropped a soft line drive onto the turf in left field. The hit probably should have resulted in another run for the Tigers, but third base coach Alex Grammas, rather conservatively, held up the runner rounding third. However, when both Gibson and Evans struck out against left handed reliever Dave Dravecky, and Parrish hit into a fielder's choice resulting in Whitaker being thrown out at the plate, Detroit had failed to take advantage of a potential knockout situation.

The missed opportunity would not prove costly though; Morris was in complete command from start to finish. He scattered five Padre hits while setting down thirteen straight batters at one point through the middle innings, and cruised to his third victory of the post season. The Tigers 4–2 victory appeared much closer on the scoreboard than it had seemed on the field, thanks to Morris' dominant performance. However, it was the Detroit shortstop who garnered the bulk of the attention afterwards.

"He's the finest shortstop in all of baseball," said his manager after the game. Anderson was even more profuse with his compliments when he said that Trammell was "the best shortstop I've ever seen." Never one to shy away from prodigious proclamations about players, Anderson even hinted at his 26-year-old shortstop's future prospects for Cooperstown. "If he plays another ten years, I'll leave that decision up to you."[14]

Trammell's three-hit, two-home run performance in four at-bats (he flied out to deep left field to end the seventh inning), easily made him the star of Game Four. He had become the 26th player in World Series history to slug multiple round-trippers in the same game, had driven in all four Tiger runs, and had scored half of Detroit's four runs. Despite the newfound power surge, Trammell still considered himself more of a table-setter for the big guns that typically followed him like Gibson, Parrish, Evans, and others. "I'm not a homerun hitter, really," he said afterwards. "This was coincidence today. I wasn't thinking homer either time."[15]

Trammell was, however, quickly becoming the undisputed offensive force of the 1984 World Series. Through four games he was batting .563 (9–16) with four runs scored and six RBI's. His nine hits had him positioned for a run at the all-time World Series record of 13. More importantly, his team was now within a single victory of achieving their season-long objective of a World Championship, something they desperately wanted to accomplish before the home crowd at Tiger Stadium. "We'd love to win it

The 1984 Detroit Tigers put together one of the most dominant single seasons in baseball history, winning 111 games before they were done, including an unparalleled 35–5 start (National Baseball Hall of Fame Library, Cooperstown, New York).

here," Trammell explained after Game Four. "We'd love to win it here for the fans and not have to go out to that craziness out there in San Diego."[16]

Sunday, October 14, proved to be the climax to the 1984 season for the Detroit Tigers when they wrapped up the fourth World Series championship in franchise history. The game followed a familiar script with the home team scoring three times in the first inning, knocking out San Diego's starting pitcher, Mark Thurmond, who was able to retire only one of the first six batters he faced. The big blow had been Gibson's towering home run into the right field upper deck with Trammell on base. It was the fourth time in the five games that a Padre starting pitcher had failed to get through three innings.

The visitors battled back throughout the game, however, tying it briefly in the middle innings, before Gibson's second home run of the game, a titanic three-run blast in the eighth inning off of Gossage, iced it for Detroit. Having rounded the bases and while making his way back to an ecstatic Tiger dugout, Gibson with pants torn at the knees and his arms raised in triumph would form the iconic image of that magical season.

"Today we played like we can normally play," said Anderson of his team afterwards. "I was hoping we could show some firepower, and we finally did today."[17] The 8–4 series-clincher was the signature win of the year for the Tigers; they finally busted out offensively and did away with a pesky Padre team. "The Tigers play the hell out of this game," said San Diego's manager, Dick Williams, from the visitor's clubhouse. "They play the way you are supposed to play."[18]

"We're the champions. We get the ring," said a happy and relieved Trammell, celebrating with his teammates. "This is what it's all about."[19] After six weeks of spring training, including 28 Grapefruit League games, a six-month regular season of 162 games—much of it under intense media attention, and then eight pressure-packed post-season games, the season had finally ended in triumph. "It's all over," Trammell added. "They can't take it away from us."[20]

Adding to the thrill of accomplishment that he shared with his teammates, Alan Trammell was recognized as the Most Valuable Player of the 1984 World Series. Despite going hitless in four official at-bats in the final game, he ended the series batting .450, which led all regulars for either team. He scored five runs and knocked in six, had a double, the two home runs, and stole a base. His nine base hits in a five-game series tied the World Series record. He committed one error, thanks to a bad bounce grounder off of the Jack Murphy infield, in eighteen total chances in the field. Perhaps even more importantly, Trammell was the ultimate tone-setter in the series, either scoring or driving in a first-inning run in four of the five games.

The award netted the Tiger shortstop a 1984 Pontiac Trans-Am for his efforts, but in his typically humble manner, Trammell downplayed the significance of the honor. "I realize I'm the MVP, and it feels good," he said. "But if Alan Trammell couldn't have had a good Series and we won, I'd be just as happy."[21]

That Trammell was named the MVP of the series might have been considered a minor upset considering the outstanding performances of two of his more attention-getting teammates. Gibson's tape-measure home runs in the season's final game were indicative of the "Big Game" type of player he would become. Gibson had also been named the MVP of the American League's Championship Series for his performance against Kansas City. Morris had turned in three outstanding post-season pitching performances, all resulting in Detroit victories, and had gone the distance in his two World Series starts. Morris' October body of work rivaled that of an earlier Tigers' great, Mickey Lolich, who had put together three complete-game victories in the 1968 World Series championship over the St. Louis Cardinals. Yet it was the Detroit shortstop that Sparky Anderson likened to "Huck Finn," that ultimately stood out on a team full of outstanding players.

"I've had the good fortune to play with people like Alan Trammell," said Lance Parrish about the teammate he had played with since they debuted together in September of 1977. "He's a super person. He means so much to this team. We wouldn't have had this year without Alan. He got the key hits, the big hits. He was particularly good early in the season when we got off to that great start. I'm extremely proud of him winning the most valuable player award."[22]

"The people really don't understand how much pain he had to play through this year," added Gibson. "A person of lesser character might have quit at any time. He's just a remarkable person."[23]

Gibson's comments about the physical toll the season exacted on his teammate were not without merit. Trammell's body was wearing down quickly as the season wound down, and the increased intensity of play through the post-season only further aggravated his weary shoulder and aching knee. Shortly after the series ended, it was announced that he would be heading to Atlanta later that week to have arthroscopic surgery on both joints. "I was disappointed," said Trammell about having to face surgery again before the celebrations had hardly ended. "I was looking forward to having a nice winter. Unfortunately, I'll have to have some rehabilitation."[24]

As the years went by, Trammell would often look back at that magical year of 1984. Late in his playing career he tried to put a finger on some of the less obvious keys to that championship season: "When we swept the Orioles in Baltimore at the end of the last (1983) season. It was just the lift we needed. We went into the off-season with the right frame of mind."[25]

That late season success, although meaningless to the eventual champion Orioles in 1983, paid dividends to a young Detroit team that found itself ahead of the next season. "Going into spring training in '84, we felt very confident we were going to be successful," he added. "Right out of the get-go, we started out 35–5. Sports are contagious. Winning or losing is contagious. We were just confident we were going to win. Whatever we needed, we got it done. Somebody coming off the bench or whatever.... Everybody was part of it."

Trammell would admit however, that the ridiculous early season success the team enjoyed, only increased the pressure later on in the summer. "We felt a little bit of pressure because we had had such a tremendous season, but if we didn't win it all, nobody would remember us. We felt like we had to win it all."[26]

Trammell's MVP performance that October, catapulted him, for the first time really, into the consciousness of baseball fans around the country. The 1984 World Series gave many casual observers their first up-close look at a player who had excelled in his sport for a number of seasons already, but had remained outside of the spotlight. His brilliant performance on the sport's biggest stage allowed followers from outside of Detroit and the Tiger fan base to recognize what a unique player Trammell had developed into. Reputations, good or bad, are often made in such settings. His Game Four heroics, where he accounted for all four Detroit runs with a pair of two-run home runs, elevated Trammell's reputation—he was looked upon as one of the clutch players in the game.

"The bottom line is I was swinging the bat well at the right time," he explained. "Like so much of baseball, it was all timing. They named me the MVP, probably because of that one game. The homeruns actually meant something. That was all our scoring, so that part was gratifying. That was the game that people remember me for."[27]

8

Back to Earth

During the winter months in the early part of 1985, Alan Trammell could reflect on being at the peak of his profession. The euphoria over a World Series championship in Detroit was still fresh in the minds of everyone involved. Players, management, and fans could all bask in the glory of the accomplishments from the previous summer that had paid in full all of the blood, sweat, and tears accumulated through previous campaigns. No longer was Trammell a member of a wishful team chasing New York, Baltimore or Milwaukee in the division. The Tigers had conquered not only baseball's strongest division, but had seized both the American League pennant and a World Series championship as well.

Trammell was no longer the skinny, fuzzy-cheeked youngster that had played with such uncommon poise while just barely out of his teens. He turned 27 years old that February, and was a key member of a championship team. To many observers, he was *the* key member of the team; the one Detroit could least afford to be without. He was one of the best players in the American League, recognized for his all-around play and ability to make clutch plays in any phase of the game. He was an off-field as well as on-field leader, not afraid to challenge teammates whose games had fallen out of line, nor did he fail to embrace pressure situations himself. He was awarded the American League's Gold Glove at shortstop for the fourth time in 1984, and had enjoyed another highly-prolific season at the plate. He and Lou Whitaker had been the catalysts to the high-scoring Tiger attack, where first inning runs had set the tone for so many of the 104 regular season victories, as well as the seven additional post-season triumphs.

The remarkable consistency that Trammell displayed with the bat during the 1984 season had been dazzling. His .314 batting average for the season held up under almost any imaginable circumstance. He batted .304 at home and .322 on the road; .320 against left-handed pitchers and .310 against right-handers; and .318 in night games versus .304 in day games. Had he not missed nearly a month of action mid-season, Trammell likely would have been a leading candidate to win the American League's Most Valuable Player Award that season. Trammell's role as a key contributor to the Tigers' magical season was recognized nonetheless by the Baseball Writers Association of America, who placed him ninth in voting when the honor had been awarded to teammate Willie Hernandez back in November.

Off the field, Trammell was busy with his wife Barbara, taking care of their two small children at their off-season home in Del Mar, California. His oldest child, Lance, had been named after close friend and teammate Lance Parrish, and was nearing three years old. Younger son Kyle was just over a year old. Those growing responsibilities allowed for some time away from the glare that had shone so brightly on Trammell and his teammates for much of 1984. The winter months allowed for much needed downtime, which included rest and rehab for Trammell's surgically repaired right shoulder and left knee. "Nobody is ever going to know," he said about the pain he endured for much of the championship season. "I was hurting, but you can overcome a lot when so much is on the line and the end is in sight. I just kept telling myself, 'it's almost over, it's almost over.'"[1]

By the time the team reported to Lakeland, Florida, for the start of spring training, Trammell reported that he was feeling fine physically. But, observers noticed early on in Grapefruit League action that the Tigers' shortstop was not really testing his arm and shoulder, seemingly shying away from cutting loose with his throws. "I know what they're saying. If I don't throw everything like a bullet, they're going to wonder what's wrong," Trammell explained, refuting speculation that his arm miseries from the previous season were not yet behind him.[2] The denial soon proved hollow when he sat out of spring training action for nearly two weeks, the organization acknowledging that his shoulder was acting up.

Trammell's ailing shoulder only added to an unsettling March in Lakeland for a veteran Detroit team trying to block out the distractions associated with being the defending champions. Sparky Anderson, in one of the most bizarre moves of his hunch-filled managerial career, tinkered with the idea of breaking up his highly-successful Trammell-Whitaker combination, just days before the 1985 season opener. Anderson was enamored with a 23-year-old switch-hitting infielder by the name of Chris Pittaro, who had hit .284 in Double-A ball the previous summer. Calling him "the best young infielder I've had come up through camp in fifteen years," Anderson inserted Pittaro as his starting second baseman, and moved Whitaker to third base, only ten days before the team would head north to start the regular season. "This isn't just an experiment for a day or two" claimed Anderson, stating that the moves were "etched in cement."[3]

Like many of Anderson's short-term infatuations, the move was aborted within days, with neither Whitaker, nor his double-play partner Trammell, comfortable with the switch. Pittaro instead was moved to third base, keeping the Trammell-Whitaker keystone intact. With Parrish behind the plate and Chet Lemon in centerfield, the Tigers would head into 1985 once again with tremendous up-the-middle strength. Kirk Gibson was being viewed as an emerging superstar, Jack Morris and Dan Petry would again form as strong a 1–2 top of the rotation combination as there was in baseball, and Willie Hernandez, the AL's reigning MVP, headed up a strong bullpen. Detroit was the overwhelming favorite to repeat as champions as the new season opened. With the core of the team entering their primes, some even viewed the Tigers as a potential dynasty.

"Obviously, we can't expect to be 35–5 or win 104 games again," pleaded Trammell as spring training drew to a close. "Those are once in a lifetime happenings. We can't duplicate them, but we can be successful." Wise beyond his years, the realist in Trammell recognized that 1984's triumph would not guarantee a championship in the upcoming season. The pitfalls that can trip up seemingly invincible teams trying to repeat, are many. "Winning once doesn't make the next time any easier," he said. "The good thing is we know what it takes."[4]

Any attempts to throttle-down the exorbitant expectations for the team quickly dissipated as the 1985 season began. Described by Anderson as "a better team than my Cincinnati teams,"[5] the Tigers won their first six games and visions of another 1984-type start ran rampant in Detroit. The strong start wouldn't last however. By the end of April they had dropped behind the Toronto Blue Jays in the Eastern Division race and would continue to lose ground as spring turned into summer. After dropping the first two games of an early June series in Toronto, the Tigers found themselves an alarming 8½ games behind the division-leading Blue Jays.

The consistent winning streaks that had been so prevalent a year earlier failed to materialize with the same regularity in 1985. No one area on the club was primarily to blame, but all areas were cause for concern. Inconsistency in the starting pitching made long winning streaks difficult to string together. Milt Wilcox's tendonitis-riddled shoulder, having been taxed for everything it could give in 1984, gave out by the end of May, his season and career in Detroit effectively over. Hard-throwing Juan Berenguer, who had so ably filled the fourth spot in the rotation a year earlier while making 27 starts, was dropped from the rotation early in the 1985 season, ineffective and with an ERA greater than five. The bullpen also took a major step back, and was no longer the stabilizing force it had been for Sparky Anderson in tight games a year earlier. Although he would accumulate 31 saves that season, Hernandez's entrance to a game no longer signaled an automatic victory. He developed a penchant for giving up late-inning home runs, a trait that would infuriate Tiger Stadium fans numerous times over the summer. By mid-season, Aurelio Lopez and Doug Bair were complete disasters pitching in relief, limiting the options Anderson could rely on to bridge the innings between his starters and the closer Hernandez.

Defensively, the club developed an aggravating tendency towards careless and sloppy errors, with many often coming at the worst possible times. The Chris Pittaro experiment failed miserably, and was aborted before mid-season. He played only 28 games before being sent to Triple-A Toledo and never again made an appearance in a Tiger uniform. Third base became a lair for inconsistent defense and weak hitting.

But perhaps the most glaring difference from the previous season was the club's mysterious inability to score runs, especially at critical moments. While players like Gibson, Parrish, and Evans were having outstanding seasons, the Tigers were not scoring runs in clusters, which had allowed them to overwhelm their opposition. The Tigers still clouted home runs at a crisp pace, running neck-and-neck with Baltimore for the major league lead, but they lacked the consistent spark that had allowed them to manufacture runs whenever they seemed to need it during the 1984 campaign. Bench players like Barbaro Garbey, Johnny Grubb, Dave Bergman, and Marty Castillo, who had contributed so much the summer before, saw their offensive production fall off considerably.

Central to the problem had been the play of Trammell, who was batting some thirty or forty points below his averages from the two previous seasons when he and Whitaker had formed the most dynamic 1–2 lineup combination in either league.

"I'm sorry, but I'm going to put it right on Alan," said Anderson shortly before the All-Star break. "He is a great player, and we all know it. Now I'm going to put him under the pressure and ask him to give us the lift we need in the second half of the season. We've got to get going, and I'm looking to Alan to do it for us."[6]

Anderson even shook up the lineup for a brief period, dropping Gibson into the cleanup spot in place of the slumping Parrish, while moving Trammell back to the number three slot. Trammell responded with a home run in the final game before the All-Star break, an 8–0 thrashing of the Twins, raising hopes that the team would respond in the second half of the season.

"I know I've got to hit better than I've hit," admitted Trammell who sat at .274 with 30 RBI's at the traditional mid-season break in the schedule, versus the .307 mark and 44 RBI's he had the year before at that time. "Lou has done his part, and now I've got to do mine. We're not going to win unless

I start contributing more than I have so far. I haven't done that poorly, but I've got to do a lot better if we're going to catch Toronto."[7]

The All-Star Game in Minneapolis that summer marked Trammell's second appearance in the game. He replaced Ripken to start the seventh inning and made his first All-Star Game plate appearance, leading off the ninth inning with the National League leading 6–1. Trammell grounded out to third base off of the Padres' reliever, Goose Gossage, contributing to a forgettable night for the Detroit-heavy contingent at the 56th mid-season classic. Anderson, as manager of the American League squad, had selected Morris to be his starting pitcher. Morris, playing in his home state, didn't survive the third inning and ended up being the losing pitcher in the contest. Whitaker went 0–2 at the plate, while wearing a souvenir uniform secured at a local gift shop because he had left his regular game jersey back in Detroit. Petry walked three of the four batters he faced before being replaced by Hernandez who then gave up a two-run double that broke the game open for the National League. "It was not our best moment," explained Anderson in a rare, for him, brevity of words.[8]

The second half of the season began with most observers holding an overriding belief that Detroit would still make a run at the division title. Things didn't get much better however. After playing well in June and pulling briefly to within 2½ games of Toronto by June 30, the team went 12–16 in July, chiefly against American League West competition, and fell to 9½ games back by the end of the month. An inconsistency in the offensive attack was held largely to blame. "We're scoring almost a run a game less than a year ago, and you can't do that and expect to win," lamented Anderson after a frustrating mid–July loss. "We've just got to start manufacturing some runs."[9]

Although it wasn't official, all hope faded for the defending champions after a two-week stretch in August when Detroit lost five games in which they held a multi-run lead entering the ninth inning. Over the final month of a hugely disheartening season, the team basically played out the string, battling Baltimore and Boston for third place. The Tigers were officially eliminated from the American League Eastern Division race on September 21, fittingly in a sloppily pitched and sloppily played game they lost in Boston, 7–6. "I think this is the worst fielding team I've ever seen," complained Anderson after a late season defeat that year. "There is just no excuse for the way we've played in the field. We've just plain stunk."[10]

The Tigers did manage to finish strong over the final two weeks and took third place in the division, saving whatever face they could on a disappointing finish. One bright spot in the final week had been a 5–1 win over Boston that essentially delegated the Red Sox to fifth place. Detroit turned three double-plays, executed two sacrifice bunts, and scored four runs on a pair of two-out hits, including a two-run homer by Trammell, in one of the cleanest games the team had played in months. "It hasn't been our year, but it sure is nice to play a good game," commented Trammell afterwards. "I'd like to have a few more games like this one, but you can't turn back the clock."[11] More typical of the season was the next day's game, when hard-luck Dan Petry pitched nine innings of two-hit, shutout ball against Boston, only to watch his team lose 2–0 when Hernandez gave up back-to-back home runs in the tenth inning.

For Trammell, the second half of the season wasn't much better than the first, and if anything—may have been even worse. He batted just .239 after the All-Star break and finished with a final batting mark of .258. His power numbers were somewhat in line with his previous two seasons, 13 home runs and 57 RBI's, but with only 21 doubles. His on-base percentage ended up at .312, down significantly from the .382 and .385 figures he had registered the previous two seasons, partly explaining why he and Whitaker had not been the same catalysts at the top of the order that they had been in 1984. "Last year we jumped out on top all the time," admitted Trammell late in the season. "We were always ahead early and that comes from Lou and me. But Lou had a good year...."[12]

Detroit's final record of 84–77 was 19½ games worse than the championship pace they had set a year earlier. A team that had been a near-consensus choice to repeat as not only division champions, but also as World Series champions, finished 15 games behind first-place Toronto, and perhaps even more embarrassingly, 13 games behind second-place New York. After holding the top spot in the standings wire-to-wire in 1984, Detroit spent exactly 17 days in first place in 1985, none after April 28. Lack of consistency was a problem the entire season. When they hit well, the pitching faltered. When the starting pitching was strong, they either failed to score runs in crucial situations or the bullpen failed. When both the hitting and pitching was clicking, they were horrendous defensively as their 143 errors, second-highest in the league, attested to. After starting the season 6–0, they never managed climb higher than thirteen games over .500 (47–34 on July 10), and were unable to string together the type of long-winning streaks that had accentuated their magnificent season a year earlier. Trammell and the rest of the Detroit organization spent a much different off-season that winter, asking themselves what had happened.

When Boston Red Sox' right-fielder, Dwight Evans, drove Jack Morris' very first pitch of the 1986 season over the left field fence in Tiger Stadium, the Tigers found themselves trailing just seconds into the new campaign. The startling beginning served as a bad omen for a Detroit organization that had convinced itself that any hangover from their championship two years prior was over, and that the 1985 season had been an aberration. The team entered the new season with a retooled bench and bullpen, and had added more speed to the lineup. However, by the end of June—approximately three months into the season–Detroit was sitting at .500 (37–37) and was in sixth place in the AL East, twelve games behind the division-leading Red Sox.

For Trammell the season had been a struggle from the very start. He dealt once again with shoulder pain that surfaced during spring training and lingered into the early parts of the regular season. There was talk about his career being in jeopardy, especially if he could not make the routine throws anymore without pain. Whether it was the physical pain he was enduring, or the pressure he felt to kick-start the team out of the doldrums it had seemingly been in for more than a year, Trammell's play suffered both in the field and at the plate. He committed seven errors in April, half a seasons' worth over most years in his career. Offensively, he continued to be well below his 1983 and 1984 production and was scuffling along with a batting average in the .230s well into June. His on-base percentage was below .300, embarrassingly low for a table-setter like Trammell, who was counted on to ignite rallies and score runs in the Detroit lineup. For the first time in his career, there were murmurs of discontent about the play of the Tigers' shortstop.

"I think because we're losing, you look at the year, and I'm not having a great year," admitted Trammell as the season neared the half-way point. "People think 'Aw, something's wrong' and all this. I'm playing as hard as I ever have."[13]

Trammell had started the season batting sixth in the batting order; Sparky Anderson hoped to make him more of a run producer. The team had acquired the speedy veteran outfielder Dave Collins in the off-season, and had planned on batting him and Whitaker at the top of the Detroit order. The idea was to inject more speed into a lineup that had become stagnant at times and overly home run dependent. The move, like most that season, did not pan out as planned. Anderson used different lineups in each of the first 22 games and Collins eventually became only a part-time player during his one season in Detroit. Within weeks, Whitaker and Trammell had been reestablished as the 1–2 batters in the Detroit lineup. "I'm not hitting as well as I'd like, but I'm contributing here and there with a few hits" said Trammell during the first half of the 1986 season. "I can look at myself in the mirror and know that I've given it my best."[14]

"His best" was proving to not be good enough for a small fraction of Tiger supporters who had become increasingly critical of a Detroit team that fell out of the race by the All-Star break. Trammell's performance over the preceding season-and-a-half made him a prime target for criticism from an audience that wasn't satisfied with just savoring memories of 1984. Those criticisms, however, were quickly defended by those who knew him best.

"I wish people could see how hard Tram tries," said Morris in mid–June that season about his teammate. "That guy puts the weight of the whole team on his shoulders. I read something last week that we should trade Trammell? I can't believe that shit. You trade Trammell, you trade the heart of this team."[15]

"I know now he's giving the very most you can give," added his manager, Anderson, who nonetheless had kept Trammell on the bench for a few days in late May while the team had been riding a short winning steak with Tom Brookens filling in at shortstop. "People look at his batting average. I don't care if he ever gets a hit."[16]

By the All-Star break, Trammell had rebounded somewhat, raising his average to .259 with seven home runs. He was starting to feel stronger physically, the early-season arm miseries seemingly abating while his all-around game improved greatly. He was throwing without pain, better than he had in a couple of years. His defensive play had risen again to a level that was as good as any in baseball at the shortstop position. "The first month was probably as rough a streak as I went through, and I wasn't happy with that," commented Trammell late that summer. "There were some weird errors. I hit a runner in the back with a relay throw. But they're still errors, and they didn't look good on the record. But I think over the last month I've been playing well and trying to contribute as much as I can, any way I can—which is my style of play."[17]

Trammell was also finding his stroke at the plate, putting together eleven multiple-hit games during one 18-game stretch in August that pushed his batting average into the .270s. More noticeably, he had discovered a power stroke and was hitting the ball over the fence with greater regularity than he ever had previously in his career. By the first of September he had already eclipsed his career high in home runs with fifteen. He swatted three more over the first two days of the month, all part of a four home runs in five days stretch that was the greatest power surge of Trammell's career up to that point. Despite the Tigers suffering through another disappointing season, the restored health and newly found punch left Trammell feeling rejuvenated. "Realistically, we're not going to win it," admitted Trammell at the beginning of September with the Tigers sitting in fourth place, nine full games behind Boston. "But until they tell us to stop fighting, we're going to keep trying."[18]

Throughout the season's final month, Trammell continued to add to his career high in home runs. He had made a technical adjustment to his stance part-way through the season, widening out the placement of his feet in the batter's box.[19] Others thought the change in Trammell's game was more mental than physical, part of a maturation process that saw the 28-year-old playing within himself, rather than taking on so much of the burden associated with the team's disappointing performance. "Earlier in the year, I thought Alan was putting way too much pressure on himself," explained Darrell Evans, the 39-year-old first baseman and DH that was generally acknowledged as the clubhouse leader during that period. "He was being too critical of himself."[20]

Trammell reached a personal milestone on September 19 in Detroit when he smashed his 20th home run of the season off of Yankees' left-hander, Dennis Rasmussen. For good measure, Trammell added another on October 2 in Milwaukee to end the season with 21. He joined his keystone buddy Whitaker, third baseman Darnell Coles, and Evans to form an all-20-home run-hitting infield for Detroit. In doing so, the 1986 Tigers became only the second team in MLB history to reach such notoriety.

That Trammell and Whitaker had both reached the 20-home run plateau for a season was astonishing to many of those who remembered the two skinny kids that had first come to Detroit almost a decade earlier. "I never would have believed he could have hit ten home runs," said first-base coach Dick Tracewski about Trammell, while thinking about the scrawny teenager he first saw in September 1977.[21] The first two hitters in the Detroit lineup were no longer players that opposing pitchers just wanted to keep off base ahead of the sluggers that typically followed in the Tigers' batting order. Whitaker and Trammell hit back-to-back home runs to lead off the game against Cleveland on August 5 that summer, the first time they had ever accomplished such a feat. "They're hitting homers like outfielders," joked Anderson at one point late that year about the 1–2 hitters in his lineup, both middle infielders.[22]

Trammell finished the 1986 season with respectable numbers for batting average (.277) and on-base percentage (.347), while setting career highs in home runs (21), RBI's (75), runs scored (107, tying his 1980 mark), and triples (7). He also collected 33 doubles, stole 25 bases, and even managed to lay down 11 sacrifice bunts. His .469 slugging percentage was just two points lower than the career high he had set in 1983, and was the highest of any shortstop in the major leagues that season.

Defensively, Trammell was bested by Toronto's Tony Fernandez for the AL Gold Glove at shortstop, but to those who were watching closely, number "3" in the Tiger jersey was fielding as well as he ever had. "Alan is playing shortstop now like before he got hurt," commented Anderson late that summer."²³ No longer restricted by the arm and shoulder miseries that seemed to wear on him mentally and physically, taking away from other parts of his game, Trammell was again making the long throws required of an elite player at the position. By the second half of the summer, Trammell was feeling so good physically that he said: "I think I was throwing better than I ever have this season."²⁴

Trammell's reclamation was one of the few bright spots in an otherwise forgettable season for the Detroit Tigers. Although they closed to within 4½ games of the division lead at one point in early August, they never seriously contended. Only a hot streak to end the schedule, where they won their final five games, allowed Detroit to reach its season-high mark of twelve games over .500 at 87–75. The Tigers finished a distant 8½ games behind the division-winning Red Sox. Injuries and off years had played a big part in Detroit's second consecutive disappointing season. Gibson missed nearly a month and a half early in the season with a badly sprained ankle. Parrish injured his back and didn't play again after July. Lemon and Petry were injured for portions of the season and were often ineffective when they did play.

A tender right elbow troubled Trammell over the last few games on the schedule, but unlike the shoulder pain he had fought through for the better part of three seasons, the elbow injury was not considered serious. "I'm not worried about the elbow. I do machine exercises to help strengthen it three times a week and I'll continue to do the same thing in the off-season. Despite another disappointing third-place finish, Trammell could find solace in his own strong completion to the season. "I thought about it and decided that this has been a pretty good season no matter what happens at the end," he said just a few days before it had ended.²⁵

His manager, Sparky Anderson, concurred, finding some solace at the conclusion of a second-straight campaign that had begun with the highest of aspirations, but ended with frustration and disillusionment. "You'd have to say he's one of the ones around here that had a good year."²⁶

9

1987

For the first time in at least four years, the Detroit Tigers were viewed as only fringe contenders for the top spot in the American League's Eastern Division heading into the 1987 season. Three years removed from their storybook championship season of 1984, most prognosticators sensed that the Tigers' peak as an American League power had passed. A panel of 163 writers surveyed from around the country by *The Sporting News*, picked Detroit to finish fifth in their division in 1987, behind New York, Toronto, Boston, and even the lowly Cleveland Indians.[1]

A changing of the guard was thought to have taken place in what most still considered baseball's most competitive division. While Milwaukee, Baltimore, and Detroit had represented the division in three straight World Series earlier in the decade, most pundits now believed that those teams were in decline, and were being surpassed by a retooled New York Yankees team led by Don Mattingly and Ricky Henderson; a Toronto Blue Jays team that had supplanted the Tigers for the division crown in 1985, and that was universally cited as having the best talent in the American League; and a Boston Red Sox club that had won the AL Pennant the previous year.

The decreased expectations for Detroit were much deeper than just reaction to disappointing seasons in 1985 and 1986 that many might have described as "underachieving." While the everyday lineup and starting pitching remained solid and mostly intact from the previous two seasons, there was considerable concern over the rest of the 25-man roster put together by general manager, Bill Lajoie. Fringe portions of the roster had been retooled, unsuccessfully, over the past two winters, while the organization tried to recapture the magic that had existed on Sparky Anderson's bench and in his bullpen in 1984. Only Dave Bergman and Johnny Grubb remained in their roles as extra position players on the team, while Guillermo (no longer Willie) Hernandez, was the only remaining member from the championship season's bullpen. However, the biggest change heading into the 1987 season, a big piece of the core lineup from that championship season had been chipped away.

9. 1987

The Tigers' organization had spent the previous two off-seasons skirting the issue of free agency with several of its highest profile stars. Kirk Gibson had played out his contract at the end of the 1985 season, only to find that the free agent market for a 28-year-old, game-changing outfielder with uncommon power and speed was mysteriously passive. With few outside options available, he re-signed with Detroit in January 1986, for three years and $4.1 million. Jack Morris had a similar experience after the 1986 season. When an apparent multi-million dollar offer from his hometown Minnesota Twins was suddenly pulled out from under him, Morris was left with no real options other than signing again with Detroit. The Detroit organization would not have the same luck, however, with their cornerstone behind the plate, catcher Lance Parrish.

Parrish had played out his contract and had been granted free agency at the conclusion of the 1986 season. He was unable to come to terms with a Tiger organization that was wary of a back condition that had forced Parrish to miss the final 71 games. Unlike Gibson and Morris who succumbed to re-signing with Detroit rather than further testing the free agency waters that had proved unusually dry during that period, Parrish and his agent Tom Reich let the January deadline pass that permitted him to sign a contract with his current team. Under the rules of free agency at that time, Parrish was not eligible to sign with Detroit before May 1, 1987. As spring training camps opened in Florida, it became increasingly clear that Parrish was not going to come back to the Tigers. When the Philadelphia Phillies emerged as the only serious suitor and offered him a guaranteed one-year, $1 million contract on March 13, Parrish signed, ending his playing career in Detroit.

The loss of the six-time All-Star catcher, who had three Gold Gloves and five Silver Slugger awards to his credit, was considered a crippling blow to a Detroit team that hadn't seriously contended for post-season play in either 1985 or 1986 *with* Parrish. The muscular catcher was among the most physically imposing players in the major leagues during the first half of the 1980s, and provided a steadying presence on the field for the Tigers. He had been the regular catcher for eight seasons, and was an impact player both as a rifle-armed backstop intimidating potential base-stealers throughout the American League, as well as the middle-of-the-lineup, cleanup hitter for Detroit who had averaged over 27 home runs and 90 RBI's from 1979–1985 (excluding the strike-shortened 1981 season). Even in his injury-plagued season of 1986, Parrish had walloped 22 round-trippers and drove in 62 runs.

With lessened expectations and a makeshift lineup that included Orlando Mercado (3 career HR's) behind the plate, Mike Heath (a catcher by trade) playing right-field, and former National League backup outfielder, Terry Harper, serving as the designated hitter, the Detroit Tigers opened the 1987 season with a meek 2–1 loss to New York. Bewildering many of the Tiger Stadium crowd of 51,315 that day, was Sparky Anderson's choice to fill the gigantic hole in the number four spot in the lineup, his shortstop Alan Trammell.

The cleanup position in a batting order is usually reserved for the top power-hitting and run producing batter in the lineup, often filled by big, burly players, capable of driving in runs in bunches when their long, powerful swings make contact. Anderson's selection of Trammell to fill the void in the lineup created by Parrish's departure was considered unconventional by some and just another wild experimentation by the whimsical manager by others. Although no longer the slender, 165-pound kid that had played regularly in the big leagues while in his early twenties, Trammell at 185 pounds and sporting a career high of 21 home runs set just the year before, was still some 40 pounds and another ten home runs light of the typical cleanup hitter in American League lineups that spring. Anderson had other ideas though, as to what he wanted from his number four hitter that summer. "With three guys hitting ahead of him and getting on base a lot," he explained with visions of the speedy trio of Lou Whitaker, outfielder Pat Sheridan, and Gibson batting first, second, and third, "he'll have tons of opportunities."[2]

"Our number four was gone," remembered first-base coach Dick Tracewski about the thought process that went into the decision. "Sparky was a stickler for driving in runs, moving over runners, scoring from third with less than two outs, cheap runs. That was something Alan could give us on a consistent basis. The only person we ever had who compared that way was Rusty Staub."[3]

A month into the season, the move looked like a failure. The team, having left Lakeland on the heels of a dismal spring training, was struggling mightily, while Trammell was battling a sore left ankle and hitting just .262 with only one home run and ten runs batted in. His slugging percentage was a lowly .333, abysmal numbers for a bat anchoring the middle of the order. Trammell's struggles were magnified by other woes the Tigers faced that spring. Gibson missed the first 24 games with a torn rib muscle—robbing Detroit of the dynamic number three hitter in the lineup that they so desperately needed, while third baseman Darnell Coles who had been such a pleasant surprise the year before when he blasted 20 home runs and knocked in 86 runs, had reported to camp overweight, batted just .136 over the season's first five weeks, and quickly found a seat in Anderson's doghouse.

After losing to Oakland on May 9 the Tigers' record stood at 10–18. They were in sixth place and already ten games behind the division-leading Milwaukee Brewers. Detroit had scored the second-fewest runs of any team in the American League, and the Trammell experiment in the number four slot seemed like it would be short-lived. Rumored interest in the exiled and enigmatic slugger, Dave Kingman, exemplified the desperate atmosphere that existed around the Tigers. The fifth place finish that had been predicted for Detroit before the season seemed realistic and possibly even their ceiling, based on the team's play through the first 28 games. Attendance sagged at Tiger Stadium, down by more than 100,000, as spring entered summer and local fan interest focused more on exciting playoff runs by the Detroit Pistons and Red Wings.

The return of Gibson seemed to spark Detroit's baseball team however. Following their season-low point on May 9, the team went on a streak that saw them win 14 of 17 games and close out May a game over .500 at 24–23. The streak shrunk their deficit in the divisional race to just six games back of New York, who had established itself as the front-runner. Trammell, like much of the rest of the team, heated up with the weather and increased his offensive production at month's end to a very respectable .331 batting average with four home runs, 22 RBI's and a .448 slugging percentage.

In June the Tigers' shortstop went on an ever more torrid streak. He hit safely in 37 of 39 games at one point, which included a career-high 21-game hitting streak. In a June 6 game in Boston that was televised nationally as NBC's Saturday *Game of the Week*, Trammell went 3–5 in a gritty 5–3 victory in 14 innings, a contest that lasted nearly five hours. He twice was the recipient of intentional walks, with both occurring during the extra frames, indicative of the increased fear and respect Trammell was generating around the league. The three hits raised his season's average to .356, which vaulted him above the Red Sox' Wade Boggs for the top spot in the American League batting race. "Boggs loans it out once in a while, just so other guys can know what it feels like," said Anderson after the game, joking about his shortstop temporarily wrestling away an honor that the Boston third baseman seemingly had a strangle-hold on.[4] Boggs was in the midst of winning five batting titles in six seasons during that period.

A week later in the opener of a return three-game weekend series against the Red Sox in Detroit, Trammell bombed a three-run homer in the seventh inning off of Roger Clemons to break a 4–4 deadlock and lead the Tigers to victory. He homered again and scored two runs the next day as Detroit won the middle game of the series 6–4. Then in the Sunday finale, Trammell scored both Detroit runs in a tightly contested 2–1 victory. He tied the game after singling and coming around to score in the seventh inning, before reaching base an inning later by walking on a full-count pitch. Trammell then took second on a Larry Herndon single, before coming around to score the eventual winning run on a Mike Heath single to right with two outs. Scoring from second was no easy task for Trammell who was suffering from a badly pulled muscle in his right thigh as well as a painfully bruised heel. "Tram can't run, shouldn't be playing, but I got to play him," quipped Anderson about the one player whose all-around play was energizing the team's resurgence. "He's our leader now."[5]

"I had my bad knee, my shoulder last year, now my thigh," said Trammell of his latest bout with the injury bug. "This leg probably won't be able to heal all season." Determined to play through the pain in what was developing into the greatest all-around season of his now ten-year career, Trammell was nonetheless frustrated at the aches and strains that had taken a toll on his career. "I don't like to be labeled like that, have that tag of always being injured. It bothers me. I'd like to be known as a guy who plays the game and enjoys it."[6]

With Gibson back in the lineup and batting in front of him, and power threats in Darrell Evans and rookie catcher Matt Nokes reaching the seats with regularity behind him, Trammell was consistently producing runs like his manager had envisioned. He knocked in runs in 15 of the 26 games Detroit played in June, part of a monstrous month in which Trammell batted .376 with nine home runs, 21 runs batted in, and 25 runs scored. He ended the month with a batting average of .350, third highest in the league behind Boggs and Milwaukee's Paul Molitor. He was riding the ultimate hot-streak of his career, one that had Anderson telling anyone who would listen that "he's turned into a dynamic hitter."[7]

"I've had my good streaks before, but never one in which I've contributed as much as now," said Trammell in the middle of June about the unprecedented production he was enjoying both in scoring runs as well as driving them home. "I know it won't continue like this. I expect good numbers, but not .350."[8]

Taking their cue from Detroit's on-field leader, the Tigers stormed through the month winning 17 games while losing only nine. They ended June five games behind the Yankees and nine games over the .500 mark. The Tigers' offense which had been so anemic through the first month of the season was now sizzling. They scored five or more runs in 18 games that month, overwhelming teams at times with their newly found firepower. They walloped Cleveland 15–3, Boston 18–8 and 11–4, Milwaukee 11–1, California 15–2 and 10–7, and Minnesota 15–7 at various points during their hot streak in May and June.

"I've never seen us score the way we have the last couple of weeks," said an astounded Anderson about his suddenly potent club.⁹ "It's almost as if it was another season," added Darrell Evans, recollecting the inept offensive attack the Tigers displayed over the season's first month. "I remember we couldn't buy a hit in Oakland. We couldn't score, but we're different now. We expect to explode every night."¹⁰

In July, Detroit continued its ascent in the division standings, winning 17 of 22 games during one stretch to close within three games of first place as they headed into August. A team that had been eight games under .500 in early May, was remarkably now 17 games over the break-even mark and squarely in the thick of a three-team race with the division-leading Yankees and second-place Blue Jays. As the season passed its midway point, it had become increasingly apparent that the 1987 season was going to be quite different from the disappointment of the two previous campaigns. "This is too long a stretch for it to be just a bubble," said Trammell when asked whether the Tigers could sustain the momentum they had gained during the middle portion of that summer. "It's not going to burst. I'd be very surprised to see us go in the tank now. We have too many guys helping out for it to happen."¹¹

The 1987 edition of the Detroit Tigers had a much different aura surrounding them than their world championship predecessors three years earlier. While the World Series champions jumped off to arguably the greatest start in baseball history, and played out their season in storybook fashion, the 1987 team had been forced to overcome obstacles from the very beginning. They had entered the season with lowered expectations and then were nearly counted out after a slow start, just weeks into the campaign. The two teams' makeup and styles of play also differed dramatically. The 1984 team was accustomed to jumping out to early leads and then suffocating teams with overpowering starting pitching, a lockdown bullpen, and air-tight defense. It boasted a lineup filled with home-grown everyday players as good as any in the game. By 1987 the Tigers' roster had been significantly transformed, with fewer star-quality players and a larger cast of role players. Cast-offs from other organizations and unproven call-ups from Detroit's minor league system played major parts in the team's turnaround and surrounded the smaller remaining core from the championship team. It was a more flawed team, but one that learned to maximize its strengths.

Jack Morris remained the ace of the starting rotation and among the best starting pitchers in all of baseball. He was 12–4 at the All-Star break in 1987, on his way to winning 18 games which would lead Detroit in that category for a ninth straight year. Dan Petry, however, was no longer the "Robin" to Morris' "Batman" role. After winning 67 games for the Tigers over the previous four seasons, Petry had fallen off to an injury-riddled 5–10 mark in 1986 and was struggling similarly again in 1987. Despite having a winning record at 7–5, Petry's performance in the early months of 1987 had been so ragged, with an ERA nearing six, that he was pulled out of the starting rotation by early August.

Instead the bedrocks behind Morris in Sparky Anderson's rotation were right-hander Walt Terrell and lefty Frank Tanana, both veteran pickups from the 1985 season. Terrell was a sinker-ball thrower that thrived when pitching in Tiger Stadium with its long and thick infield grass, and Trammell and Whitaker manning the middle-infield behind him. He battled from the mound with a bulldog's tenacity and was an innings-chewing constant on the pitching staff, rarely leaving a game before the seventh inning. Tanana was no longer the flame-throwing left-hander he had been in his early 20s while pitching for the California Angeles. 34-years-old that summer, he had transformed himself into a junk-ball throwing extraordinaire, baffling hitters with an assortment of curve balls, screwballs, and changeups, thrown from multiple angles and at varying speeds. Rounding out the rotation was six-foot six-inch rookie, Jeff Robinson. The hard-throwing Robinson was expectedly inconsistent as his 5.37 ERA that season attests, but he provided a number of quality outings for Detroit that summer.

The bullpen was a patchwork affair all summer. Guillermo Hernandez was well past his MVP form of 1984 and had been injured for much of April and May. When he was able to pitch, he was often ineffective, and entered June with a loss, no saves, and an ERA over twelve. Right-hander Eric King was a second-year player that had been picked up in a swap for Juan Berenguer after the 1985 season. By 1987, he was a trusted member of Anderson's pen and was often used in a swing-role, pitching long or short-relief, and often for multiple innings per outing. Mark Thurmond, whom the Tigers had roughed up twice as a starting pitcher for San Diego in the 1984 World Series, had come to Detroit a year earlier and was now pitching strictly in relief. The lefty appeared in 48 games in 1987. The real find in the Tigers' relief-corp that summer was Mike Henneman, a 25-year-old Missouri native, who had been called up from the minor leagues on May 11. Henneman was a hard-throwing right-hander with a three-quarters motion delivery that proved to be a godsend to the Detroit bullpen. He had unflappable poise in tight situations for a rookie, and was 8–1 as a reliever, with two saves and a 2.38 ERA through his first two-and-one-half months in the major leagues.

Overall, the restructured pitching staff of the Tigers would allow nearly 100 more runs than they had permitted in their championship season in 1984. However, the game had changed greatly since then. Scoring had increased considerably over the three year span since 1984, and had spiked noticeably again in the first half of 1987. Runs scored had increased by nearly seven percent from 1986, and home run totals in particular were skyrocketing, up by over 15 percent in the American League. An astonishing 20 players would hit 30 home runs or more in the AL that season, led by a rookie first baseman for the Oakland A's, Mark McGuire. Although nothing was ever proven, most attributed the inflated home run rate to a juiced up ball which Sparky Anderson called "that nitroglycerin ball."[12] Regardless of the cause, higher-scoring games became much more commonplace in 1987, and no team took advantage more than the Detroit Tigers.

Detroit's in-season turnaround in offensive production that year was astounding. A team that had struggled to score runs with a feeble, under-manned lineup during the first six weeks of the season, was lighting up American League pitching staffs with regularity by early summer. By the end of July, the Tigers led the American League in runs scored and were second only to the St. Louis Cardinals in all of major league baseball. By season's end they would not only lead the majors in runs scored with 896, but would establish the highest team total since baseball adopted a 162-game schedule in 1961. Included was a team record 225 home runs, nearly 40 more than the 1984 team had socked, a team mark that has existed well into the 21st century.

While Trammell was easily the offensive leader, offensive production oozed from nearly every position player on the Tiger's roster. Lou Whitaker, although batting only .265 for the season, remained a highly-effective lead-off batter—walking 71 times and scoring 110 runs, the third highest total in the AL. Once Gibson returned from his rib muscle injury in early May, the fleet left-fielder was soon terrorizing opponents with his game-changing power and speed. Despite missing the first five weeks of the schedule, Gibson was on his way to a 24-home run, 26-stolen base, 95-run season. His return to the three-slot in the batting order coincided with Trammell and the rest of the Detroit lineup turning red-hot offensively.

Darrell Evans and Matt Nokes were the primary power sources hitting behind Trammell. Evans was enjoying another of his typical seasons as the Tigers' regular first-baseman. The consummate professional hitter was socking home runs with a regularity that would give him a season total of 34, while also picking up 99 RBI's. He also chipped in 100 walks, contributing to numbers that would be much more appreciated in later decades, when his eye-popping on-base percentage that approached .400 that season, and his OPS of nearly .900 were more fully valued. Nokes, a rookie catcher, possessed a classic left-handed swing at the plate and was the surprise find for an organization that had braced for the pain and ridicule anticipated from losing Parrish to free agency. Instead, a player initially targeted for a year in Triple-A, was having a Rookie-of-the-Year caliber season that would see him hit 32 home runs and bat .289 while starting 94 games behind the plate. He platooned with the veteran Mike Heath as the Tiger backstops. While neither was the defensive presence Parrish had been, Heath was a very solid receiver with a quality throwing arm and chipped in with eight homers and 33 RBI's. Together, the combination of Nokes and Heath gave Detroit offensive production at the catcher position that exceeded anything Parrish had ever produced individually.

Chet Lemon, Pat Sheridan, and Larry Herndon were the primary sidekicks to Gibson in the Detroit outfield. Lemon, although no longer the Gold-Glove caliber centerfielder he had been in the championship season, was still a quality defender covering the vast spaces in Tiger Stadium's deep center field. Offensively, he chipped in with a fine 20-home run, 75-RBI season. Sheridan was a tall, lanky outfielder with good speed and occasional power that had come to Detroit from the Kansas City Royals. He shared right field with Herndon who rebounded from a trio of sub-par seasons to bat a sizzling .324 with nine home runs and 47 RBI's in just over 200 at-bats.

Tom Brookens emerged once again as the survivor in the annual battle for Detroit's third base job, after the disappointing Darnell Coles was shipped to Pittsburgh in early August. Brookens responded with one of his more productive offensive seasons, batting .246 with 13 home runs and 59 RBI's. Veterans Dave Bergman and John Grubb were productive options coming off the bench for Anderson, and between the two combined for eight home runs and 35 RBI's.

A key to the club's offensive turnaround was the acquisition of National League veteran Bill Madlock in the first week of June. Madlock was already 36-years-old and on the downside of a 15-season career when he was signed by Detroit after being released by the Dodgers. He had been a four-time National League batting champion however, and still swung a dangerous, and much needed, right-handed bat. Madlock also played with fire, exemplified by his nickname, "Mad Dog," and by the eighteen career ejections he had received from major league umpires. Madlock provided Sparky Anderson with a right-handed hitting alternative at first base, who could spell Evans when facing a tough left-hander. He also proved valuable as a designated hitter option that was effective against all types of pitching. Madlock would bat second in the lineup for much of the summer.

"The type of year we had in 1984, I don't think we'll ever duplicate," said Trammell when comparing the relative cakewalk the Tigers had in their championship season versus the dogfight they now found themselves in with Toronto and New York. "A 35–5 start, winning 104 games, sweeping the playoffs, winning the World Series four games to one—that was a script that can't be improved on. This year it's been more of a struggle. We're not a team with a lot of stars. The secret of our success is that we get production from a lot of different people."[13]

Over the first two weekends in August, Detroit continued its assault on first place in the division. After losing two of three in New York to the first-place Yankees, the two teams concluded their season series the next weekend in Tiger Stadium. The Tigers bombed the Bronx Bombers in three of the four games, winning by margins of 12–5, 8–0, and 15–4, while seemingly deflating New York's balloon. The Yankees left Detroit having fallen out of first place, a decline they would never recover from. The team that had been the front-runner in the division for most of the season, would finish 23–27 over their final 50 games and quickly fall off the pace being set by the torrid Tigers and Blue Jays. Trammell did his part in insuring the Yankees' demise, scoring five runs and driving in three over the weekend series in Detroit.

The Tigers followed up the New York series by winning eight of their next ten games and moved into first place for the first time that season on August 19, when they inched ahead of the Blue Jays by one-half game. For the remainder of the month, Detroit and Toronto would eye each other from a distance, the two teams never separated by more than one game at the top of the division, as both clubs feasted primarily on American League Western Division competition. "You play a hundred games to have fun the last 62," said Darrell Evans that August. "The fun is starting."[14]

By month's end Detroit's record stood at 77–52, good for first place in the division and the second-best record in all of baseball. Toronto was 77–54, only one game behind the Tigers. New York trailed by four games and was fading fast—with injuries and a shaky pitching staff taking their toll as the dog days of the major league schedule endlessly ground on. As September dawned, the Tigers and Blue Jays had clearly emerged as the two best teams, not only in the division, but in the entire American League. The race between two clubs locked into a blossoming rivalry looked destined to go down to the wire.

Alan Trammell continued to roll along through the best individual season of his career. Although his batting average had dropped from its high water mark of .362 on June 16, to an August-ending .323, he was still ranked among the top 5 hitters in the American League batting race. He had also matched his career high in home runs set just the year before, with more than a month left in the regular season, and was positioned to obliterate his previous high in RBI's as well.

One home run in particular had special meaning for the ten-year Detroit shortstop. On June 19 in Baltimore, Trammell connected off of journeyman right-hander Dave Schmidt, sending the ball soaring into the left field bullpen in Memorial Stadium. The homer was the one-hundredth of his career, a milestone not lost on a player with a keen sense of baseball history. "It means my baseball card will look a lot better with three digits instead of two," Trammell joked with the media after the game. "I knew the minute I hit it that it was number 100 for me. That's why I asked for them to return the ball from the bullpen."[15]

On July 14 in Oakland, Trammell played in just his third All-Star Game, pinch-hitting for the American League in the third inning of an eventual 2–0 National League victory. That Trammell had finished fourth in the fan balloting at shortstop was a disappointment in itself, considering the type of season he was having. He shrugged off the perceived slight in typical fashion, saying "It's not that big a deal. I don't always seek attention, and I'm not a flashy person."[16] Trammell's pinch-hitting appearance was his lone activity for the game, as Boston Manager John McNamara elected to split the shortstop duties between Baltimore's Cal Ripken, Jr., and Toronto's Tony Fernandez. Batting against NL righty Rick Sutcliffe, Trammell grounded a hard-hit ball through the middle that St. Louis' whiz Ozzie Smith failed to field cleanly when trying to short-hop the ball, moving to his left from his shortstop position. The do-or-die play that Smith failed to come up with was ruled an error, denying Trammell of what arguably should have been his first All Star Game hit. "This was only my second at-bat in an All-Star Game and you never know how many chances you are going to get in one of these things," he portended afterwards.[17]

While the numerous nagging ailments he played with that summer may have robbed him of a half-step in the field, Trammell remained a superior defensive player at his position and was the undisputed on-field leader for Detroit. Now in his tenth full season in the major leagues, Trammell knew the circuit and his competition as well as any player in the league. He was able to compensate for any physical limitations he might have been dealing with due to injury and fatigue, by cheating a step here and there defensively, or reading a situation ahead of others. Trammell had always looked for the little edge that could make the difference in a tight game, but never more so than in the 1987 season. Whether it was making a clutch play in the field, driving home a runner, or scoring a run himself, he was a unique player for the Tigers, impacting all aspects of the game. "I'm not your prototype cleanup hitter," Trammell acknowledged about himself. "But I can do some things other cleanup hitters can't do. I can run, steal a base.... I don't clog up the middle of the order."[18]

Not everyone was in agreement though that the Detroit shortstop would be able to hold up as the focal point of the Tigers' lineup, both offensively and defensively, through the rigors of a tight September pennant race. Detroit's local television broadcaster at the time, George Kell, a Hall-of-Fame player himself in the 1940s and '50s, thought too much might be expected from Trammell that summer. "I worry about a shortstop hitting fourth and thinking too much about his hitting. Because shortstop is such a vital position, I want him concentrating on defense. He'll get his hits, but I don't want the pressure on him." Kell would concede however that Trammell had "handled it extremely well" and that he was a "rare individual."[19]

Sparky Anderson, who had masterminded the unconventional placement of Trammell in the center of the Tiger lineup, would ride out the rest of the season with his team's chances largely dependent on his all-everything shortstop. In reality, he had no other choice. "You have to remember that when I got here, Trammell wasn't as strong as he is now. He dumped a few hits in right-center, but didn't do much more than that. Now he's a strong person. I've seen him grow up and fill out."[20]

With summer turning to fall, Trammell's play was getting accolades all across the league. His name was being prominently mentioned as an MVP candidate, which seemed a distinct possibility if he could finish strong and lead Detroit to the post-season. Nearly 130 games into the 1987 schedule, there was little doubt that Trammell was closing out his career year in the major leagues. "I can't say anything really complicated," he tried to explain about his unprecedented production at the plate. "I'm just seeing the ball really well, taking good swings, and hitting it hard."[21] That same approach would be needed for Detroit to be successful in their remaining games. Over the next five weeks, Alan Trammell was about to experience the pennant chase of his life.

10

Race to the Finish

Those who expected Alan Trammell to cool off that September were quickly proven wrong. Some believed that the cumulative fatigue from playing shortstop nearly every day of the schedule, along with the increased amount of time he had spent on the base paths during that long, hot summer, would finally take its toll as the days grew shorter. Instead the player that had been counted on the most to produce runs in the Detroit lineup, went on another hot streak. He batted .417 over the first nine days, including two more home runs, ten runs scored, and seven driven in. The hot streak raised his season's average nearly twenty points to .342, which was third in the league.

More importantly, the Tigers won seven of the first nine games that month to maintain first place in the American League Eastern Division, staying just ahead of the Toronto Blue Jays who remained just as hot, only 1½ games behind. A little over a week into September, both teams settled into their remaining schedules which featured games exclusively against divisional opponents. The Tigers and Blue Jays wouldn't face each other, however, until the final ten days of the season, when they would meet seven times. That stretch included a season-ending, three-game series in Detroit scheduled for the first weekend of October. Until then, the two rivals would compete only on the out-of-town scoreboards, with each winning with a high rate of regularity while waiting for the other to blink.

A new face in the Detroit uniform was playing a major role in the Tigers' efforts to remain a step ahead of the Blue Jays. General Manager Bill Lajoie had made a key late-season acquisition, without whom the team likely wouldn't have been able to keep pace with Toronto. Sensing that his club needed an additional arm in the starting rotation, Lajoie had traded with the hapless Atlanta Braves on August 12 to acquire veteran starting pitcher, Doyle Alexander. In Alexander the Tigers were gaining an experienced right-hander closing in on his 37th birthday. Getting traded was nothing new to Alexander, as Detroit would be his eighth organization at the major league level, having been included in seven previous trades. His reputation was that of a wily craftsman, relying on pin-point control and changing speeds, rather than challenging batters. To be successful, Alexander had to keep the ball away from hitters in predicable situations where his less than overpowering stuff could be exploited. He had been 5–10 with a 4.13 ERA in Atlanta that season, so his addition was generally viewed with indifference. At best he was considered as an alternative as Sparky Anderson's fourth starter, who otherwise chose between a struggling Dan Petry and rookie Jeff Robinson.

The Tigers wildest dreams couldn't have encapsulated what they got from Alexander over the final two months of the 1987 season. Baseball history is littered with instances of a late-season pickup by a contending club that swung a pennant race: the veteran slugger that rises up on old, tired legs to deliver hits at crucial moments, the journeyman infielder that steps in for an injured regular and plays above his head for a couple of weeks, the savvy pitcher that settles a pitching staff that is fading as summer turns to fall. Few acquisitions of that type though, have ever matched the boost that Doyle Alexander gave Detroit when it needed it most that summer.

His first win came at Minnesota on August 20, when he pitched eight scoreless innings in an 8–0 washout of the Twins. Over his next four starts, Alexander pitched two other complete-game shutout victories and allowed only a single run in another game while pushing his Detroit record to 5–0 with a 1.75 ERA. His phenomenal streak would continue on for the remainder of the schedule, as he won four more decisions against no losses, while never lasting fewer than seven innings per start or allowing more than three earned runs. A pitcher whose pattern over his career suggested a slightly better than .500 record most seasons, instead went 9–0 for Detroit over the final seven weeks of the season. With Morris, Terrell, and Tanana already in place, the addition of Alexander gave the Tigers a formidable starting rotation for the stretch run.

After their hot start to the month, the Tigers were ambushed in Milwaukee by a surging Brewers club that was pushing New York for third place in the division. The Tigers lost the first three games of a four-game weekend series to Milwaukee, and desperately needed to salvage the final game on Sunday. Once again it was Trammell that turned things around, breaking a scoreless tie in the fourth inning with a solo home run. When Milwaukee tied the game in the bottom of the eighth, Trammell led off the ninth inning with a single and eventually came around to score the game-winning run, stopping the slide and moving Detroit back into a first place tie with Toronto. The next night, Trammell had three hits, including the

RBI hit that drove the previous season's AL Cy Young Award winner, Roger Clemens, from the game as the Tigers beat Boston, 3–0.

Trammell went on another tear starting with the win in Milwaukee on September 13, and lasting through September 21, where he knocked out multiple hits in seven of eight games including four more home runs, which gave him 27 on the season. The Detroit shortstop's clutch hitting keyed a stretch where the Tigers won eight of ten games following the three-game losing skid against the Brewers. The last of the victories during that streak was a 4–0 win over Boston with Alexander tossing a two-hit shutout. The team then left Fenway to fly north of the border for a showdown series in Toronto.

The Toronto Blue Jays had just completed their first decade of existence the previous summer. An expansion team in 1977, they had averaged 103 losses over their first four campaigns in the American League and had taken up a regular residency in the basement of the AL East. However, General Manager Pat Gillick had slowly improved the talent level of his fledgling franchise, often delving into Latin American countries to sign prospects, a tactic ahead of most teams of that era. By the early 1980s, managers Bobby Cox and then Jimy Williams, fielded competitive teams—winning 89 games in 1983 and 1984, before breaking out with 99 victories in 1985 and dethroning the Tigers as Eastern Division champions. The 1987 team had shaped up as the best Blue Jays squad in their short history, and was generally acknowledged as the most talented team in all of baseball.

While the first winning teams in Toronto were built on strong starting pitching and a lineup filled with players more reliant on speed than power, the 1987 edition of the Blue Jays was admirably well-rounded. The starting pitching remained stout but was also backed by a deep bullpen filled with hard-throwing young arms. The lineup had speed, power, and an abundance of athleticism. After blowing a three games to one lead to lose the 1985 American League playoffs to Kansas City, followed by a disappointing fourth-place finish in 1986, Toronto was both hungry and experienced.

Veteran right-handers Jim Clancy (31) and Dave Stieb (30) had been the Blue Jays' stalwarts in the starting rotation for many seasons. They had been joined late that season by a grizzled grey-beard from Baltimore in 35-year-old lefty, Mike Flanagan. The star of the rotation was a fourth-year left-hander, Jimmy Key, who was on his way to seventeen wins while leading the league in ERA that season. Toronto was also breaking in another left-hander, 24-year-old David Wells, who would go on to win 239 major league games over a 21-year career. A deep and balanced bullpen was led by workhorses Mark Eichhorn (89 appearances), Jeff Musselman (68), and Tom Henke (62 games, 34 saves).

The Blue Jays collection of athletic position players was second to none. It was exemplified by the outfield trio of Lloyd Moseby, Jesse Barfield, and George Bell, all three having been born within two weeks of each other and now in their prime at 27-years-old. The threesome could run, throw, and hit for power—combining for 101 home runs and 47 stolen bases in 1987. Bell had emerged as a superstar that summer. The Dominican Republic native entered the series against Detroit with a .312 batting average and league leading totals for home runs (47), RBI's (132), and runs scored (109).

While Bell was an obvious league MVP candidate, he may not have even been the most valuable player on his own team. Tony Fernandez, Toronto's 25-year-old shortstop, was a do-everything type player having the same type of season that Trammell was having with Detroit. Fernandez was considered by that point to be the premier defensive shortstop in the American League, on his way to winning the second of four straight Gold Gloves he would collect. He was enjoying a breakout season at the plate as well, batting .322 with gap power. Fernandez had also stolen 32 bases and was a catalyst at the top of the potent Toronto lineup.

The rest of the Blue Jays' lineup was deep and dangerous. Willie Upshaw was a veteran power-hitting first baseman and run producer. Kelly Gruber was an up-and-coming everyday third baseman who could hit and field his position. Veteran infielders Rance Mulliniks and Garth Iorg were excellent role players and thrived as platooned players that wielded threatening bats. 35-year-old catcher Ernie Whitt was the steadying presence on the team. An excellent defensive catcher, the native Detroiter also swung a powerful bat as his 19 home runs and 75 RBI's could attest to. For good measure the Blue Jays had on their bench a pair of young sluggers in 23-year-old Fred McGriff who would go on to hit nearly 500 home runs, most of them in the National League, and the large and powerful 24-year-old Cecil Fielder, whose prodigious slugging would create a name for himself in the near future.

The schedule makers had done their jobs well, matching the two winningest teams in baseball in 1987 against each other seven times over the final 11 days of the season. Nearly a decade before the term "Wildcard" became part of major league baseball's vernacular with the expanded playoff field, the Tigers and Blue Jays met knowing that the stakes were winner-take-all. Despite posting an impressive win total, one of them wouldn't be playing in the post-season. Toronto entered the penultimate weekend of the schedule with a 93–59 record, one-half game ahead of Detroit who had played one less game and was 92–59. "I definitely think now the cream of the crop in baseball is the Tigers and Blue Jays," said Trammell on the eve of the series opener. "I think right now they are playing a little better than we are. It will come down to pitching. They may have a little advantage because our bullpen has been a little suspect. Overall that's their only edge, and I'm not conceding that either."[1]

Despite the tiny deficit, the odds-makers favored Detroit to finish the season in first place. In a poll of AL East managers done just before the series in Toronto got underway, each liked the Tigers' chances. Boston manager John McNamara seemed to sum up the general consensus when he said, "Toronto has the best all-around talent in our league, but Detroit has the chemistry—the knowledge of what it takes to win."[2] Both teams entered the series playing well with the Tigers racking up a 15–7 mark in September, while the Blue Jays were even better at 16–5. Trammell summed up the feeling of most when he said "everyone has known for a long time that it would come down to this."[3]

The series opened on Thursday, September 24, in Toronto's Exhibition Stadium, a venue designed for, and better suited to, Canadian-style football. It had a hard artificial turf as its playing surface, a huge foul territory that surrounded the infield and an unusual outfield configuration with grandstands running parallel to the left-field wall, well beyond the curvature of the actual playing field. The right-field wall, which was nothing more than a temporary fence, cut perpendicularly across from centerfield with an open expanse and no grandstand behind it.

The already-heightened intensity level was raised even more early in the first game of the series. The Tigers scored twice in the top of the third inning, but the key play came on an out. When Kirk Gibson grounded into a force-out at second base with Bill Madlock running from first base, Madlock took out the Blue Jays' shortstop, Tony Fernandez, with a cross-body block that would have made an NFL coach proud. When Fernandez, who had been flipped into the air, landed awkwardly on the tip of his elbow, Toronto had arguably lost its most indispensable player for the remainder of the season with a broken bone in his arm.

The Blue Jays and their fans were infuriated at the ruffian tactics coming from the player known as "Mad Dog," who seemed more intent on taking out the shortstop, than staying in the base path. Fernandez, to his credit, was not bitter at the time saying only of Madlock, "he was just doing his job, trying to win."[4] The play seemed to inspire the Jays though; in the bottom of that same inning they turned four hits, two walks, and a wild pitch into four runs while taking the lead. The score stayed at 4–2 into the seventh inning when Trammell singled-in Whitaker to cut the lead to 4–3, and knock Flanagan from the mound for Toronto. That was as close as Detroit would come, as Henke struck out the final two Tiger batters in the ninth to finish off the Toronto victory. Detroit hadn't been able to overcome a gritty, but trouble-filled night for Morris, who gave up seven hits and eight walks while taking the loss.

Things didn't get much better the next night as Detroit again jumped out to a 2–0 lead, which they then nursed into the bottom of the ninth inning. With one out and a Toronto runner on first base, Willie Hernandez took the mound in relief and promptly gave up a double to former University of Michigan quarterback and the former Tiger first baseman-outfielder Rick Leach. Jays' backup shortstop Manny Lee then tied the game 2–2 with an opposite field triple into the right-field corner. Detroit brought in Mike Henneman to replace Hernandez, and then elected to load the bases intentionally in order to create a force-out at home plate. With one out and the potential winning run on third base, Sparky Anderson moved his infield in while Toronto center-fielder Lloyd Moseby stepped to the plate. Moseby grounded a sharply hit ball to Whitaker who fielded the ball cleanly, but then unleashed a low throw towards home plate. Tigers catcher Mike Heath was unable to field the ball cleanly, and the ball bounded away while Lee slid safely across the plate with the winning run.

"It was just what we wanted," said a frustrated Whitaker in the Detroit clubhouse.[5] The hard hit ball off of the bat of Moseby should have resulted in a force-out at home plate, but instead resulted in another Toronto victory. "We've put ourselves in a hole before, that seems to be the way we play better," said Trammell, who at least outwardly was putting a brave face on the situation before adding, "Of course, we're running out of games."[6]

If the Tigers and their followers thought the first two games in Toronto were lost in maddening fashion, then the Saturday afternoon game forced them onto the ledge. Detroit again had jumped out to the early lead, with Trammell doubling in Gibson in the first inning, before riding home himself on a Matt Nokes' home run. But, the three-run lead didn't last even a full inning as Walt Terrell allowed the tying runs to score in the bottom of the frame. Detroit struck big again in the third inning when Nokes homered for the second time that day, a grand slam that put the Tigers up 7–3. When Darrell Evans hit a leadoff home run in the fifth inning, the Tigers had increased their lead to 9–4, and seemed to be on their way to the much-needed victory. The Blue Jays, however, chipped away with single runs in the fifth, sixth, and seventh innings, and came to bat in the bottom of the ninth inning, down 9–7.

The rookie Henneman, who had been Anderson's most consistent reliever for the last two-thirds of the season, had come into the game in the sixth inning, but whether due to nerves or fatigue, started coming apart in the ninth. He gave up two hits and then hit a batter without recording an out, and was replaced by journeyman Dickie Noles who had been acquired from the Chicago Cubs just days earlier in a waiver deal. Toronto manager Jimy Williams sent up his 37-year-old veteran, Juan Beniquez, to pinch hit for Lee. After working the count full, Beniquez lined a fastball just over a leaping Trammell at shortstop for what looked like a game-tying, two-run single. As the ball landed in left-center field however, it seemed to disappear from sight in the late afternoon shadows, and bounded along the artificial turf by Gibson who was desperately trying to cut it off. The ball rolled all the way to the fence, clearing the bases, as Leach scored all the way from first base with the winning run.

"It was a foot from being a triple play," said Beniquez after the game, knowing that the line drive off his bat had just barely eluded the six-foot Trammell's leaping effort, before landing and rolling to the left-field fence on the hard outfield carpet.[7] Toronto's stunning 10–9 victory was their third straight come-from-behind victory, and their second consecutive walk-off win. More importantly, it had given the Blue Jays a commanding lead in the division, with only eight games remaining in the regular season. Toronto was 3½ games in front and clearly in position to deliver a knock-out punch if they could beat Detroit the following day.

The Tigers' clubhouse was understandably quiet in the aftermath. The pitching staff had just been shredded for 17 hits and four walks, while forfeiting separate three, four, and five-run leads. The bullpen had blown it's twelfth save opportunity in the past 22 tries, leaving nearly everyone in a Detroit uniform to wonder if any lead would be safe the rest of the way. "We don't have any semblance of using people out of the bullpen," said Anderson in his own unique way about the lack of trust he had in his relief corps 154 games into the schedule.[8] Lady Luck also seemed to be on the side of the Blue Jays, as their ninth-inning rally had started with a bloop double to center field by Barfield and an infield dribbler off of the bat of Upshaw. When asked after the game if Toronto appeared to be the team of destiny, after the events of the preceding three days, Trammell tersely stated, "The thought has crossed my mind."[9]

After the writers had collected their last quote and the cameras had been packed away, a piece of Tigers' lore was born in a quiet corner of the Exhibition Stadium visitor's clubhouse. A core group of hardened veterans—Trammell, Gibson, Evans, Brookens, Petry, Grubb—while sipping beer and in no particular hurry to leave, talked about the dire situation they were in. That shared moment forged a steely resolve to continue to pressure the Blue Jays and win the division. They all agreed that the next game was the key. They had to win or the race would effectively be over. Gibson would later be credited with the tag line for that group's collective vision which was setting "the biggest bear trap of all time."[10]

On Sunday afternoon the two rivals engaged in a contest which could best be described as a death struggle, where both teams recognized the immense implications of a win or loss for either side. George Bell singled in a Toronto run in the first inning before the two starting pitchers, Alexander for the Tigers and Clancy for the Blue Jays, locked horns with neither giving an inch. "The first eight innings just kind of flew by," said Trammell afterwards about the all too real sense that the game, and very likely the season, were slipping away. "Before you knew it we were down to our last shot."[11]

Trailing 1–0 in their last at-bat, Gibson timed a Henke fastball and drove it into a stiff wind well beyond the temporary fence in right field, the ball bouncing down the football field towards a faraway end zone. The home run served as a stay of execution for the Tigers and tied the game at 1–1, forcing extra innings. In the top of the 11th inning, Evans homered to give Detroit their first lead, 2–1, but the Tigers were unable to hold the lead. Beniquez reached base when Trammell bobbled his ground ball, and then pinch-runner Kelly Gruber eventually scored on a two-out hit to spoil 10⅔ innings of stellar pitching from Alexander, who was then removed with the game tied again, 2–2.

Taking advantage of their inflated September rosters bolstered by minor league call-ups, both managers pulled out all the stops, trying to gain any edge that might lead to victory. Anderson used five pitchers and 13 position players in the contest, while his counterpart, Williams, used six pitchers and nearly emptied his bench—using 17 Toronto position players. Finally in the 13th inning, Detroit rookie Jim Walewander reached base on a leadoff walk, advanced to second on a sacrifice bunt, and then came around to score on a pop single by Gibson that gave Detroit the lead once again. The Blue Jays put a runner on first with one out in the bottom of the inning, but two batters later, Barfield hit a grounder to Trammell who flipped the ball to Whitaker for the force out, giving the Tigers the victory they so desperately needed. "I'm just emotionally drained," said an obviously fatigued Trammell in a much-relieved Tigers' clubhouse ahead of the return flight to Detroit. "I've been sick all day with a cold. It's been a hell of a day."[12]

It had also been an emotional weekend in far greater ways for the Tigers' star. Before Saturday's game he had received word that his wife Barbara had given birth to a baby daughter. The Trammell's third child, Jade Lynn, was born in San Diego where his wife and two small sons could be supported by family and friends while Alan remained focused on the pennant race. A beaming Trammell had been the center of congratulations and good natured ribbing as the news spread in the Detroit clubhouse. He had spent much of the season on his own already, as first his wife and sons were tied up in San Diego well into June with school related activities, and then more recently when his expectant wife had gone back to California to await the baby's birth. Trammell said about his reluctant bachelorhood that he "couldn't cook anything" and jokingly attributed his greatest statistical season to the steady diet of fast food and takeout he had been living on.[13]

One of the hard realities of professional baseball is the cruel grind of the relentless schedule that has a game scheduled nearly every day. Following what many players described as four days of the most intense play they had ever experienced, both teams had to immediately refocus for games the next night against a different opponent. Detroit came home for a four-game series with the Baltimore Orioles, a team mired in sixth place in the division, 31½ games out of first place. Almost predictably, the Tigers dozed through a 3–0 loss against an Orioles team that sported a team ERA over five.

"I'm not going to lie—we were flat tonight," admitted Trammell afterwards. "It's only human nature. Not to take anything away from (Baltimore starting pitcher) Mr. Habyan, he pitched a fine game. But that series against Toronto was the four most emotional games I've ever played. There's no way the atmosphere in the clubhouse tonight matched that. We were tight tonight. We fell behind and when it was the fifth or sixth inning, I know I started feeling some tension—like we didn't have much time left."[14]

The baseball world seemed to return to normalcy the next night when Detroit rolled to a 10–1 victory, but the Orioles won the third game 7–3 and then jumped out to a first-inning 2–0 lead in the fourth game of the series. Staring at a potentially disastrous three losses in four nights against the lowly Orioles, the Tigers quickly came back with Trammell playing a key role in the turnaround. He singled in the bottom of the first inning and then scored right behind Madlock who had slid hard into home plate. When the ball got away from Baltimore catcher Terry Kennedy, Trammell raced home with some heads-up base running to tie the score. The play sparked a four-run inning for the Tigers, and paved the way to an eventual 9–5 win.

The disappointing split in the four-game series with the Orioles was softened with the news that came out of Toronto. The red-hot Milwaukee Brewers followed Detroit into Toronto and swept a three-game series from a Blue Jays team whose collective collar seemed to be tightening. Toronto had been the recipient of a few fortunate breaks the previous weekend while taking three out of four from the Tigers, but found their luck changing in the season's final week. The Blue Jays offense had gone stagnant, having totaled only nine runs in the three games with Milwaukee. Worse yet, they lost their on-field leader when Ernie Whitt injured his ribs in the Milwaukee series, leaving the catching duties to Brewer castoff Charlie Moore and rookie Greg Myers. With Fernandez and Whitt both out of the Blue Jays' lineup, slugger George Bell no longer had the protection he was used to, immediately ahead and behind him, in the Toronto batting order. "We aren't as loose as we usually are," said first baseman Willie Upshaw about his teammates that week. "At this stage, every day is a tough day. You can see the signs that things are a little tense around here."[15]

Toronto flew into Detroit for the final three games of the season with a 96–63 record, their lead trimmed to one game over the Tigers who were 95–64. All the eyes of baseball would be following the series that would decide the American League's Eastern Division championship. The Minnesota Twins, St. Louis Cardinals, and San Francisco Giants had already clinched their divisions and were just playing out the schedule, readying themselves for post-season play. The Tigers-Blue Jays series also looked like it would determine the American League's MVP for that season, as Trammell and Bell appeared to be far and away the lead candidates.

"Bell has been great for them. He has to be one-two in the MVP vote along with Alan," lectured Anderson in late September. "There's only the two of them. No one else comes close."[16] Trammell tried to downplay the MVP talk, but admitted that he was excited about the possibility: "Hey, I may never be in this position to win it again, so I'm excited about the chance."[17] Turning his focus to the series at hand, Trammell succinctly described it as "the showdown that everyone wanted."[18]

In the Friday night opener, Toronto jumped out to a second-inning 3–0 lead on a Manny Lee three-run homer, in front of a juiced-up Tiger Stadium crowd of over 45,000 fans. Rookie outfielder, Scott Lusader, one of Detroit's September call-ups, banged a two-run homer of his own in the bottom of the inning, and then Trammell tied the game with his 28th home run an inning later. The Tigers added an unearned run later in the inning and then watched Alexander hang on to that 4–3 lead into the eighth inning, before he handed the ball over to Henneman who closed out the victory. The story of the night though, was the five double-plays turned by the Tigers, including inning and game-ending twin-killings in both the eighth and ninth innings.

The plays everyone was talking about both involved Trammell. The first came in the fifth inning with one out and a Toronto runner on first, and the tying run on third base. Lance Mulliniks' ground ball through the middle of the diamond was cutoff to the right side of second base by Trammell, who had fielded it while cutting behind the bag. Without stopping, he flipped the ball with a backhand flip to Whitaker at the bag, who then whirled and threw out Mulliniks at first base. Inning over—no run. In the ninth inning with one out and the tying run at first, Henneman fielded a grounder to the mound, but then threw wildly towards second base. Trammell speared the high and wide throw with his glove, while at the same time touching second base with his left foot, and then completed the throw to first base to nip the batter. "Timing. We've been doing it for ten years now," explained Trammell to an inflated press corps in the crowded Detroit clubhouse, about the nifty plays he and Whitaker made. "There just haven't always been so many people around."[19]

The game-ending double play moved Detroit into a first place tie with Toronto, with both teams now at 96–64. Nearly counted out as dead just a week ago, the team had caught the Blue Jays once again at the top of the division. "Now, it's a best two out of three," stated an increasingly confident Anderson afterwards.[20] His "two out of three" comment made reference to the likely scenario of the two teams splitting the remaining pair of games on the regular season schedule, and ending in a tie. The league had already accounted for that possibility by tentatively adding a one-game playoff date for Monday afternoon in Detroit, if that were necessary.

The Saturday afternoon game was another in a quickly growing list of classics between the two clubs. Toronto scored a run in the first before Detroit tied it in the bottom of the third. The teams swapped runs in the fifth inning, before settling into a tension-filled, pitching duel between two old war horses, Morris and Flanagan, that both had well-deserved reputations as big-game pitchers. Morris worked out of jams throughout the late innings, as the Blue Jays had constant traffic on the bases. Flanagan, meanwhile, was mowing down Tiger batters, seeming in complete command of his entire arsenal of pitches. "A pitcher senses the duel factor with another pitcher," Morris would explain afterwards. "And Flanagan was so great that I felt he couldn't be beaten. So it was a matter of survival."[21]

Through nine innings and a 160-pitch effort he described as being fueled by "sheer adrenaline," Morris kept the game tied at 2–2 before turning the ball over to Henneman. The two teams battled past the eleventh inning before Flanagan finally stood aside and let Jimy Williams go to his bullpen. Left-handed reliever Jeff Musselman got the first out of the twelfth inning, but then gave up singles to Whitaker and Madlock before walking Gibson. That brought up Trammell with the bases loaded and the division lead on the line.

Williams, not wanting Trammell to bat against the left-hander, surprised everyone by electing to go with right-hander Mark Eichhorn rather than his relief ace, Tom Henke. Trammell responded by hitting a hard, skidding drive that seemed to handcuff Toronto's fill-in shortstop Manny Lee, ricocheting off the inside of his leg and into short left field. The play which would be scored a hit, scored pinch-runner Jim Walewander with the deciding run in the Tigers' 3–2 victory, catapulting them ahead of Toronto and into first place as Tiger Stadium erupted into bedlam.

With just a single game left on the schedule, Detroit needed only to win to complete an amazing season-long comeback and finish atop the division. Sunday, October 4, 1987, was sunny and cool as 51,005 fans filled Tiger Stadium. The day was breezy, and a dark shadow spread across the infield—cast from the upper heights of the stadium—making visibility for batters less than ideal. Trammell had come to the ballpark off of a short night, as he had welcomed his wife and newly-expanded family which included his new daughter, from a late night flight arriving out of San Diego.[22]

As had been the pattern over every game they had played over the previous ten days, the Tigers and Blue Jays settled into an intense, drama-filled contest. Frank Tanana and Jimmy Key, both left-handers, opposed each other that day. Key was sharp the entire game, mixing his trademark curve ball with a fastball and changeup, and allowed only three hits on the day. One, however, came in the second inning when Larry Herndon lofted a fastball that had caught too much of the plate towards deep left field. Bell, the Toronto left fielder, tracked the ball while drifting towards the left field line, and appeared to be positioned to catch it. At the last second though, the ball seemed to catch in the stiff breeze that was blowing towards right field. Bell suddenly reversed his direction and moved back to his left towards center field. He had no chance however, as the ball carried just over the left-field screen and into the first row of seats for a home run. The wind-blown homer off of the bat of Herndon had given Detroit a 1–0 lead.

Tanana, meanwhile, had won only once in his last nine starts, and was struggling this day to throw his collection of breaking balls over the plate with any consistency. Instead he fooled a surprisingly passive lineup of Blue Jays' batters by relying more on his pedestrian-speed fastball which they frequently took for strikes. Surviving on guile and the craftiness he had developed while transforming himself from a power thrower into a junk-balling, finesse pitcher, Tanana managed to avoid trouble, keeping Toronto runners to a minimum.

When the eighth inning began, Detroit still held a 1–0 lead. The outcome of the entire season was coming down to the final two innings, and it was the Blue Jays turn to show desperation. Moseby started the inning by singling sharply to right field. That brought up Bell who had struggled over the final week, managing only two hits in his previous 21 at-bats. Ahead in the count 2–0 and looking to make amends for his weak showing down the stretch, Bell appeared to be over-anxious and chased an off-speed pitch that Tanana had spotted down and away. Bell managed only to flick his bat at the well-located pitch and lifted a lazy fly ball into center field where

Chet Lemon made the easy catch. The Tiger Stadium crowd exhaled as much as cheered. With one out, Moseby stole second base and then moved to third on a fly out, but was stranded there when Barfield grounded back to Tanana for an easy out at first base.

In the ninth, Tanana struck out Fielder and then got Lee to ground out to third base. With the crowd roaring and the Blue Jays down to their final out, Garth Iorg took a half-hearted swing at Tanana's first offering and trickled a ball halfway between the mound and the first base line. Tanana pounced on the weak grounder, whirled and underhanded the ball to Evans at first base for the final out. Evans leaped in the air as he rushed towards Tanana. Just seconds later they were engulfed by the rest of the Tigers in a giant mob near the mound.

Detroit's 1–0 victory had clinched the American League East title in one of baseball's greatest divisional races. The Tigers final record of 98–64 was the best in major league baseball in 1987, made even more remarkable when considering the slow start the team had been forced to overcome. From their low point on May 9, when they found themselves eight games under the .500 mark, Detroit had amassed an 88–46 record, winning at a sizzling .656 clip.

While the celebrations following the Tigers' division, pennant, and World Series victory three years earlier had seemed more like "mission accomplished," the raw emotion displayed following the victory over Toronto was pure exuberance. "This is the most fun I've ever had in baseball," said Evans after the clinching victory. "It is also the year and the team I'll never forget."[23]

"I've never been involved in seven games like this," said Trammell while surrounded by writers and cameras in a standing-room-only Detroit clubhouse. "A week ago, we were really down, trailing Toronto by 3½ games. But we never gave up and now ... this. I'm so emotionally drained right now. But it's the greatest feeling."[24]

11

Disappointment × 2

For the second time in four seasons, the Detroit Tigers would face a seemingly overmatched opponent in the American League Championship Series. In 1984 they had been forced to dispatch a Kansas City club that had won 20 fewer games in the regular season, in order to advance to the World Series. And although Detroit had swept the Royals in October of that year, two of the games had been very tight—with one game going to extra-innings and another being a 1–0 contest—proving that anything was possible in a short series.

The Tigers' reward for winning the American League East in 1987, while compiling the best record in the major leagues that summer, was to travel to Minnesota for the first two games of the American League playoffs. The Twins, winners of 85 games—thirteen fewer than the Tigers—had come on strong in the second half of the season to nip Kansas City for the Western Division title. It was the first winning season in eight years for a Minnesota club that was quietly putting together a solid roster of talented young players. Detroit was a prohibitive favorite to roll past a relatively inexperienced Twins team that was just starting to come into its own. Most observers had already penciled the Tigers into the World Series where they would face their only real post-season challenger, which in all likelihood appeared to be the 95-win St. Louis Cardinals.

What transpired in the six days beginning on Wednesday, October 7, would turn into one of the greatest disappointments of Alan Trammell's career. Coming off the emotional rollercoaster they rode over their season-long comeback and through the hotly contested divisional race with Toronto, the Tigers weren't prepared for the buzz saw they were heading into within the confines of the Hubert H. Humphrey Metrodome in Minneapolis. Twins fans hadn't experienced post-season action by the home team since the very beginning of divisional play back in 1969 and 1970. But they got behind their young team in a big way, filling their indoor stadium with over 53,000 screaming fans for Game One, while waving their white hankies at any opportunity.

The tenor for the series was set in the very first game. Trailing 4–1 in the middle innings, and with everything seemingly going Minnesota's way, Detroit battled back with single runs in the sixth and seventh innings before scoring two in the top of the eighth inning to take the lead, 5–4. Trammell had scored the go-ahead run on a sacrifice fly off the bat of Lemon, after doubling earlier in the inning. However, in a replay of the horror-filled, first three games in Toronto just a week and a half earlier, the Tigers failed to hold the lead. Four Detroit pitchers combined to give up four hits, including two doubles and two walks, as the Twins scored four times in the bottom of the inning. When Jeff Reardon, one of the league's top relievers during that era, finished off the Tigers in the ninth, Minnesota had taken a surprising 8–5 decision in the first game of the series.

A similar pattern played out in Game Two, only in much earlier fashion. When the Twins trumped Detroit's two-run second inning with three runs of their own in the bottom of the frame, the Tigers were completely on their heels. Minnesota added three more runs in the middle innings and sailed to a convincing 6–3 victory. Morris gave up all six runs to take the loss, the first time in his career he had been beaten in his home state, after eleven straight wins. The humbling defeat was crowned by former Tiger Juan Berenguer, who struck out four of the five batters he faced to earn the save. With their top two starters, Alexander and Morris, having already dropped games in Minnesota, Detroit returned home knowing they were in considerable trouble.

The Tigers averted further trouble in the best-of-seven series, by pulling out a dramatic victory in Game Three on Saturday in Tiger Stadium. They jumped all over Twins right-hander Les Straker, scoring five runs in the bottom of the third inning to the delight of just under 50,000 supporters. But as they had all series, Minnesota battled back, scoring multiple runs in both the fourth and sixth innings against Terrell to draw within one run, 5–4. When Gary Gaetti, who had bullied Tiger pitching the entire series, scorched a two-run single in the top of the seventh inning—the Twins had taken the lead, 6–5. In danger of blowing a game in which they once held a five run lead, and falling behind in the series three games to none, Detroit mounted their own comeback. Outfielder Pat Sheridan homered to right field with a runner on base in the bottom of the eighth inning allowing the Tigers to regain the lead. Henneman, the only reliever in Sparky Anderson's bullpen with even a shred of trustworthiness at that point, finished off the 7–6 victory for the Tigers with a 1-2-3 ninth inning performance.

Game Four would be the death knell for Detroit. Trailing two games to one, but with a chance to tie the series with a win, and two games yet to be played in Tiger Stadium, the Tigers lost to Minnesota 5–3 in a game of missed opportunities. Trailing 4–2 in the bottom of the sixth inning, Detroit was the beneficiary of three hits, a walk, and a wild pitch, yet managed to score only one run. The key play came with a run already in, and runners still on second and third with just one out. Evans was picked off third by Twins' catcher Tim Laudner, a base running gaffe that deflated Detroit's momentum and took much of the wind out of the sails of the Tiger Stadium crowd. Making things even worse, the play occurred just moments ahead of a Berenguer wild pitch that would have scored the tying run. When Berenguer coaxed the third out two batters later, Detroit still trailed in the game. Minnesota added a run in the eighth and the crucial contest was decided. The Twins held a shocking, and commanding, three games to one lead in the series.

The end for Detroit came the next day, when Minnesota rolled to a 9–5 victory to clinch the American League pennant. Alexander was bombed for six hits and four runs and was pulled before he could complete the second inning. The Tigers tried to battle back, coming within one run midway through the game, but couldn't contain the hot Twins' bats. It was a frustrating series loss for a Detroit team that had battled so hard over the last five months of the regular season to win the AL East race. No matter how desperately they tried, when they reached back to find that extra boost of adrenaline needed to match a highly-charged Minnesota team that was clicking on all cylinders, there just wasn't anything there.

As the final out was recorded and the Twins celebrated just behind the mound on Tiger Stadium's infield grass, the NBC Television cameras honed in on the Detroit dugout where Trammell was found staring out at the field in stunned disbelief. "Some of the classiest athletes in all of sports, the Trammells, Evans…" said longtime NBC color commentator Tony Kubek while the picture on the screen depicted the finality of season-ending defeat.[1] Trammell, like many of the Tigers, never found his groove in the series—going four for twenty at the plate with only two RBI's. "I'm supposed to come up with a hit here and there to drive in runs, and I haven't done that," he had said before the final game.[2] Detroit batted only .240 as a team in the series and was outscored 34–23, with the pitching being equally at fault for the series loss.

"We're the best team in the American League, but we ain't the best team in post-season play," said a philosophical Anderson in the dour Tigers' clubhouse after the game. When asked if the back and forth battle with Toronto over the last two months of the regular season had taken everything out of his team, the Detroit manager was hesitant to use that as an excuse. "It would be an easy thing to hide behind," he said. "The Twins just came after you and they never stopped."[3]

As the succeeding days passed, the players and coaching staff scattered for the off-season, and the sting of a missed chance at a second world championship in four years began to subside—the enormity of Trammell's season could finally be absorbed. The Tigers' shortstop had put together one of the greatest individual campaigns in franchise history. It was a season rivaled only by some of the greatest names in the team's illustrious 87-year history—Cobb, Gehringer, Greenberg, and Kaline. Trammell set career highs in nearly every offensive category that year, including batting average (.343), home runs (28), doubles (34), and RBI's (105), while placing in the top 10 in the American League for batting average (3rd), on-base percentage (.402–5th), slugging percentage (.551–8th), runs scored (109–5th), hits (205–3rd), total bases (329–4th), RBI's (10th), and stolen base percentage (21-23, 91.3 percent–2nd).

Post-season speculation concerning the American League's MVP candidates focused on Trammell and Toronto left-fielder George Bell. While waiting for the official results to be released, most pundits all but awarded the honor to Trammell. He played the far more demanding position defensively (and played it at an elite level) many reasoned. Trammell was also cited for his leadership and clutch play throughout the season, and was often portrayed as having carried Detroit on his back that summer. Head-to-head comparisons between Trammell and Bell were also being made, especially the candidates' play during the stretch run of the divisional race. While Bell struggled over the last weeks including going 2-22 over the final week, Trammell had batted .417 over the final five weeks of the regular season. In fact, Trammell would be named as the American League's Player of the Month for September for his .416, 6 home run, 17 RBI heroics.

November 17 was the date that the Baseball Writers Association of America would announce the results for the American League's Most Valuable Player Award. It was an exclusive honor that distinguished a professional baseball player's career and placed them in the very select company of those great players who had won the award previously. Trammell spent the morning golfing from his off-season home in San Diego, admittedly trying to keep his mind free of the pending results. He and his wife had, though, intentionally kept the calendar cleared for the following days, anticipating the potential demands required if he were to win the award.[4]

When the news came, Trammell was dealt his second blow in a little over a month's time. In one of the closest votes in the award's history, George Bell was awarded the 1987 AL MVP award. Trammell finished a close second, with Minnesota center fielder Kirby Puckett finishing a distant third. Bell's margin of victory was only 21 points (332–311). Bell gained 16 first place votes to Trammell's 12. Nobody else received a first place vote.

As always, Trammell was diplomatic about the matter despite the bitter disappointment that came with the news. He gave credit to Bell and said the voting had been based on the "course of the year" rather than just the final weeks. "Sure I'm disappointed," he admitted. "But George is very deserving. He had an excellent year."[5]

The voting came as a surprise to many baseball observers and outraged Tiger fans and local media. Bell winning the award over Trammell would continue to be debated for years and even decades thereafter. "It would have been overwhelming to see your name alongside some of the great names in baseball, but you know—it didn't happen," Trammell said about the results. "I feel honored to be considered the second best player in the American League this year."[6]

While Bell's credentials were unquestioned, there was no shortage of individuals who quickly came to the defense of the shortstop who was often credited with being the heartbeat of the Tigers. "In 500 plus at bats he's struck out 42 times (actually 47)," pointed out Anderson while building his case for Trammell. "Two of the last four years he's had the league's best average for a right-handed hitter. He's hit at least .280 lifetime and this is his fourth .300 season. We're talking Hall of Fame here. We're talking not too many better in the history of the Detroit Tigers. We're dealing with eternity with this guy, every day, and that's kind of scary."[7]

"A lot of people are afraid to be as good as they can be," added Evans. "He's not."[8] Morris summed up the feelings of many Tiger players when he said "He's been my MVP for ten years."[9]

The most meaningful testament to Trammell might have come from one of the least-vocal sources in the Detroit organization. Whitaker, who had played alongside Trammell for more than a decade at that point, had the presence of mind to pull second base off its moorings on the Tiger Stadium infield, shortly after the final out was recorded in the last game of the regular season against Toronto. Before handing the memento over to his double-play partner in the celebratory Detroit clubhouse, Whitaker inscribed on the base: *To Alan Trammell, 1987 AL MVP. From, Lou Whitaker.*[10]

Lost at the time was the lasting impact that missing out on a second World Series championship and finishing second in the Most Valuable Player Award voting would have on Trammell's baseball legacy. He was not quite yet 30 years of age, and most expected that both he and the Tigers had many more productive seasons ahead. But the window of greatness was quickly closing on a Detroit franchise that had been ultra-talented for many years, and had experienced considerable success throughout the decade. Injuries would become more and more of the storyline for Trammell in the years ahead.

"Right now, I think I'm just starting to come into my own and put some numbers on the board that I'm capable of," he said shortly after his career season of 1987 had ended. Then he added a statement that would eerily portend the future: "I don't know if I'm going to hit .343 or 28 home-runs again, though."[11]

12

End of the 80s

When the Detroit Tigers played the 1988 season opener on April 4 in Boston, onlookers might have experienced a sense of déjà vu by the time it had ended. Jack Morris and Roger Clemens had battled to a 3–3 stalemate through the first nine innings; Clemens fanned 11 Tiger batters on the day. But with two outs in the tenth inning and the new Detroit center fielder, Gary Pettis, on second base, Alan Trammell lined a Lee Smith fastball into the left field screen above Fenway Park's famed "Green Monster." The two-run home run would prove to be the difference in Detroit's opening day victory and Trammell, like he had for much of 1987, provided the heroics. "I always considered Trammell one of the best five players in baseball," said a charged-up Sparky Anderson after the season opening win. "I'm changing my mind. I think now that he might be the best."[1]

While Anderson's statement about Trammell being the "best" player in baseball might have been arguable, there was little disputing the important role he played for the Tigers. A columnist for *The Sporting News*, Moss Klein, would write that summer that "Detroit's Alan Trammell is the league's most indispensable player, because no player is more important to his team than Trammell is to the Tigers."[2] That opinion had been further validated following the defection of another core member from Detroit's championship-contending teams.

A January 18, 1988, decision by labor-management arbitrator Robert Thomas shook the baseball world, and no part of that world was impacted more than Detroit. Ruling on a complaint brought forward by the Major League Baseball Players Association, he said that owners had colluded against players that had tested the free agent market following the 1985 season. The belief was that organized efforts took place, curtailing the competitive bidding between teams for players on the open market. Stating that "a strong indication of concerted action" had taken place, Roberts awarded damages to several impacted players, including Kirk Gibson, who were granted the immediate right to negotiate as "new look" free agents, without risk to their current contracts.³

Gibson had tired of the drama that had colored negotiations with the ball club in recent seasons. It was no secret that Tigers' owner Tom Monaghan wasn't a big fan of the fiery, stubble-bearded outfielder, and Gibson's exploration of the free agent market for two years hadn't been well received.⁴ Detroit had even tried to trade Gibson earlier in the off-season to the Los Angeles Dodgers in an attempt to receive value ahead of the anticipated free agency that many believed Gibson might receive. The trade fell through, however, and when granted the opportunity, Gibson spurned Detroit and signed a three-year, $4.5 million contract with the Dodgers as a free agent.

For the second straight year the Tigers had suffered a devastating personnel loss via free agency. The pundits once again predicted Detroit to be a "pretender" rather than contender in the American League East. "We didn't shut down shop when Lance (Parrish) left and I don't expect us to this year with Gibson gone," said a defiant Trammell. "We'll be dangerous, and if other teams don't think so, they're going to be surprised."⁵

Trammell was coming off an outstanding spring training at the plate, having batted .431 in the Grapefruit League in Florida before

Outfielder Kirk Gibson was a teammate of Trammell's for 12 seasons over two different stints in Detroit, and was a huge part of the successful Tiger teams of the 1980s. The two were also close off the field, and later each served as the other's bench coach, first during Trammell's managerial regime in Detroit, and later when Gibson was manager of the Arizona Diamondbacks (National Baseball Hall of Fame Library, Cooperstown, New York).

suffering another slow start to the regular season in the cold April temperatures. By May 20, however, he had climbed back to the .300-mark after a four-for-five day against Chicago. The team had heated up along with Trammell's bat, moving into first place after an exciting 2–1 walk-off victory at home against New York on June 20.

The next night provided even more excitement. Trailing 6–1 to the

Yankees as they came to the plate in the bottom of the ninth inning, Detroit loaded the bases with nobody out. New York manager Billy Martin then called upon his ace left-handed reliever, Dave Righetti, who got two outs before walking consecutive batters to force in runs and make the score 6–3. Righetti, who had been within one strike of ending the game on the previous two batters, then faced Trammell who was the eighth Tiger batter of the inning.

After Righetti pitched ball one to Trammell, Martin made the highly-unusual move of replacing a pitcher partway through the count on a batter. Into the game came right-hander Cecilio Guante, who had given up a walk-off, game-winning home run just the night before. The 28-year-old journeyman pitcher from the Dominican Republic battled the Tigers' shortstop to a 3–2 count before making another costly mistake.

Trammell belted a waist-high fastball into a high arc that just missed landing in Tiger Stadium's upper deck in left field. Instead, the ball fell well behind the lower deck fence for a grand slam home run, capping off Detroit's improbable come-from-behind 7–6 victory. As what remained of the original crowd of 26,535 fans went crazy with delirium, Trammell ran out his blast in customary manner; head down while trotting at a quick pace around the bases, until when he rounded third and headed for home plate, a huge grin broke out on his face. There, the Tigers players and coaches pounded Trammell with congratulatory slaps and hugs; their on-and-off-field leader once again having come through when the opportunity presented itself. "I never even expected to bat in the ninth, let alone hit a grand slam," he said in an upbeat Detroit dressing room afterwards. "That's the greatest feeling in the world, to have your teammates waiting at home plate for you."[6]

The win caused a two-game swing in the standings between the Tigers and Yankees. Instead of New York reclaiming the division lead by one-half game, Detroit had increased their lead to one-and-a-half games. Trammell's game-winning grand slam not only sustained a Tigers hot streak that saw them win 18 of 27 games in June, but set off a patented Martin tirade in the Yankee's clubhouse where he overturned the tables filled with the post-game spread of food and drinks.

As the schedule reached July 1, the Tigers were once again the front-runners in an extremely competitive division. The team was buoyed by a strong starting rotation with Jack Morris, Walt Terrell, Doyle Alexander, Frank Tanana, and Jeff Robinson leading the way. Trammell was having another outstanding season, batting .330 with ten home runs and 40 RBI's, his power numbers just slightly behind his pace from the year before. His star had never been brighter, and he was generally considered among the best players in the game, having nudged ahead of Cal Ripken, Jr., as the premiere shortstop in the American League. *Sports Illustrated* called him "simply the best shortstop in baseball."[7] He was the unanimous pick in a poll of AL general managers as the league's All Star shortstop, and for the first time in his career he had won the fan voting for the All Star game that summer, having garnered over 917,000 votes.

On June 19 Trammell's fortunes changed for the worse. He was struck on the left elbow with a pitch from Toronto's Todd Stottlemyre. For several days afterwards, he tried to play through soreness in his elbow with fluid building up around the joint. Nearly a week later, he was finally taken out of the lineup with what was diagnosed as a bad bruise, but no break was found. The injury ended up keeping Trammell out of the lineup for nearly three weeks, and forced him to miss his start at shortstop in the All Star game in Cincinnati. Once again, he had been denied his chance to shine on stage with the game's greatest players.

When Trammell did return, Detroit went on a hot streak, winning 13 of 18 games during one stretch. By August 21, the Tigers had increased their lead in the division to four games over the second place Boston Red Sox. It was the biggest lead they had held that late in a campaign since the 1984 championship season. "We don't look that impressive, we don't blow you out," he said about the 1988 squad. "We just win."[8]

Detroit was running on fumes though. Following the All Star break, the Tigers suddenly went cold and they labored to score runs, with each game seemingly becoming a struggle. The makeup of the team had changed greatly in one year, and they no longer overwhelmed teams offensively as they had on many nights in 1987. General Manager Bill Lajoie had tried to replenish the roster again during the preceding winter, picking up role players to replace what they had lost from the year before.

There was no replacement for a player of Gibson's magnitude, however. Instead they had traded Dan Petry to California for the fleet Gary Pettis, who was a superior defensive center fielder and a legitimate base-stealing threat. Pettis played well in the outfield and stole 44 bases on the season, but batted only .210 and hit just three home runs, making no one forget about Gibson who was having an MVP season in the National League. Lajoie had also tried to replace Madlock, whom the Tigers had failed to resign, with journeyman veterans such as Ray Knight and Luis Salazar. The 35-year-old Knight hit only .217 in what turned out to be his final year in the big leagues. Salazar, although he played well at times as a one-man jack of all trades, did not make up for the fire and intensity Madlock had brought to the team, a trait that was sorely missed in 1988.

There were big drop-offs in offensive production elsewhere as well;

players like Darrell Evans, Matt Nokes, and Larry Herndon failed to produce as they had a year earlier. Evans struggled all season, batting .208 with only 22 home runs, while looking every bit of his 41 years of age. Meanwhile Nokes, who had been such a pleasant surprise when he hit 32 home runs as a rookie catcher, could muster only half as many long-balls and saw his batting average drop by more than 30 points. The fall-off in production was far greater than what the new additions could make up for. The result was a decrease by nearly 200 runs scored for the Tigers, a startling one-year decline by the team coming off major league baseball's highest run total since 1953.

Despite the offensive struggles, the Tigers continued to win at a steady clip while holding off the hard-charging Red Sox. Boston had won 19 of 20 games at one point in late July into early August, and had nearly erased the nine game deficit they had faced in the standings at the All-Star break. Thanks in large part to Trammell, who had contributed a five-RBI game on August 4 in an 11–6 romp over Boston in Tiger Stadium, Detroit won four times in a five-game series with Boston, which helped rebuild their lead to the high-water mark of four games on August 21.

But two wins in a seven-game road trip was the preamble to a disastrous four and 19 stretch for Detroit that extended into mid–September. By the time the team came out of its funk, the Tigers were in third place and 5 ½ games behind the front-running Red Sox. Trammell had missed more than a week of time during the losing streak due to a pulled groin, an injury that would hinder him the remainder of the season. While sitting out with the injury, he ended one six-game skid by delivering a game-winning, pinch-hit single in the bottom of the ninth inning against the Blue Jays. "I guess if they're going to go with anyone, they'd go with Trammell," said Toronto reliever Todd Stottlemyre who had given up the game winning hit. "If he's not the best player in the league, he's up there."[9]

Trammell had no sooner worked his way back into the regular lineup, when he was hit in the right forearm on a pitch from the Blue Jays' Dave Stieb. He tried to play with the painfully bruised muscle, but was ineffective at the plate. With only a week left in a season that had slipped away, Anderson took his star shortstop out of the lineup. Although he pleaded with the Detroit manager before the season's final game, Trammell would not play again that year.

Unlike the previous year, when he had carried the ball club on his back during the stretch run that lasted through the first weekend in October, Trammell had not been able to duplicate those kinds of heroics in 1988. An injury-plagued September saw him bat only .196, causing his season average to plummet from .325 entering the month, down to a final figure of .311. For the season he had hit 15 home runs and drove in 69 runs while playing only 128 games; respectable numbers, but nowhere near the superhero effort the offensively-starved Tigers needed. Detroit finished one game behind Boston in the division, a misleadingly narrow margin considering the Red Sox had matters well in control before losing six of their last seven contests.

When Trammell reported to Lakeland for spring training in 1989, he was on the final year of the two-year contract he had signed before the 1988 season. It had been the first agreement he had signed since the seven-year deal he made as a 22-year-old player for the Tigers back in 1980. At the time it was signed, Trammell's long-term deal was viewed as one that was mutually beneficial. He had secured a lucrative contract in only his third year, with a commitment from Detroit's management for seven years. The Tigers were locking up one of the cornerstone pieces of the rebuilding phase the franchise was undergoing, at a rate considered fair to both sides. Before the contract had reached the end of its term, however, the market place in baseball for a player of Trammell's caliber far exceeded the $400,000 average salary the seven-year contract was worth.

"I know other players passed me in salary," Trammell said later about the long-term deal he had signed in 1980. "But I gave the Tigers my word. I had the security of a seven-year deal. If I had gotten hurt, they would have still had to pay me." The stance Trammell took was not always a popular one with some of his teammates. As he had developed, turning into one of the premier players in the American League by the mid–1980s, several of the players encouraged him to ask for more, to renegotiate the contract he was still bound to. "We would sit around and talk contract," Trammell remembered. "A lot of my teammates said I should ask for more. I just said, 'That's your opinion.'"[10]

While teammates like Parrish, Gibson, and Morris had all explored the market and eventually left the club for greener pastures via free agency, Trammell remained patient. The contract he signed in 1988 was worth a little more than $1.2 million per season and brought him in line with what star-caliber players were making then. But even in 1988, when Trammell was at his career height, acknowledged universally as one of the top dozen players in the major leagues, there were still 45 players making more money that season.

Looking to rectify the situation and to help insure that he remained a career Tiger, both Trammell and the ball club were ready to discuss a deal that would be the biggest of the star shortstop's career. A deal came together very quickly. While standing on the practice field during batting practice at Lakeland's Joker Marchant Stadium, Trammell and Lajoie negotiated a three-year, $6.5 million extension to his contract, which otherwise would have expired at the end of the 1989 campaign. By all accounts the deal was sealed with a handshake less than ten minutes after the two started talking.

"I spoke with some people, talked with the Players Association," said Trammell after news of the signing had been released. "I know what other middle infielders are making. I had a couple of figures in mind. I threw one at him and he said, 'Yes.'"[11]

The deal locked up Trammell's services with Detroit through the 1992 season. Despite disappointing finishes to the previous two seasons, he still expected the team to be a regular contender for the American League pennant into the future. "I don't think this team is on the downswing at all. We still have a lot of talent, and I can see us contending indefinitely if the nucleus stays the same."[12]

By the time the 1989 season opened, the Detroit Tigers were only a sliver of the team that had been a perennial contender in the American League East for most of the decade. Defections to free agency, poor trades, injuries, and concessions to Father Time all contributed to the bottom falling out on a proud franchise that season. Detroit lost eight of their first ten games, never reached .500 at any point in the entire season, and had settled into last place in the division by June 7, a position they would never recover from.

The patchwork roster cobbled together by the team's management over the previous two seasons had finally come undone, while the lack of a productive farm system also caught up to Detroit. Gone were stalwarts such as Evans, Brookens, Terrell, Hernandez, and Grubb; age and ineffectiveness finally catching up to most of them. Players like Keith Moreland, Rick Schu, Gary Ward, Ken Williams, Rick Brumley, Tracy Jones, and Chris Brown had been brought to Detroit as stopgap measures, but failed to sustain the high level of play the Tigers had grown used to in previous years.

A 14–0 loss at home to Minnesota in the season's fifth game was just a preview of the long summer to come for the Tigers that year. The situation got so bleak early, that after just 37 games and with Detroit already eleven games under .500, Sparky Anderson left the team and went home to California for a few weeks, having been diagnosed with mental exhaustion. "It's not a good season when you're out of it by June," he said at the time.[13]

Trammell's season mirrored that of the team; miserable in every aspect. He pulled a thigh muscle in spring training and missed a significant amount of time in Florida before starting the regular season with an ice cold two for 18 at the plate. No matter how hard he tried, Trammell just couldn't duplicate the feats that had become so common in previous seasons. Perhaps the loss of his close friends, Evans and Brookens, from the team, removed an important element critical to his comfort zone. Others suggested that without the protection afforded by so many big bats in the Detroit lineup, opposing pitchers were able to pitch him more carefully. When that started to happen, Trammell then tried to do too much to compensate.

When a bad back started to plague him partway into the season, an already dreadful season turned into a nightmare. Trammell hit a walk-off home run in the bottom of the ninth inning to beat Kansas City 2–1 on May 20, but otherwise the highlights were few and far between. The back injury prevented him from swinging the bat with any authority, depriving the Tigers of the player that had been so crucial to their success over the preceding seasons. He struck out three times in a game against Baltimore on June 3, the first time in nearly two years that had happened to him. "I won't play until I'm 100 percent. I'm tired of not contributing," vowed a frustrated Trammell.[14]

Trammell was placed on the 15-day disabled list on June 8, whereas the team won only four times in 16 games during his absence. He returned to the lineup later in the month, but with little effectiveness. Anderson finally had no choice but to remove him from the cleanup spot in the batting order in late July. By the time Trammel found himself back in his old familiar second spot in the batting order, Detroit's erstwhile number four hitter had only three home runs and 24 RBI's.

As the unsightly season ground towards its final month, hamstring woes afflicted the Tiger's shortstop, causing him to miss even more games. Late in the season, with little to play or hope for, Trammell stated simply: "My goal for the season is to play two entire weeks without getting hurt."[15]

The Tigers finished the 1989 season in last place in the AL East with only 59 wins. Their 103 losses was an embarrassing total and left them 30 games behind the division-winning Toronto Blue Jays. It was arguably the worst regular season in Detroit's history. Trammell played a career low 121 games that summer (excluding the strike season of 1981), while also posting a personal low batting average of .243. His production figures, which included five home runs and 43 RBI's, were the least he had put together since his rookie year. "It's been a year in which nothing meshed, individually or as a team," explained Trammell after the season had ended. "We just never got anything going. I can't blame my back for everything, but I couldn't do the things I'm capable of at the plate this year."[16]

The disastrous season put an ugly blemish on what had otherwise been a splendid decade of baseball in Detroit. While the 1984 season had been the obvious pinnacle, with a World Series title and some of the greatest moments in franchise history, the Tigers had consistently fielded contending teams throughout the 1980s. Prior to 1989 they had amassed winning records each year of the decade, a streak that actually extended back to the 1978 season (coinciding with Trammell's first full year). The Tigers had jockeyed with the New York Yankees for the little-recognized honor of "winningest team of the decade" across the entire major leagues, with both teams entering the 1989 campaign tied for that distinction with 780 victories. But the lowly 59-win season left Detroit well back of New York, who despite its own troubles that season, finished 15 games better than the Tigers with 74 victories, sewing up the tag as the decade's winningest team.

As the 1980s came to a close, Trammell was one of just 14 players in the American League to have played the entire decade with the same team. He joined teammates Whitaker and Morris as part of that short list. What Trammell would only begin to realize at that point in his career was how much was about to change with Detroit's baseball landscape. The team was no longer a perennial contender for the American League pennant. Instead the club was in a full rebuild mode, coming off the 103-loss season. Turnover in the roster would become commonplace. Gone were the days when Detroit would roll out a familiar everyday lineup that equaled any in the game. More recognizable faces would be leaving in the days ahead, and a revolving door of players, seemingly brought in on a trial and error, or stop-gap basis, would replace them. The franchise would be sold again within two years, with accompanying repercussions. What was increasingly clear was that opportunities had been missed in both 1987 and 1988; opportunities that didn't appear likely to repeat themselves again anytime in the immediate future. Alan Trammell's best days in a Tiger uniform were slowly drifting behind him.

13

Lost Seasons

Alan Trammell turned 32-years-old shortly before reporting to spring training for the 1990 season. Appearance-wise, his torso may have thickened some, the face was a little more weathered, his hair thinning and receding slightly, but otherwise he was still "Tram," entering his thirteenth season as the Detroit Tigers' shortstop, where he was already entrenched as one of the most familiar figures in franchise history.

For the first time in his career though, doubts began to surface about his capabilities on the field. He was still regarded as one of the finest players in baseball when healthy, and was as well-rounded a player as there was in the game, capable of leading his team to victory in the field, at the plate, or on the base paths. But staying healthy had been a problem for Trammell throughout his career, and especially so the past two seasons. He was either out of the lineup or playing hurt much of the time in August and early September in 1988, when the Tigers lost the grip they had held on first place for much of that summer. Back woes heavily contributed to Trammell's horrific 1989 season, where he was of little help in preventing the complete collapse the team had suffered on the field. Some thought he would never be able to stay healthy again over an entire 162-game schedule, nor could he be counted on the way Detroit's talent-starved franchise still did.

Rumors surfaced during the off-season about a potential blockbuster deal that would see Trammell return to his hometown of San Diego to play for the Padres. While there may have been some minor buyer's remorse on the Tigers part regarding the three-year, $6.5 million contract they had doled out a year earlier, especially for a player coming off of consecutive injury-plagued summers, it is doubtful that Detroit's management gave any serious consideration to actually trading Trammell.

Age-wise, he was still comfortably within what most considered the prime years of a major league baseball career, quite capable of stringing together another four or five highly productive seasons. He had received MVP votes in six of the previous nine years, including top-ten finishes in three of those seasons. For the past half-decade he had been casually mentioned as a possible, if not probable, Hall of Fame candidate provided he continued to put together the types of years he was producing from 1983 through 1988. With health and a return to his pre-1989 form, career plateaus such as 250 home runs, 500 doubles, and 1,200 RBI's were within his reach. If Trammell could accumulate base hits for five more seasons at the roughly 175 hits per season pace he attained from 1984 through 1987, he would exceed 2,600 career hits. With health and extended longevity, the 3,000 hit mark, a traditional baseball gold standard, was not impossible for him to reach.

"It's a nice compliment," he had said one summer in the late 1980s when asked whether his career was on a Hall of Fame-worthy path. "Right now I have to continue at this pace for the next four or five years for me to be considered. If I go on and have 200 homeruns and 2,500 base hits, and being a shortstop.... My approach is I don't look too far down the road. If I could put together what I did in '86, '87, and this year, there's potential. And I think another world championship would help. I'd love to see it, but I've got some work to do to be in that category."[1]

As the 1990 season began, the prospects for "another world championship" appeared to be a pipe dream at best. Following a last place finish in which the Tigers had seemingly quit on the second half of the year, winning only 29 games from July 1 onward, respectability was the more immediate goal. Besides Trammell, Detroit still had household names from its recent glory days in Lou Whitaker, Chet Lemon, Jack Morris, Frank Tanana, and Dave Bergman. None of them, however, was the same caliber of player they had been just a few years earlier. During the off-season the Tigers tried to resuscitate a moribund offensive attack which had produced its lowest run total in over a decade by adding veteran outfielders like Gary Ward and Lloyd Moseby, although both were clearly on the downside of solid careers. Tony Phillips had been signed in the off-season as a free agent for the intent purpose of batting leadoff while playing third base, a troublesome position for Detroit in 1989, where eight different players combined to make 43 errors while contributing little offensively.

The biggest hope for offensive improvement came with the signing of Cecil Fielder, the former Toronto prospect, to play first base for the Tigers in 1990. Fielder had been a promising player as a reserve and spot starter for the Blue Jays for four years in the late 1980s. He tired of that role though, having never accumulated more than 175 at-bats in any one season, and signed a million-dollar contract to play the 1989 season for the Hanshin Tigers in Japan. Playing every day, the powerfully built, six-foot three-inch Fielder, who weighed somewhere north of 250 pounds, hit 38 home runs in the Japanese Central League. Detroit's signing of the still unproven Fielder, who had never hit more than fourteen homers in a major league season, was indicative of the desperate state the team was in to add a power source to a club that had hit its fewest number of round-trippers since the 1976 campaign.

"When you lose 103 games, you kind of expect to be picked last," said Trammell on the eve of the 1990 season. "It's going to be easier to play the underdog role and try to sneak up on people. Certainly we don't think of ourselves as a seventh place ball club. I'd be surprised if we were."[2]

With Fielder cemented into the lineup as the everyday cleanup batter, Sparky Anderson returned Trammell to his accustomed spot as the number two batter in the Tigers' lineup. Trammell started the new season with a ten-game hitting streak, longer than anything he had managed to piece together during the entire 1989 campaign. His batting average hovered around the .300 mark for most of the first half, and by the midway point on the schedule, he had already surpassed his home run and RBI totals from the previous season. Most importantly, the back injury and other ailments he had suffered through the year before, appeared to be behind him. "I feel good right now, but you never know at this point," he said during the season's first half. "I've been hurt a lot in my career. If I could change one thing that would be it."[3]

Meanwhile, the team which had wobbled out of the gate, falling ten games below the .500 mark at one point, had rallied to close within sight of the break-even mark by the beginning of July. Fielder was exceeding Detroit's wildest hopes as the middle of the lineup presence they had lacked the preceding two years. He hit three home runs in a game two different times before the All-Star break, and was leading the major leagues in home runs with 26, and RBI's with 65, by the time June ended.

Shortly before the mid-season break, Anderson shifted Trammell to the number three spot in the batting order, where he batted behind Whitaker and Phillips who were each getting on base with regularity. With the terrifying specter of Fielder looming on deck behind him, Trammell was consistently getting pitches to hit from American League hurlers that no longer had the luxury of pitching around the Detroit shortstop. The result was that Trammell revisited the form he had played with in his near-MVP season of 1987, hitting the ball with authority and driving in runs with regularity. He had four hits, including a walk-off home run, to beat the Chicago White Sox in a game in mid–July. He swatted fifteen doubles in only 96 at-bats over one stretch of games starting in late-July and lasting into early-August, rediscovering the pop that hadn't existed during an injury plagued second-half of 1988, or any of 1989. Trammell's average climbed to near .320 in late-August when he hit .425 over a ten-game stretch, coming within just four percentage points of the American League's batting leader, Rickey Henderson of Oakland.

"Right now my goal is only to keep my average above .300," Trammell stated in early-September when asked about the prospect of capturing a batting title. "And to remind everyone about what went wrong last year. I was hurt. I hope everyone thinking I'd lost it, now thinks otherwise."[4]

Overshadowing Trammell's impressive comeback was the hitting prowess of Fielder who was the talk of baseball. Before the end of August, the giant first baseman surpassed the 40 home run and 100 RBI marks, threatening to be the first major leaguer in more than a decade to reach the 50-home run plateau. By September 15, Fielder's home run total had reached 46, with just over two weeks left in the schedule. His pursuit of 50 home runs kept Detroit fans interested in the Tigers through the waning days of a second consecutive season where they never really contended in the American League East. While much improved over the laughingstock club that had worn Tiger uniforms the year before, Detroit was still seven games under .500, and battling Milwaukee, Cleveland, and Baltimore for third place as best of the "also-rans."

"We've got a lot of new faces here," Trammell said late that summer. "One year isn't enough to develop good chemistry. I don't think we've ever been in sync together. We're rebuilding. It takes time. That's just the way it is."[5]

Fielder entered the season's final game in Yankee Stadium with a season total of 49 home runs. Anderson batted him second in the order that final day in order to eke out every possible turn at the plate as the Tigers' slugger made a final run at the 50-mark. In the fourth inning, Fielder blasted a towering drive to left field off of Yankee rookie pitcher Steve Adkins for his 50th round-tripper of the season. Two innings later Fielder blasted another one—giving him 51 home runs—the highest single-season total since Cincinnati's George Foster hit 52 in 1977. Greeting Fielder at home plate both times was Trammell, who was batting just behind him. "I never saw a guy who could hit home runs as far and as often as he did," Trammell would later say.[6]

Detroit's 10–3 victory over the Yankees in the 1990 season finale secured third place in the division for the Tigers who finished with a 79–83 record, nine games behind the division-winning Red Sox. In spite of the team's mediocre final mark, most followers felt pretty good about a Tigers season in which they improved their win total by twenty games from a year earlier.

Trammell went one for four at the plate in that final game in New York, giving him the .300-season he had so dearly coveted. Alan Trammell's comeback year in 1990 is probably the most overlooked and underappreciated of his entire career. He finished with a .304 average, hit 14 home runs, and amassed a career-high 37 doubles. With Phillips and Whitaker getting on base regularly ahead of him, and Fielder batting behind him, Trammell also drove in 89 runs that season, the second-highest mark of his career. To really put his season in perspective, a comparison must be made to Trammell's peers that played regularly at shortstop in 1990. Only the Reds' Barry Larkin was able to join Trammell as a .300 batter at the position (.301), while Cal Ripken, Jr., (85) was the only other shortstop to come even close to Trammell's RBI total. Perhaps the most telling statistic from Trammell's season was the 146 games he managed to play in that summer. It was his highest total in three years, and a mark he would never approach again the rest of his career.

The correlation between Trammell's excellent season individually and the 20-game improvement by the Tigers was not lost on baseball's keen observers. For the seventh time in 11 seasons he received votes in the MVP voting, and was named yet again by *The Sporting News* as one of the games Most Indispensable Players. "If you look back over the years, I guess it's true that if I have a good year the team usually does well too," admitted Trammell, drawing the same relationship that many others were quick to point out. "I think that's because my teammates have been able to feed off of my success and vice versa." The veteran shortstop fell short of taking credit for carrying the Tigers however: "I've always said I'm not a carrier. I don't put a team on my back and carry it the way someone like Cecil can. I'm not a spectacular player offensively or defensively—I don't try to be. But I think when other players on the team see I'm doing well, they pick up on it."[7]

Trammell's strong comeback in 1990 not only helped Detroit, but also held at bay those critics that felt the team needed to clean house and bring in an entire new wave of ballplayers. The long-time double-play combination of Trammell and Whitaker was not immune to the clamor some raised for a sweeping youth movement by the Tigers. "If we continue to go down in the standings, they're going to have to bring in some young kids and I understand that," said Trammell. "But I would like to stay with the Tigers. I want to be with the new regime when we get back up in first place again."[8]

One young player that had caught everyone's eye was a 21-year-old, hard-hitting infielder named Travis Fryman, who had been Detroit's first round pick in the 1987 amateur draft. Fryman was a shortstop-third baseman that had fast-tracked his way to Detroit the previous summer, and was easily the most impressive young prospect the Tigers had on the roster. He stemmed the criticism the organization had been receiving for some time—for not having produced an everyday player in more than a decade. In Fryman, the team's scouts and front office personnel envisioned a power-hitting shortstop in the mold of Cal Ripken Jr.; someone the team could rebuild around. And while Fryman wasn't yet ready to threaten the job security of a player with Trammell's stature, no one could blame the incumbent for at least sneaking a look now and then over his shoulder. "I'll know when it's time, and it isn't time yet," said a defiant Trammell late in 1990 before admitting, "Eventually, he'll be the shortstop."[9]

As good as the 1990 season had been for Trammell, 1991 couldn't have been any more frustrating. After getting off to a good start while batting over .300 into early May, a nagging wrist injury caused him to slump badly. He batted less than .200 over a two-month stretch of games, causing his average to dip below .240. Then he hurt his left knee and missed two weeks in early July. The fear at the time was that Trammell had torn ligaments, but after resting for a period he was able to return to the lineup much sooner than originally expected. Upon Trammell's return, he went on a mini-tear, registering nine hits in 21 trips to the plate before badly spraining an ankle in just his fifth game back. The ankle injury landed Trammell on the disabled list where he stayed until August 13.

When Trammell finally returned from that setback, he wasn't able to sustain any sort of consistency and the rest of the season became a struggle. "Every time it seems I get something going, something else happens," he said.[10] He hit only three home runs the second half of the year, failed to drive in runs with any regularity, and clearly wasn't the player he had been a year earlier. Trammell finished 1991 batting .248 with 9 home runs, 55 RBI's, and 57 runs scored. He played in only 101 games, the fewest he had played in since becoming a regular for the Tigers in 1978. It marked the third injury-plagued season in four years for the veteran shortstop. "Alan probably is never going to play 150 games again," said Sparky Anderson near the end of the disappointing campaign.[11]

In 1992 bad turned to worse. After missing most of spring training with a variety of ailments, Trammell had gotten off to a slow start with the bat in the regular season—but was coming on strong five weeks into the schedule. Then on May 15 in Kansas City, he felt something pop in his lower right leg while running out an infield single on Kauffman Stadium's artificial surface. X-rays later disclosed a broken ankle. "Luckily, it's early in the season," said Trammell, trying to remain optimistic. He was determined to return to the fold as soon as possible.[12]

Instead the season became an exercise filled with frustration. First, he and the team waited for the ankle to properly heal, a process that didn't happen as quickly as originally anticipated for the 34-year-old veteran. As the weeks and months passed, it became a matter of if, rather than when, Detroit would activate its injured star. The team was going nowhere that summer, curtailing any urgency the organization might have had for Trammell's return. Losers of their first six games, the Tigers had quickly plummeted to the lower regions of the standings where they would remain the entire year. With nothing really to gain, the Detroit brain trust seemed in no hurry to dislodge Fryman, who had settled nicely into the everyday shortstop role. Fryman was in the midst of a second straight 20-home run, 90-RBI campaign and was already entrenched as the young star of the Tigers.

As the season stretched into its late stages, the decision was made to hold Trammell out for the rest of the campaign. His season was over, having played just 28 games. As the waning days of another miserable season wound down, Anderson started to turn an eye towards the next year, and he had Trammell start taking ground balls at third base during pre-game workouts. Whether Trammell, whose contract expired at the end of the 1992 season, would be back in Detroit, though, was far from certain.

There had been significant changes in the Detroit Tigers organization since the glory days of the 1980s, most of which had resulted in turmoil and the degradation of a model major league franchise. General Manager Bill Lajoie, who along with President and CEO Jim Campbell, had been credited as the architect of the perennial contending team that eventually won a World Series in 1984, left the front office after the 1990 season. Campbell meanwhile, had been removed from actual baseball operations, replaced by Bo Schembechler, the legendary former football coach of the University of Michigan. As if that puzzling change wasn't enough, the Tigers fired radio broadcaster Ernie Harwell, one of the most popular and well-known figures not only with the organization, but across the entire state of Michigan. Amidst the turmoil and chaos created by his new front office management, owner Tom Monaghan sold the ball club at mid-season in 1992 to business rival and fellow-pizza mogul, Mike Illitch. As a condition of the sale, both Campbell and Schembechler were fired by the outgoing regime along with numerous underlings in the Tigers' front office. The new owner wanted to start with a clean house as he rebuilt the once-proud organization.[13]

Against this backdrop, a 15-year veteran that had been making over $2 million per year, was coming off consecutive injury-shortened seasons and was without a contract. Taking matters into his own hands, Trammell approached new general manager Jerry Walker in early December after an off-season workout at Tiger Stadium. "Do you want me back?" Trammell reportedly asked. When Walker indicated that he did, the negotiations began in earnest. Two short meetings between Trammell and Walker resulted in an incentive-laden deal for 1993 that could range from a $1.2 million minimum, all the way up to $2 million. The contract also included a $2.4 million option for the 1994 season.[14]

"I could have had an agent come in and tell the Tigers how great I am, how much I've done for the club over the years and all that B.S.," said Trammell when asked about his negotiating directly with the Detroit general manager, rather than involving an agent. "But the truth is, I've been hurt lately. I know it. They know it. They were willing to guarantee me substantial money even if I get hurt again. And if I play a lot and perform well, I'll get paid even more. I think that's fair."[15]

Trammell reported to Lakeland in the spring of 1993 without a starting position in the Detroit lineup, nor any clear role. Sparky Anderson was evasive about how much playing time his long-time star would get, saying only that Trammell would see spring training action not only at shortstop, but for the first time in his career at third base, and possibly even in the outfield as well. Throughout the spring, Trammell was adapting well to third base and to his short stints in the outfield, until a groin injury sidelined him over the final days of the exhibition season. His exasperating trend towards nagging injuries appeared ready to continue into another campaign. He would start the regular season on the disabled list. "I realize this could be it for me," Trammell said dejectedly, facing the growing perception that he could no longer remain healthy.[16]

He returned after missing the first 12 days of the season, and was inserted into the lineup at third base. His first day back the Tigers beat the Seattle Mariners 20–3, the second time in less than a week they had registered a 20-spot on the scoreboard. Trammell didn't get a hit in the game, but walked twice, stole two bases, and scored a pair of runs. He didn't get a hit in any of his first four appearances, but then clustered five hits over his next two games, including his first home run of the season.

Meanwhile, the Detroit ball club was reeling off winning streaks of five and six games, pushing themselves into first place in the division on April 23. It was a position they would hold on to for the next 57 days. Coming off losing seasons in three of the previous four years, including a sixth-place finish that was 21 games worse than the division-winning Blue Jays in 1992, the Tigers early season run atop the American League East was a gust of fresh air for a franchise that had gone stale. Fueling the surge was an explosive offensive attack that was lighting up scoreboards with irregular totals throughout the early weeks of the season. They scored ten runs or more in a game ten times in the first half of the season alone, and averaged nearly eight runs per game in April. By the beginning of June, the Tigers were still averaging over six runs per game, an historic pace for that era.

The lineup Detroit rolled out that season was filled with muscular power hitters that fit an all-or-nothing, home run or strikeout profile, featuring the likes of Fielder, catcher-DH Mickey Tettleton, and outfielder Rob Deer. Each was capable of hitting mammoth home runs, and could break open a tight game with one swing of the bat. However, they also struck out nearly 30 percent of the time, even more if they were in the midst of a slump, making the attack highly explosive, but also vulnerable to being shut down.

Whitaker, Fryman, Phillips, and catcher Chad Kreuter were also capable of hitting the long-ball, but were much more consistent in getting on base (Phillips would register an astounding .443 on-base percentage that season). A new, but old face also contributed to the Tigers' hot start. Kirk Gibson was back in a Tiger uniform after a five-year absence mostly in the National League. Although he was 36 years old, and was no longer the same explosive player he had been when he originally played in Detroit, Gibson still swung a dangerous bat and played with an edge that made him highly effective.

Early in the season, Trammell found himself in the role of a semi-regular, platooning with the left-handed hitting Scott Livingstone at third base. Trammell was also being used by Sparky Anderson as an occasional DH, and even made a handful of starts in both left field and center field. In his first major league game as an outfielder on May 9, Trammell made four putouts, including a nice running catch on a ball hit off of the bat of New York's Pat Kelly. As spring turned to summer, Trammell heated up at the plate. A month after coming off the DL, Trammell was batting .300. In June he continued to hit well, raising his average even more to .308 by month's end. Then he went a torrid ten for 19 in the four games leading up to the All-Star break, and raised his average to a sizzling .321.

On June 20, Detroit's record stood at 43–25. They led the division by two games in the standings and could seemingly slug home runs and outscore teams at will. It would be the high point of the season. A disastrous nine-game road trip to Baltimore, Boston, and New York, closed out June and saw the Tigers go winless, sinking to third place. A month later their record had deteriorated such that they were only one game over .500, and they had fallen all the way to fifth place. Just five weeks after holding the division lead, they were effectively out of the race.

Pitching and defense had remained concerns all through the season's first half, even while the team had been winning. On the return flight to Detroit from Kansas City, just ahead of the All-Star break, Anderson and his coaching staff made the decision to return Trammell to shortstop and move Travis Fryman over to third base.[17] Fryman was an excellent offensive player, on his way to a .300–22 home run–97 RBI-season. However, he was error-prone, as the 19 errors he had committed to that point of the season attested. The Detroit brain trust was looking to tighten up the league's shabbiest defensive team any way they could, and turning to the 35-year-old Trammell was an obvious move.

Back at his familiar spot in the infield, Trammell thrived in all aspects of the game. He immediately solidified the infield, making all of the necessary plays with the usual efficiency that exemplified his play. Offensively, his average dipped below .300 for a few days in mid–August before he departed on a 16-game hitting streak in which he batted .475. The rest of the Tigers also seemed to respond to the switch, winning seven-straight games at one point. By the end of August, Trammell had raised his average to .330 for the season, and had gone from an aging, injury-prone question mark heading into the season, to a revitalized offensive force and the team's defensive glue. He played so well that Anderson delayed plans he had for an extended look at another shortstop prospect, Chris Gomez, who instead spent time most of his time playing second base in August and September.[18] "It's just such a great feeling to have nothing wrong with me physically at this point in the season," said Trammell late in the summer.[19]

Detroit finished the season in fourth place, ten games behind Toronto which was on its way to a second straight World Series triumph. The Tigers' 85 wins were their most in five years, as was the home attendance mark, which was just under two million fans. Trammell finished the season on an upswing, ending with a highly-impressive batting mark of .329. A strong September netted him totals of 12 home runs, 25 doubles, 60 RBI's, and 72 runs scored. His .388 on-base percentage and .496 slugging percentage were each the second-highest of his career. Despite registering only 401 official at-bats in 112 games played, it was one of his finest seasons. Unfortunately, it would also prove to be the last truly productive season of Trammell's career.

Nineteen ninety-four was not a good season for him or the Tigers. The club was unable to duplicate the hitting prowess that led to their great start in 1993, and scored almost 250 fewer runs in 1994. The team faltered in the early going, losing their first four games and quickly dropped into last place where they remained as a non-factor in the AL East race the entire summer. Their lineup was suddenly viewed as one of the oldest in baseball, with only two regulars under the age of 30. Whitaker (37), Trammell (36), Gibson (36), Phillips (35), and Tettleton (33) were all at, or quickly approaching, the advanced stages of a professional baseball career. With little to lose, and trying to infuse a youthful presence into the playing group, Anderson started playing Gomez more and more as his regular shortstop, significantly cutting into Trammell's playing time.

Trammell spent much of 1994 as a platoon infielder of sorts, sitting out against right-handed pitchers and playing shortstop primarily against left-handers, while the right-handed hitting Gomez slid over to second base in place of Whitaker. Trammell and Whitaker often found themselves pinch-hitting for each other that summer, in what was their 17th full season in the major leagues. Trammell still flashed the ability to make the clutch play at times, such as the mid–June night in Milwaukee when the Brewers put the winning run on third base with two outs in the bottom of the twelfth inning. The next batter then hit a ball to Trammell deep in the hole behind shortstop, where Trammell fielded the ball and twirled in the air to throw the batter out at first base, ending the Milwaukee threat. The defensive gem proved to be decisive as Detroit scored four times in the top of the thirteenth inning, leading to a victory.

For the most part, however, the season was a struggle for Trammell. Scrambling for at-bats while getting irregular playing time, he watched his batting average deteriorate as his days as a full-time player receded into the past. After a strong start at the plate, he began to struggle more and more with his mechanics as the mid-summer weeks passed by. With the team a non-contender once again, Trammell's personal woes only added to an already depressing season that had an even more ominous dark cloud hanging over it.

Labor tensions between the Players' Association and owners were coming to a head that summer. The dispute in 1994 was the culmination of years of hostility and mistrust that had been building between the two parties. Major league baseball's owners claimed the game had reached a financial crisis, and that a large number of small-market teams were either unable to compete with their richer counterparts, or worse yet, would eventually fold due to financial hardships. The owners believed that the answer had to come from a system of revenue sharing between teams from sources such as broadcast rights and merchandise licensing. They also believed that a salary cap for players was justified, similar to what had occurred in other professional leagues such as the NFL and NBA. Additional adjustments to the game's financial structure were also being proposed, such as the elimination of salary arbitration, free agency eligibility, and the implementation of a team's "right of refusal," given to a team whose player(s) had solicited offers from other clubs.

Working against any possibility of the owners swaying the MLB Players Association into such an agreement, was their recent history of actions.

Since the inception of free agency in the mid-1970s, owners had been trying to find ways to curb unrestricted player movement and the proliferation of salaries. In 1981, owners had pushed for a form of compensation that would be awarded to teams losing a player to free agency, triggering the players' in-season strike that cut two months out of the schedule that summer. More recently, owners had been found guilty of colluding in the mid-1980s in an attempt to shrink, if not eliminate, competitive bidding on free agents such as Kirk Gibson and Jack Morris. By reducing the bidding wars that typically accompanied an open market for that caliber of player, the free agent had few options and often ended up settling for their current club's offer. By 1994 the Players Association viewed the cries of competitive disparity between large- and small-market franchises, and the need for a salary cap in baseball, to be further ploys to take back from players what had been gained nearly two decades prior.

With the 1990 Collective Bargaining Agreement set to expire on December 31, 1994, and owners insistent on the inclusion of a salary cap as part of any new agreement—the players set an in-season strike date of August 12, trying to get movement in the owners' negotiation stance. The owners countered on August 1 by declining to make a $7.8 million payment to the players' pension and benefit fund. By refusing to pay this annual contribution, the owners demonstrated they were prepared to call the players' bluff and forced them ever-closer to the edge.

When the strike date came, the players felt they had no recourse and walked away from their ball clubs, convinced the owners would not let the season, and more importantly the post-season, be squandered. Both sides were willing to wait out the other. An elongated negotiation session led by federal mediators on August 31 produced no new results and the season fell into jeopardy. Commissioner Bud Selig set September 9 as a tentative deadline to end the walkout and salvage the remainder of the season. A counter-proposal by the Players' Association offering the concept of a tax on the higher-payroll teams that could be distributed among the lower-revenue clubs in order to equalize markets—was dismissed by owners as being far short of the corrections the game's financial structure required. Sadly, on September 14, Selig announced the cancelation of the remainder of the 1994 regular season and its post-season; the first time in history that a season had not been played out to its conclusion.

"How do you explain this to a kid?" asked Trammell in rhetorical fashion at the time of the strike. "You can't. We don't expect fans to be sympathetic, we really don't. But we're being forced into this."[20]

Detroit's season was mercifully cut short after only 115 games. Their truncated 53–62 record consigned them to last place in the division, eighteen games behind New York. The longer than normal off-season also brought many question marks for an organization that clearly was in need of a face-lift. No one on the roster faced more questions about their future during that uncertain off-season than Trammell. He played only 76 games in 1994, with just 61 starts at shortstop. While his .267 batting average, eight home runs and 28 RBI's were respectable numbers for a player with only 292 official at-bats, it was becoming strikingly clear that he was slowing down. His .307 on-base percentage was the lowest of his career; lower even than his miserable 1989 and 1991 campaigns. His three stolen bases were the fewest he had swiped since his rookie season in 1978.

The 1990s had not been kind to Trammell. After establishing himself as one of the premiere players in baseball over the previous decade, he had positioned himself well to rack-up offensive career marks that would be among the greatest in history at the shortstop position. However, that was possible only *if* he could continue that late 1980s pace for an additional five to six years, or into the mid to late-1990s. What happened instead is that between the ages of 32 and 36, still prime years for many players of the modern era, he had been snakebit. Trammell played in only 464 of a possible 763 games (61 percent) for the Tigers from 1990 through 1994. After a very productive 1990 campaign, knee and wrist ailments had hampered him in 1991. A broken ankle cost him nearly all of 1992. He started the 1993 season on the disabled list with a severe groin injury. Then at age 36, a strike cost him most of the last two months of 1994. Having entered the decade with just over 2,000 career hits, he added only 249 in the five seasons that followed, which was about the equivalent of what he had produced every one-and-a-half seasons during his prime years between 1983 and 1989. Similar patterns had played-out in other categories as well, such as home runs, doubles, stolen bases, and runs scored; categories that Trammell had been distinguishing himself in prior to 1991.

As the autumn season absent of a World Series in 1994 took shape, the likelihood that Trammell's playing career in Detroit had concluded was very real. With no end in sight to the strike, serious doubts remained as to whether the 1995 major league baseball season would start on time, if it was even played at all. For a soon to be 37-year-old shortstop that had been injury-plagued in recent years, and had seen declining production when he was on the field, there was no guarantee that another contract would be offered by the Tigers. Alan Trammell's future in baseball was in limbo.

14

The Long Goodbye

The contentiousness between baseball's players and owners that had resulted in the early termination of the 1994 season, continued throughout the winter months of 1994 and 1995. In December the owners proceeded with the implementation of a salary cap without the consent of the Player's Association, a move that shortly afterwards was challenged, and then revoked, when the players filed a complaint with the National Labor Relations Board. Despite intervention by Congress and President Bill Clinton, the impasse continued well into the new year. With little optimism towards the 1995 season being played, the owners' Baseball's Executive Council approved on January 13 the use of replacement players for the 1995 season. Commissioner Bud Selig declared, "We are committed to playing the 1995 season and will do so with the best players willing to play."[1]

However, as the teams went to spring training in Florida and Arizona with their collection of minor leaguers, former players, and others castoffs willing to cross the Player's Association figurative picket lines, the first cracks in the unity of baseball's management started to appear, including one very large one within the Detroit organization. Peter Angelos, owner of the Baltimore Orioles, was both cognizant of fan reaction as well as protective of Baltimore's native son, Cal Ripken, Jr., who was within a year of breaking Lou Gehrig's consecutive games played record, and refused to field a team of replacement players. Angelos was the first to break the unity owners had thus far displayed in issues related to the handling of the strike. Detroit manager Sparky Anderson, despite technically being part of baseball management, took his own stand and refused to take part in any on-field activities involving replacement players. Anderson's departure from the league's company line was no doubt embarrassing for the Tiger organization. Trying to avoid a messy public spat over the decision to use replacement players, Anderson was placed on administrative leave by the Tigers. Other teams, such as the Toronto Blue Jays, tried to separate their managers and coaches from the labor issues and any potential post-strike fall-out that might result, by assigning them to work only with minor league players within the organization's system, and not with any replacement players. Some local labor organizations around the U.S. and Canada banned the use of replacement players at stadiums and venues, further weakening the owner's tactic of trying to play the 1995 schedule without the regular unionized players.

By late March the owners had been cited for unfair labor practices by the NLRB and an injunction was filed and upheld days later by future Supreme Court justice, Sonia Sotomayor, of the U.S. District Court of New York. Justice Sotomayor returned the players to work under the terms of the recently-expired basic agreement that had just lapsed on December 31. With the regular players ordered to report, the 1995 season was set to resume on April 25, with an abbreviated spring training commencing ahead of it.

The strike ended without the adoption of either replacement players or a salary cap. There also was no new labor agreement in place. Major league baseball would resume under its previous basic agreement until a new one was forged, something that wouldn't occur until 1997. It would be eight more years before the "competitive balance tax," largely known today as the "luxury tax" would finally be agreed upon and implemented.[2]

Meanwhile organizations all across baseball had waded through the off-season cautiously; not knowing if or when a 1995 season would be played. Teams were hesitant to commit contracts to players when the financial structure of the game faced so much uncertainty. The Detroit Tigers were no exception. Wanting to make room for young players on the major league roster, the organization allowed productive veterans such as Mickey Tettleton, Bill Gullickson, and Eric Davis to walk away to free agency, without any serious attempt to re-sign any of them. A larger dilemma presented itself with Trammell, and to a lesser extent, Gibson. The contracts for both had run out at the conclusion of the previous season. The club hadn't offered salary arbitration for either player on a new contract for 1995, making both of them free agents. However, the abrupt ending to the schedule in 1994 had not allowed the Detroit organization to give a proper send-off to either of these iconic symbols from more successful times. Gibson was coming off an extremely productive summer in which he smashed 23 home runs by the time the strike commenced on August 12. When the strike finally ended in March, re-signing Gibson, who at age 37 had no intentions of playing anywhere else but Detroit, made sense for the Tigers.

Trammell's status, on the other hand, was much less clear cut. His preference was always to play at least one additional season in Detroit. However, with the organization committed to Chris Gomez at shortstop and Travis

Fryman at third base, and with Lou Whitaker still under contract for another year at second base, there wasn't an obvious role for the 37-year-old Trammell. Torn by the longtime, mutual loyalty that had built up between an organization and player, Trammell was left to twist in the wind that spring, while resolution to the strike played out and debate continued over what to do with an aging relic for a Detroit organization that desperately needed to move into a new era. "Is he going to be a hang-around guy?" Trammell asked about himself when explaining his situation to reporters. "I've got to decide. Whether or not they want me, they've got to decide. If they don't, I'll pack it in."[3]

As the long off-season wore on, he became more resolute in his desire to continue playing. Trammell began listening to offers his agent, John Boggs, fielded from other teams. The San Diego Padres, Cleveland Indians, and New York Yankees all showed interest in adding a veteran of Trammell's caliber to their roster. The interest by the Yankees was two-fold: They wanted a veteran shortstop that could step into an otherwise loaded lineup short-term, but also one who could mentor their hotshot prospect, 21-year-old Derek Jeter, who had been New York's first round selection in the MLB 1992 June Amateur Draft and was rated by *Baseball America* as the game's fourth best prospect heading into the 1995 campaign. "There will be a lot of soul searching done by Alan," said Boggs during the middle of the 1994 and 1995 off-season. "He's played his whole career in Detroit, but he's a baseball player too, and his competitive juices are flowing."[4]

In the end, Trammell and the Tigers settled on a one-year deal for $1.3 million for what most assumed would be his 19th and final season. He took a considerable cut from the $3 million he had made in his previous contract, but understood that the climate had changed. "My deal is fair," he said. "The owners are finally getting their act together. They mean business—and everybody can see it."[5] A shortened 144-game schedule had been agreed upon, a concession to the late conclusion to the strike. The season began three weeks later than normal, but once again, injury forced Trammell to start on the disabled list, this time with a pulled left hamstring.

When he was finally able to play, he started off hot, getting seven hits over his first three appearances while driving in three runs. He played regularly in the early going, playing exclusively at shortstop through much of May and into June. While his batting and on-base averages were still respectable—he was batting over .300 into early August, with an on-base percentage running about 75 points higher—the pop in his bat was gone. Trammell was no longer driving the ball for extra-bases with any regularity, or driving in many runs. He would finish the year with only two home runs and 23 RBI's in 223 at-bats, with his .350 slugging percentage one of the lowest marks of his career. His playing time was significantly cut into as the season wore on, as Anderson committed fully to the younger players. Trammell batted only 23 times in September, collecting just three hits, finishing with a .269 batting mark.

Among the personal highlights that summer was a game-winning grand slam home run against Milwaukee on June 25. Trailing 3-1 in the bottom of the eighth inning, the Tigers pushed across one run before with two outs and the sacks filled, Trammell homered off of Brewers' righthander Ron Rightnowar. In addition to giving Detroit an eventual 6-3 victory, the home run was noteworthy in that it tied him with Tigers legend Charlie Gehringer for 12th place on Detroit's all-time home run list with 184. Three weeks later, Trammell collected hit number 2,300 of his career in a game against California.

The personal accomplishments masked what otherwise had turned into a depressing second half of the summer. The team had played respectably over the first two months of the year, before putting together a hot-streak starting in late June that saw them win 13 of 18 games, and pull within three games of first place with a 37-33 overall record. However, a cold streak followed in which Detroit lost 14 of 17 games, resulting in them falling to 8½ games out of the lead by the end of July. At that point, the Tigers' organization, led by general manager Joe Klein, threw in the towel on the 1995 season. They traded away their best starting pitcher, former Blue Jay David Wells, to Cincinnati at the July trading deadline. Ten days later, the Tigers sent their veteran relief pitcher, Mike Henneman, to Houston in a post-deadline waiver deal. The organization was committed to young players like Fryman (26), Gomez (24), and outfielders Danny Bautista (23), and Bobby Higginson (25). The moves seemed to not only gut the roster of top-end veteran talent, but killed Detroit's morale for the rest of the campaign. The team collapsed from that point on, finishing 24 games under .500, and 26 games behind the division-winning Boston Red Sox.

On August 10, following a 7-2 throttling in Arlington, Texas, by the Rangers, the losing atmosphere finally got to one of Detroit's old warriors. Trammell was sitting on the team bus, waiting for the return trip to the hotel, when Gibson slid into the seat next to him and offered his longtime teammate and friend a beer he had brought onboard. After Trammell initially declined, Gibson chided him with a "What, you're not going to help me celebrate my retirement?"[6] The veteran shortstop was in disbelief for a few minutes before finally being convinced that his teammate of 12 seasons was actually leaving the team. Citing the losing atmosphere, a decrease in his personal commitment to the game, and above all—a desire to be with his family, Gibson was walking away from the Tigers for good, retiring at age 38.

With Gibson gone, assumptions increased that the last two members of the 1984 champions would soon be joining him in retirement. Although Whitaker was still performing at a high level, and had not yet announced anything, his demeanor and body language indicated that 1995 would be his final season with the Tigers. His contract expired at the end of the season, and little interest seemed to exist from either side about getting another deal done. Sparky Anderson's future in Detroit was even more tenuous. The stance he took in the spring, declaring that he would not manage replacement players, had not been well-received by the baseball establishment, nor had it been looked upon favorably by Detroit's management, including owner Mike Illitch. Anderson essentially served as a lame-duck manager throughout the 1995 season, with his contract also expiring at the end of the year. With every game crossed off the schedule that summer and fall, Anderson's 17-year tenure in Detroit was unceremoniously winding down.

Trammell had been much more ambiguous about his future, and quickly voiced displeasure over premature reports of his pending retirement. One story circulated that he would become a scout and minor league instructor within the Tigers' organization at season's end, a story that Trammell refuted with some disdain. "There's probably a pretty good chance this is going to be it, but I want to wait until the season is over before I finally sit down and make my decision," he said.[7]

As the final games played out early that fall, fans got their final look at what was universally acknowledged as one of the greatest double-play combinations in baseball history. "Trammell-Whitaker," like Tinker and Evers, Ruth and Gehrig, Williams and DiMaggio, or Koufax and Drysdale, were already names linked together forever in baseball lore. They were winding down their 19th season in the Major Leagues, their 18th as Detroit's regular shortstop-second base combination—the longest such combination in history.

Few things in team sport are as harmonious as a well-turned ground ball double-play between the shortstop and second baseman. The crack of the bat sends a white blur whirring along the ground at a rapid clip towards the middle two-thirds of the infield cutout. Leather and flesh meet as the ball is stopped and redirected with the flick of a wrist towards the second base bag. There, a keystone companion doesn't gather the sphere, but rather converts it to an object seemingly already on its way with even greater velocity towards the waiting first baseman. The maneuver is completed in three to four seconds at most, as the choreographed movements around the base occur while evading an oncoming runner that comes boring in. No duo ever performed this object of baseball beauty better than Trammell and Whitaker.

Although the two were separated by only a year in age, and despite rooming together on the road early in their careers—beginning in 1977 at Double-A Montgomery and through their first few season in the major leagues—they were not necessarily close. Trammell was outgoing, a team prankster, and looked upon as one of the team's leaders on and off the field.

Lou Whitaker (shown relaying a throw to first base during the 1978 season) would team with Trammell to play 19 seasons in the major leagues, and form the longest running, and arguably the best, double-play combination in baseball history (National Baseball Hall of Fame Library, Cooperstown, New York).

Whitaker was quiet and kept to himself, content to do his job at the ball park while seeking privacy off the field.

"We've kind of separated over the years, Lou and I," said Trammell late in their careers. "We very seldom do anything together off the field. But there's a special feeling when we get on the field. It's like eye contact. We don't even talk. We just look at each other. And that relationship, well, there aren't too many of those around..."[8]

The relationship on the field was some part chemistry and a large part hard work. "Infield practice never stopped," said Trammell. "Timing is so important. Lou and I wanted to keep that edge. It was second nature where Lou would be (on the double play). That's where the timing comes in. If someone else was playing second base, I had to take that split second to look at second base and that could cost you the double play."[9]

"That's one of the little things you get by working together so much," added Whitaker about their on-field magic around the bag. "You don't see us stepping on each other, or bumping into each other. Like when Tram is directly behind second base, making a throw, I'm never blocking his way. Or if he's going to make the play himself, I'm never in the way of the bag."[10]

On September 13, before a Tiger Stadium turnout of fewer than 9,000 patrons, Trammell and Whitaker set the American League record for the most games played together at 1,915. They sheepishly doffed their caps while standing out near second base as the momentous feat was announced to the sparse crowd before the start of the second inning. They broke the mark set just a few years earlier by the Kansas City Royals' George Brett and Frank White. "I'm the only manager in history to have two guys that good their whole careers together," said Sparky Anderson afterwards. "It'll never happen again."[11]

If it hadn't already, the record sparked comparisons with other notable double-play combinations in baseball history. In sheer longevity, the Detroit duo dwarfed anything that had come before them. The famed Joe Tinker and Johnny Evers played ten seasons together for the Chicago Cubs in the very early days of the 20th century. Other famed pairings from the more modern era (loosely defined as play following World War II) include the 1940s through 1950s Brooklyn Dodgers' tandem of Pee Wee Reese and Jackie Robinson, the Chicago White Sox' Luis Aparicio and Nellie Fox (late-1950s through early 1960s), the Cubs' Don Kessinger and Glen Beckert (mid–1960s through early 1970s), and Sparky Anderson's Cincinnati Reds keystone from the 1970s "Big Red Machine" of Dave Concepcion and Joe Morgan. Yet, none of those pairings even reached ten full seasons together serving as the primary middle-infielders for their clubs. When factoring longevity with the defensive excellence and offensive production displayed throughout their careers, the Trammell-Whitaker combination has to rate as the greatest shortstop-second base combination in baseball history.

Former major league pitcher, Jack Billingham, a 145-game winner over his 13-year career, had a unique perspective for comparison of two of the greatest double-play combo's in history. His best seasons were served pitching for the Reds from 1972–77, during the peak years of the Cincinnati dynasty when Concepcion and Morgan roamed the middle of the infield behind him. However, he finished his career with two final seasons with the Tigers in 1978 and 1979, Trammell and Whitaker's first full seasons in the majors. "I didn't think Joe and Davey could ever be matched," he said near the close of the 1995 campaign. "But I played with Lou and Alan for two seasons and they just got better and better. They added two years to my career. Being a sinkerball pitcher, and having Lou and Alan backing me up allowed me to win 20-some games (25) my last two seasons."[12]

As a fervent student of baseball history, Trammell didn't have to go further than his Southern California roots to gain his own viewpoint on where he and Whitaker placed in baseball annals. "I look at the 19-year record of ours and look at Davey Lopes and Bill Russell who played together for nine years," said Trammell of the longtime Los Angeles Dodgers duo from the 1970s. "Lou and I more than doubled that. Will it ever be broken? I don't know. I think it's highly unlikely the way the game is today with free agency. I will say those 19 years are something both Lou and I can be proud of."[13]

"You know, you can talk about DiMaggio's 56-game hitting streak and some of these other records that will never be broken," said Anderson. "Well you'll never see two players spend 19 years together like Lou and Alan did. They were raised by the Tigers, brought up by the Tigers, played their entire careers with the Tigers, and had a love for the city and the uniform."[14]

By season's end, the pair had tacked on three additional games to their American League record, making a total of 1,918 games the two had appeared in together. The mark fell just short of the major league record held by the Chicago Cubs' Ron Santo and Billy Williams who appeared in 2,015 games together. "When you think about it, we've been together longer than a lot of husbands and wives," commented Whitaker.[15]

The season finale in Baltimore's Camden Yards was for all intents and purposes a celebration of the "retirements" of Trammell, Whitaker, and Anderson. The Orioles were gracious hosts and staged moments to honor their long-time combatants. A nostalgic Anderson inserted the Whitaker/Trammell combination in the 1–2 slots at the top of the batting lineup that day, with plans to then pull them after their initial at-bat. The two ran out to their positions at the bottom of the first inning, while the rest of the

14. The Long Goodbye

Tigers held back in the dugout. Cal Ripken, Jr., and Baltimore second baseman Jeff Huson, then presented bases to their Detroit counterparts, while the Baltimore crowd saluted the Tiger keystone paring. As Trammell and Whitaker headed back to the dugout, most assumed they would never be seen as active players again. "They've had enough," pronounced Anderson after the game when talking about the two. "They've had good careers and long careers, but they've had enough."[16]

Despite no official announcement at the conclusion of the season, and overtures from several teams that off-season, Whitaker's career was over. He finished his 19 years as one of the best players in franchise history, and more than 20 years later still ranks on the club's all-time list in games-played (3rd), at-bats (4th), runs scored (4th), doubles (5th), home runs (7th), RBI's (8th), walks (2nd), and stolen bases (10th).

Anderson, meanwhile, made official on his own terms what everyone had long supposed. "I ain't here no more!" he told a media gathering in typical upbeat fashion the next morning at Tiger Stadium.[17] After seventeen seasons and 1,331 victories managing from the Detroit dugout, he was moving on. He said that day that he wanted to manage again, but never did. Some suspect that the stance he took against the owners' plans to use replacement players that spring got him blackballed from ever managing another major league club. Anderson's legacy was secure nonetheless, cemented as the first manager in history to win World Series titles with teams from both leagues. His 2,194 total victories are the sixth highest total in baseball history. He was elected to the Baseball Hall of Fame in 2000.

Trammell, however, remained non-committal about his presumed retirement. As the off-season stretched on, his yearning to play another season won out. "I still have a desire to compete," he explained in simplistic terms.[18] Whether he came back to complete a rare 20th season in the major leagues, or to transition into his post-playing career by becoming a player-coach of sorts, or maybe to just delay the inevitable for one more year, Trammell decided to return to the Tigers for the 1996 season. The organization had little choice but to welcome him back, his status as one of the greatest players in team history firmly established. He signed for around $650,000, a paltry sum for a player of Trammell's prestige, but the money wasn't the motivating factor in his coming back. "Money's not really the issue. Just being back is what makes me happy."[19]

"I know I'm not the player I was ten years ago, but I'm not going to be asked to do the things I did ten years ago," he explained when asked about the role he would fill on a rebuilding Tigers team. "We're trying to develop kids here, and I'd like to help out with that."[20] Trammell's return was clearly a major step in finishing an outstanding career on his own terms. While he went along with much of the pomp and circumstance that surrounded the endings of the careers of Whitaker and Anderson, Trammell had never submitted to the popular belief that he too should quit the game. "When someone retires, it should be because it's what they want, not what someone else wants. Even though I don't know how much I'll play, I'm looking forward to the season. The game is in my blood. I'm a lifer."[21]

For the first time since reporting to spring training in 1979, Trammell was greeted by a manager other than Sparky Anderson. Buddy Bell, 44-years-old and a veteran of 18 Major League seasons as a player himself, had been appointed as the new skipper for the Detroit Tigers. Bell was only seven years removed from the end of his playing career, and had been a contemporary of Trammell's during many of their peak years, which he had spent primarily as a hard-hitting third baseman for the Texas Rangers. Among the storylines of Bell's first spring training in Lakeland that March was the surprisingly strong play of the 38-year-old Trammell. Expected to be no more than just a part-time player and pseudo coach, Trammell played so well during the Grapefruit season that he gained the starting nod when the team headed north.[22]

Although he opened the campaign with the familiar number '3' on his back as the Tigers' starting shortstop, things were not the same for Trammell, who was in his 20th season in Detroit. Bell batted him in the ninth position on the lineup card for the season opener, and then pinch-hit for him in the eighth inning of an 8–6 loss to Minnesota. Three days later he was pinch-run for in the 12th inning of a 9–9 game in Oakland. Once recognized as one of the American League's clutch players, Trammell was no longer viewed as the Tigers' "indispensable player," and was often being substituted for in crucial situations as if he were a journeyman utility infielder.

Trammell got off to a solid start at the plate, batting .323 in April with a home run and seven RBI's, while playing in 36 of Detroit's first 54 games. But, he started to tail off in May, his power was non-existent and he wasn't driving in many runs. In June the club acquired another shortstop, Andujar Cedeno, jettisoning Gomez to San Diego in the process. With Cedeno in the fold, Trammell's appearances became relegated mostly to pinch-hitting duties or the occasional start at second or third base.

In early July, Trammell suffered from an injured left ankle that landed him again on the disabled list. Loose fragments in the joint were causing the ankle to lock up. Orthoscopic surgery appeared to be the only viable option, but would seemingly signal the end of Trammell's career. "He gives us credibility and identity, but he's struggling physically," said Bell about his hobbled veteran.[23]

While Trammell watched from the sidelines that summer, he was witness to a changing landscape from what he had come to know over his twenty seasons at the major league level. Divisional re-alignment, an expanded post-season field, inter-league competition, and a proliferation in scoring, had either already taken place or was looming on baseball's near horizon as the 1996 season unfolded. Each of those moves represented a significant shift in the game as it had been played during Trammell's long career.

The two leagues had already watered down the long-standing divisional makeups, parting from the established East and West sets that had been in place since the inception of divisional play in 1969. Now each league had added a Central Division, and with an expansion team set to begin play in Tampa, Florida, in 1998, Detroit was being shifted to the newly-formed American League Central Division. The move would break ties within what had unquestionably been the most competitive division in major league baseball during Trammell's time. Longtime rivalries the Tigers had established with AL East clubs such as Baltimore, New York, Boston, and Toronto would wither away. Instead, Detroit would compete with the Cleveland Indians, Chicago White Sox, Minnesota Twins, and Kansas City Royals, clubs that didn't have the same cache for either the Tigers' players or fans.

Three-division leagues also necessitated a fourth post-season team, which would come in the form of a wild card entry. The wild card position allowed for the best second-place club in each league to qualify for a shot at the World Series. While this stimulated late-season interest in many additional cities around each league, with the opportunity to reach the post-season, the move also eliminated the time-honored tradition that had always differentiated major league baseball from other professional leagues. Previously, only a first place finish, earned over a grueling 162-game schedule, had qualified a team for a chance to play in the post-season. The addition of a wild card entry removed that highest of standards. No longer would there be the type of high-stakes drama and heightened play such as Detroit and Toronto played over the final two months in 1987 when they finished 1–2 not only for the AL East title, but also the best record in baseball. While only Detroit advanced to the American League playoffs in 1987, if the two teams would have played under the revised post-season format that was instituted in 1995, both Detroit and Toronto would have qualified for post-season births.

The summer of 1996 also marked the final season of intra-league-only play at the major league level. Limited inter-league play would be introduced in 1997, breaking customs that had existed since the game's earliest beginnings, where National and American League teams played exclusively within the vacuum of their own leagues prior to the World Series. The implementation of inter-league play would create opportunities for fans in each city to see the great teams and stars from the opposite league (a quaint notion already being chipped away by the increased television coverage of games on ESPN and other national cable outlets), but it also eliminated the intrigue that came by not seeing or competing against the "other" league on a regular basis. Other than spring training exhibition games, the All Star Game, and World Series, the two leagues operated independently of each other, spawning countless bar room discussions about the relative strengths of each league.

While the realignment of divisions, inter-league play, and the addition of a wild card team to each league were artificial stimulants to the game, undoubtedly meant to regain fan interest following the damaging season-ending strike in 1994, the play on the field was also undergoing change. Scoring was up dramatically in both leagues, reaching highs it had not seen since the 1930s. Home runs on a per-game basis were at an all-time high. Slug-fests with scores like 9–8 or 12–7 were becoming commonplace. The American League's cumulative earned run average in 1996 would be 4.99, its highest mark in nearly 50 years.

While the specter of steroids and other performance enhancing drugs was just coming to light at that time, there was no doubt that players were bigger, stronger, and faster than ever. A myriad of reasons were often mentioned as plausible explanations. Better nutrition, advanced strength and fitness training, and advancements in technologies such as video analysis used for training and preparation, were all factors that seemed to nudge the game's balance away from the pitcher and towards the hitter throughout the 1990s. Whatever the reasons, the game itself was changing, as managers, particularly in the American League, loaded up their lineups with fence-busting, swing-from-the-heels hitters, capable of launching the long ball. This took away from subtleties in the game such as base running, the stolen base, sacrifice bunting, and hitting behind a runner—qualities that a well-rounded player like Trammell exceled in.

The proliferation of offense was especially noticeable at the shortstop position, where a pair of 21-year-olds was revolutionizing a spot on the diamond normally reserved for slick-fielding glove men that didn't always bring a threatening presence to the plate. In the summer of 1996, the Seattle Mariners' Alex Rodriguez and New York Yankees' Derek Jeter were both playing their first full seasons in the American League, threatening to blow apart any previous conceptions of what a shortstop might be capable of.

Six-foot-three and built like an NFL tight end, Rodriguez was the prototype for the modern infield superstar. He batted .358 to lead the American

League that summer, becoming the first shortstop in over 30 years to win a batting title in either league. He also blasted 36 home runs, 54 doubles, scored 141 runs, and drove in 123, in what was arguably the greatest offensive season by a shortstop in major league history. Jeter, meanwhile, was also 6-foot-3, but played with instincts and an ease seldom seen in the game's history. Jeter would be named the American League's Rookie of the Year in 1996 while batting .314 with 10 home runs, 104 runs scored, and 78 RBI's, as the Yankees won the first of the five World Championships they would earn with him as their shortstop. That September, 23-year-old Nomar Garciaparra made his major league debut for Boston, just ahead of a Rookie of the Year campaign in 1997 that saw him put together a 30-game hitting streak and blast 30 home runs.

As the schedule wound down that year, the Detroit Tigers' first season under the direction of Buddy Bell had not gone well. They were on their way to losing 109 games, the most in franchise history. A franchise known for being one of the most healthy in baseball just a decade before, was now void of talent across the board and playing in a deteriorating stadium that had lost its charm. Meanwhile, the Tigers' passionate fan base slowly eroded, as attendance and local television ratings dwindled. Despite the bleak outlook for the club late that summer, Trammell continued to rehab his injured right ankle and remained steadfast in his refusal to retire from the game as an active player.

"…A rebuilding team doesn't want to clog up its roster with a no-offense, 38-year-old infielder with no pop," wrote Craig Carter and Mark Newman with much derision for *The Sporting News* late that season. "So why do the names Mays, Mantle, and Carlton pop to mind? 'Yo Tram' know when to say when."[24]

He quietly returned in September when the rosters limit opened up beyond 25-players. Trammell was brought back slowly, and played irregularly as the team played out the string on another disappointing season. Despite there being no formal announcement, most thought for sure this time, that the end was nearing for the iconic Tiger. With little fanfare, it was announced that Trammell would start at shortstop in the season finale in Tiger Stadium against Milwaukee. A crowd of just 13,038 turned out that Sunday afternoon and watched him beat out an infield hit and contribute a sacrifice fly during regulation of a 5–5 tie with the Brewers. He had been greeted by long ovations before each at bat that day, especially after it had been announced that Trammell would address the crowd after the game.

With one out in the bottom of the tenth inning and Detroit trailing 7–5, Trammell lined a sharp single to center field off of Milwaukee relief-ace Mike Fetters, bringing the tying run to the plate. Bell sent Shannon

Penn in to pinch-run, affording Trammell the opportunity to receive a standing ovation from the small crowd, while he trotted back to the dugout. When Travis Fryman followed just moments later by grounding into a game-ending double-play, it became official: The season, as well as the career, of one of the greatest players in Detroit Tigers' history had drawn to a close.

Trammell had made the decision to retire about two weeks earlier, informing Bell and general manager Randy Smith, but otherwise keeping the decision to himself. After initial hesitation on his part, but with the gentle prodding of the Tiger organization, it was decided that Trammell would personally make his decision public following the final game. While a microphone was being setup out on the Tiger Stadium infield grass just in front of where the shortstop is normally positioned, Trammell slipped down the tunnel leading from the Detroit dugout, as the day's emotions caught up with him. "I went down in the tunnel and lost it," he later admitted about the tears that flowed during that private moment; the finality of his playing career ending, having sunk in.[25] After he composed himself, it was time to share the news with everyone else.

"Today was my last day," he announced to what was left of the crowd that afternoon. "And as much as it hurts to say that, it is somewhat of a relief. One thing I am most proud of is that I did it with one club my whole career."[26]

"I've had two bad years in a row. It's like Sparky said almost a year ago today: 'It's time.' I've been struggling big-time. I was hoping to contribute a little bit, and it just wore me down. I couldn't find my niche. I wish I was stronger. I wish I could have given the club a little more lift, but now I want to turn the page as quickly as I can and get on."[27]

In his final season as a player, Trammell batted just .233 with a single home run and only 16 RBI's. He batted .191 after May 1, and finished with a batting average, on-base percentage, and slugging percentage, all below .300; telling indicators that he had nothing more to give as a player. "I knew my role was to be a role player, but handling it was a different matter. So a couple weeks ago, after a combination of a handful of at bats against guys who got me out, against guys who I knew I should get good contact (against)...."[28]

"It's a sad day," said Detroit president John McHale. "It's a sad day to see a great player decide enough is enough. But he did it on his terms."[29]

Watching the announcement from the visiting dugout with the rest of his players and coaches was Brewers manager Phil Garner. "It's sad to see him hang it up," he said. He's a consummate player, and guys like that belong in a class of their own, and it's called the Hall of Fame."[30]

When word spread to Toronto where Cal Ripken, Jr., was wrapping up another season with Baltimore, he added his own comments about his longtime peer. "It's always sad when you see a player leave the game, especially one you know and watched closely. You don't want to see the good ones go away."[31]

When the ceremony had concluded, Trammell dressed quickly and headed for the players' private parking lot with a collection of bats and balls and his youngest son, Kyle, in tow. A gathering of reporters waited to capture the scene. Without lingering, he threw the keepsakes into the backseat before hopping into his white Pontiac SSE, ready to leave his workplace of the past 20 years. "Take care. See you," he uttered to those that remained, before he eased out of the Tiger Stadium parking lot for the final time as an active player, and drove away.[32]

15

"Bringing Back a Hero"

By the fall of 2002, the Detroit Tigers organization, as well as its fan base, was in desperate need of hope. It had been ten years since owner Mike Illitch had purchased the team from fellow-pizza mogul Tom Monaghan. Over that period of time, Illitch had enjoyed immense success winning three Stanley Cups with his Detroit Red Wings NHL franchise, but had not attained anything near that level of prosperity with the flailing Tigers. His biggest success had come off the field when he had successfully steered the organization away from its decaying relic of a home in Tiger Stadium, to the club's new base at shiny Comerica Park.

Three years into its residency at Comerica Park, the novelty of a new ballpark was wearing off for a following that was becoming increasingly disengaged from the Tigers less-than-stellar play on the field. Attendance had dropped by more than a million paying customers in 2002, from the 2.5 million fans that attended games at Comerica Park in its inaugural season of 2000. The team wasn't competing on the diamond, nor did it have any star power.

A new manager would be needed for 2003, something that had become a regular occurrence since Sparky Anderson's departure following the 1995 season. While Anderson suffered through an extended lean period himself, and had developed detractors over his last years in Detroit, the alternatives had not turned out any better. The Tigers had averaged 95 losses in the seven seasons since he had vacated the Detroit dugout, and none of his successors—Buddy Bell, Larry Parrish, Phil Garner, or Luis Pujols—had lasted even three full seasons in the position. Losers of 106 games in 2002, Detroit needed a miracle worker.

Instead they turned to a familiar face, a personality recognized, known, and beloved by a Tiger Nation waiting anxiously for a return to glory days that were now more than a decade past. Alan Trammel had emerged as a front-runner for the Tigers' managerial position soon after Pujols was released at the merciful end of Detroit's season. Trammell was one of four candidates general manager Dave Dombrowski intended to interview, along with the current manager at the Tigers' Triple-A affiliate at Toledo, Bruce Fields, Yankees coach Willie Randolph, and Oakland coach Ken Macha.[1] After Trammell interviewed on Friday, October 4 before a panel that included among others, Dombrowski, and former Detroit greats Al Kaline and Willie Horton, the greatest shortstop in Tigers' history was the clear front-runner for the job.[2]

Since retiring as a player six years earlier, Trammell had remained in baseball in a variety of roles. He had served for two years in the Tigers' organization as an advisor, scout, and minor league instructor, working mainly behind the scenes. In 1999 he had returned to uniform in Detroit as the hitting coach under manager Larry Parrish. However, when Phil Garner replaced Parrish that fall, Trammell was not retained and instead went home to San Diego where he became part of Bruce Bochy's staff as the first base coach for the Padres, a role he had remained in for three years.

Despite a lack of managerial experience at any level of professional baseball, there was considerable pressure for the Detroit organization to hire Trammell as its manager. The Tigers' position was not considered one of the plumb openings in the major leagues that off-season, and none of the other candidates was considered to be a "can't miss" hire. Once his name had surfaced publically as a serious applicant for the position, it became very difficult for Detroit to consider choosing anyone else. Public sentiment wasn't going to allow it.

On October 9, 2004—Trammell was announced as the 35th field manager of the Detroit Tigers. He was given a four-year deal to turn around the fortunes of a fran-

Trammell (shown late in his career in this 1995 photograph) played 20 seasons in Detroit, joining legends Ty Cobb and Al Kaline as the only players to reach that milestone while wearing a Tiger uniform. Trammell would come back to manage Detroit for three largely unsuccessful seasons between 2003 and 2005 (National Baseball Hall of Fame Library, Cooperstown, New York).

chise that had struggled mightily on the field for more than a decade. "He's class personified," said Dombrowski at the introductory press conference. "He's someone who represents the best years of the Tigers."[3]

"This is a day I'm very proud of," said Trammell, shedding his suit jacket in favor of the familiar number "3" jersey upon being introduced. "This Olde English "D" will always be a part of my life. I'll be a Tiger wherever I happen to be."[4]

"To put into words what the opportunity to manager the team I love so much is almost impossible. It's a privilege beyond anything I could imagine. I know only one way to succeed in baseball. That's to give it everything I've got. That's the way I played, and that's the way I'll manage. That's a promise I can easily give to every Tiger fan."[5]

Trammell understood that a massive rebuilding effort faced him. Despite being three time zones away and coaching in the National League, he had continued to follow closely what was happening in Detroit. In fact, it was part of the motivation he cited in returning to his adopted hometown. "We've got to get some respect back," he said. "It means as much to me as anything. It's probably the number one reason I'm back. It hurt me for this team to not do well."[6]

Trammell's hiring was clearly a win in the court of public opinion in Detroit and across the Tigers' regional fan base. He was *the single player* from that core group that had won a World Series and rejuvenated baseball in the Motor City—that seemed destined to wind up in this role. Trammell standing in that traditional position on the first step of the dugout meant the natural plan of succession had finally been followed. The chasm formed since the ending of the Sparky Anderson era had finally been bridged. "He's the guy I hoped for," said Tiger legend Al Kaline after the press conference. "The guy we had to have here."[7]

The day after Trammell's introductory press conference, *The Detroit Free Press* offered an editorial piece titled "Welcome Home, Alan Trammell" which encapsulated the sentiment of much of the Tiger following: "After several years of bad choices and false dawns, the Detroit Tigers finally have decided to restore the legacy of an historic baseball franchise by bringing back a hero. If the Tigers organization allows Trammell to put together a first class coaching staff and gets him the players he needs to compete, this may be the beginning of the end of the long baseball famine in Detroit."[8]

Not everybody, however, was willing to lap up the good vibes that were resonating from the hire. *The Detroit News'* Joe Falls, the godfather of Detroit sportswriters, openly questioned whether the new manager would be tough enough on his players. Falls' colleague, Rob Parker, called the hiring a "feel good public relations move," and intimated that the club should have hired a more experienced candidate for the managerial position.[9] Even Sparky Anderson's warning from Trammell's last days as an active player were dredged up again and offered for public consumption. "I hope he never becomes a manager here," he had said at the end of the 1995 season. "Because I want fans to remember him as he was."[10]

The cries of any doubters were soon drowned out as Trammell got busy putting together a coaching staff that was long on star power, if not always on experience. Bruce Fields was the first hire as his hitting coach. Fields was a three-time minor league batting champion and had managed at Toledo, bringing solid credentials to the role. Juan Samuel and Mick Kelleher had both enjoyed long careers in the major leagues as players, and had been teammates of Trammell's for a couple of years each. The 57-year-old Bob Cluck was an experienced pitching coach at the big league level, and would serve as the elder presence on the staff. But the hires that really ignited the passion of success-starved Tiger fans were the appointments of Kirk Gibson and Lance Parrish, who were brought back by Trammell to return the club to its former glory. Gibson would serve as Trammell's right-hand man as bench coach, while Parrish would be the bullpen coach.

The reunion of Trammell, Gibson, and Parrish created a giddiness in the fan base that defied level-headedness. Unrealistic expectations were formed based on fans' memories of iconic players from a past generation. That the trio was made up of men, each now in his mid-'40s and no longer playing on the field, seemed to get lost in the jubilation of the hires. In reality the staff was inheriting a miserable baseball team, a point that was masked by what in hindsight can only be described as an unfortunate marketing campaign by the Detroit organization. The three Tiger stars from the 1980s were cast in various media advertisements ahead of the 2003 season while wearing dark sunglasses, and exuding rock star personas, while spewing slogans like "It's time!" and "Let's go!"

When Trammell welcomed his troops for the first time to Lakeland for spring training, he found a club with few strengths, and a multitude of flaws, including a thin starting pitching rotation, weak hitting, and poor defense. Those weaknesses and more were apparent to Anderson who visited Trammell's first camp as a valued advisor. "I look at five years," he said about the rebuilding job in front of his one-time protégé. "When I came to Detroit, I had more available to me. I had some pretty good players. They had some talent. He's going to have a bigger job on his hands...."[11]

Tigers' radio broadcaster, Ernie Harwell, who had seen nearly everything in his 60 years in the game, was of the opinion that Trammell "gave (Detroit) a link to the past" and would "have a slightly longer honeymoon than someone from the outside," but was a realist when he added that the new manager "can't catch and throw and hit for them."[12]

What Trammell found as the regular season began was a team that was even worse than feared. They lost their first nine games, and 19 of their first 21, to quickly drop out of contention for even respectability in 2003. At one point in early May, Detroit had a 3–25 record and had been outscored by an astonishing 81 runs in those first 28 games. They wouldn't reach the ten-win plateau until nearly Memorial Day.

"I look at this year as being a learning year for myself and my players," he said early in the season, trying to stay optimistic. "I'm going to make some mistakes; the players are going to make some mistakes. But we're going to learn from them."[13]

Trammell used 34 different lineups in the first 38 games, trying anything he could to patch together a combination that gave the team a chance to win. Second base, third base, center field, and left field were positions that remained in flux throughout most of the season. He tried to play the hot hand whenever and wherever possible, and put together lineups by feel some games, while following matchup histories in others.

One night when the percentages didn't pay off came on May 13 against Oakland, when Trammell's most consistent starting pitcher, left-hander Mike Maroth, was locked up in a 1–1 deadlock in the seventh inning, before walking a pair of batters to load the bases. Trammell replaced Maroth with knuckle-baller Steve Sparks, who had gotten the A's next batter, Miguel Tejada, out 24 times in 27 previous matchups against each another. On that night however, Tejada doubled off of Sparks to score the eventual game-winning runs in a 3–1 Oakland victory. The hit was the only one allowed by Sparks in two and two-thirds innings that evening, spoiling one of the best pitched games the Tigers would get all season.

Things improved somewhat in May, when Detroit won 11 games and lost 18, the only month they would reach double figures in victories. It would prove to be the high point of the season. The Tigers would win only five games in June and continue to spiral downward at a similar pace throughout the rest of the summer.

Offensively, the only real run producers on the club were outfielders Dmitri Young and Craig Monroe, third baseman Eric Munson, and first baseman Carlos Pena. However, of the four, only Pena was considered to be something other than a defensive liability in the field. Just three regulars hit above .250 that season, leaving Trammell on all too many nights filling out a lineup card that included the likes of catchers Brandon Inge (.203) or Matt Walbeck (.174), shortstops Ramone Santiago (.225) or Omar Infante (.222), infielder Shane Halter (.217), and outfielder Andres Torres (.220).

15. "Bringing Back a Hero"

Pitching-wise, his top six starters combined for 86 losses, compiling a sickly 6.01 ERA. The bullpen wasn't much better; only Jamie Walker, who sported a 3.32 ERA in 78 appearances, was consistently effective amongst the relief corp. Franklyn German and Chris Mears were the co-leaders on the club in saves with five each, an amazingly low total for a major league club in 21st century baseball.

As the summer wore on, the losses continued to mount at a staggering rate. By mid-season, comparisons were being made between the Tigers' record and the pace that had been set by the low-standard bearer of futility in modern major league history, the 1962 New York Mets. The team even became the butt of jokes by NBC's *Tonight Show* host Jay Leno, who poked fun at them in his monologue one night. Throughout it all, Trammell continued to put on a brave front. "After a game, it grinds on him a little bit," explained a former teammate and the manager of the Seattle Mariners that season, Bob Melvin. "But the next day, he puts it away completely."[14]

By September, the media was tracking daily the losing pace of the Tigers as they threatened the all-time record of 120 losses in a season. On September 21, they plunged into a tie with the '62 Mets, having the same number of losses through 155 games played. When asked if he was aware of the historically bad record his team was amassing, Trammell admitted "I know what the number is, but I don't feel any different."[15] A night later, Detroit fell 12–6 to Kansas City for its tenth straight loss, and 16th out of its previous 17 games. The Tigers' record stood at 38–118, an unfathomable 80 games below the .500 mark.

The stress Trammell might have felt about avoiding a dubious record-losing season was dwarfed by the death of his mother during the last week of September. Trammell left the team for a short period afterward, traveling back to San Diego to be with his family, while the team rallied to hold off, at least temporarily, what seemed to be a certainty: the 2003 Detroit Tigers were going to become the losingest team in major league history.

When Trammell returned to the club for the season's final games, the Tigers continued to stave off the infamy that would be associated with such a record. They won five of the last six games, including coming back from an 8–1 deficit in the penultimate game of the schedule, when they rallied for eight runs over the game's final three innings to beat Minnesota, 9–8. That win ensured they could do no worse than tie the Mets' record of 120 losses. The next day, the final game of the regular season, Detroit ensured they would not share in that lowly distinction, as they scored seven runs in the sixth inning, beating the Twins again, 9–4.

The Tigers' final record was 43–119, one loss better than the 40–120 mark set by the New York Mets 41 years earlier. "Really, in all honesty, how much better is 119 than 120," asked Trammell to the media after the final game. "It's been a very difficult year, one of the toughest anybody's ever been through. But I'm glad we didn't tie or surpass the Mets' record. To have that off our back is a relief."[16]

As Trammell readied for a getaway trip with his wife to Italy that fall, the sobering reality of the 2003 season sunk in for the Detroit organization as well as its fans. The club had lost the second-most games in major league history, and its .265 winning percentage was the sixth lowest of all time, second only to the '62 Mets squad among teams since World War II. To further illustrate the non-competitive standing of Detroit that season, they finished an almost unbelievable 47 games behind the American League Central champion Minnesota Twins.

The Tigers rankings in various statistical categories were consistent with the club's horrendous record. They finished with the worst team batting average out of the 30 major league teams (.240), scored the second-fewest runs, allowed the second-most earned runs and the second-most runs overall. In the field, they committed the second-most errors of any team, and had the second-lowest team fielding percentage.

While there was no doubting the obvious lack of talent on Detroit's big league roster, the question had to be raised about how much of the ghastly season lay at the feet of the manager? The team had gotten off to such a bad start, and had been on the losing end of so many one-sided games, Trammell's in-game strategy hadn't really come under the normal scrutiny and second-guessing that most managers face. On that point, he had admitted around mid-season that "I haven't really had to manage a whole lot."[17] While most fans and media types were willing to give a lot of leeway to a favorite son who had walked into a difficult situation, the shine had started to rub off of Trammell's appointment as manager. Lack of talent could be understood, but the appallingly poor play and lack of improvement in fundamentals and execution was disturbing.

Others wondered about the construction of the "dream team" coaching staff, especially the appointment of Gibson as bench coach.[18] The bench coach is generally the second-in-command, the person the manager leans on as a sounding board for in-game strategy, lining up substitutions, defensive positioning, and other tasks the manager can either off-load to, or take input from—a trusted advisor role. The fact that Gibson had no coaching or managerial experience was questioned very early on in Trammell's first year—where the norm for a first-year manager, especially one with no previous experience in the position like Trammell—was to hire a long-time coach or former manager to that position.

"It's going to force me to get it together too," Trammell said when asked about improvements that would need to be made ahead of the next season. "I'm not afraid of that, I'm not afraid of any challenge. I think I'm the right man for the job. I really do. But I have to get better myself and I'm willing to get better. So I'll do a lot of soul searching as far as ideas. But I look forward to that."[19]

Determined to transfuse the Detroit roster with a significant upgrade of talent, Dave Dombrowski and the Tigers' front office worked aggressively in the off-season. They acquired shortstop Carlos Guillen in a trade from Seattle, giving stability to a position that had long been a problem. They fortified the pitching staff with free agent signings such as starter Jason Johnson and reliever Ugueth Urbina, who had saved 32 games in 2003. Outfielder Rondell White came from Minnesota, and brought a veteran bat to the offensively-starved lineup.

But the big addition was the late-winter signing of superstar catcher, Ivan "Pudge" Rodriguez, to a four-year, $40 million contract. That a player of Rodriguez' stature would sign with a downtrodden franchise like Detroit, surprised nearly everyone. He had gambled a year earlier, signing a one-year deal with the Florida Marlins when the long-term offers he coveted in free agency were not forthcoming. The gamble seemingly paid off; Rodriguez led the Marlins on a fairy tale run through the 2003 post-season, resulting in a World Series title in Miami. However, once again, teams were unwilling to risk long-term contracts on a 32-year-old catcher with high mileage. Detroit saw its opportunity and offered the additional years and dollars necessary to add a marquee player. Rodriguez brought a strong offensive presence to the middle of Trammell's batting order, an elite defensive presence to the team, and credibility that had been lacking in recent years.

Coming off the disastrous 119-loss campaign in Trammell's honeymoon season, there were guarded expectations in Detroit entering 2004. But the team surprised everyone by winning their first four games and 11 of its first 18, while looking much improved. Rodriguez was everything the Tigers had hoped for, batting .334 that season while driving in 86 runs, but perhaps more importantly, he helped stabilize a pitching staff that had been awful the year before. That pitching staff included Maroth, the reliable, soft-tossing left-handed starter, while 21-year-old Jeremy Bonderman continued to improve in his second season in the big leagues. Jason Johnson was the innings-eating starter that was so desperately needed, and a pair of young pitchers, Nate Robertson and Gary Knotts, who had been acquired from the Florida Marlins in a trade a year earlier—proved to be valuable starters in 2004.

Offensively, in addition to Rodriguez, White played left field and was a solid run producer, while Guillen surprised everyone batting .318 with 20 home runs and 97 RBI's, establishing himself as one of the better shortstops in the American League. Infante shifted to second base and became a quality all-around player, while Pena, Monroe, and outfielder Alex Sanchez all had improved seasons. The bench was deep with power-laden bats like Inge, Young, and outfielder Marcus Thames. The improved lineup helped the Tigers improve their team batting average by 32 points and their runs scored by 236 on the season.

The team stayed just below .500 for much of the first four months of the schedule, before falling off in August and September. Their final record of 72–90, placed Detroit twenty games behind Minnesota, while moving up to fourth place in the division, ahead of last-place Kansas City. Their 29-game improvement from 2003 was remarkable, the second most in baseball history, surpassed only by the 1989 Baltimore Orioles. As an added sign of the team's improved overall strength, they were outscored on the season by only 17 runs, as compared to the previous year when they had been outscored by nearly 300 runs.

Two more high profile free agent signings by the Tigers fueled even greater expectations for 2005. Reliever Troy Percival was added to fill the closer's role in the bullpen, while Detroit also added the power bat it had been lacking in the middle of its order when it signed outfielder Magglio Ordonez. The 31-year-old Ordonez was coming off of a surgically-repaired left knee, but had been a perennial .300-hitter, with a career resume filled with 30 home run and 125 RBI seasons. When the Tigers exploded for an 11–2 rout of Kansas City on Opening Day behind Dmitri Young's three home runs, Detroit's status as a dark horse contender in the American League Central appeared legitimate.

Nothing went according to plan for the rest of that season, however. Ordonez played only three games before being sidelined until July with a sports hernia. Percival was largely ineffective in 23 appearances before he was lost for the rest of the schedule with a strained forearm. The loss of both of the Tigers' high-profile acquisitions was only the beginning of a string of bad luck that would haunt Detroit that season. Nagging injuries to Guillen and White, as well as sub-par performances from Rodriguez, Young, and others, curtailed an offense that never approached its potential. Bonderman, who was quickly developing into the Tigers' top starting pitcher, was hit by a line drive shortly after the All-Star break, and was never as effective afterwards. Injuries were only a part of the problem in Detroit that summer. In games the club was hitting and scoring runs, the pitching and defense fell apart. When they pitched well, the team didn't hit. The only thing that appeared to be consistent with the Tigers that summer was sloppy play.

Sitting with a record of 61–62 on August 23, post-season play was no longer a realistic possibility. However, a .500-season, something the Detroit organization hadn't accomplished in 12 years, was still within reach. But a series of off-field events contributed to an on-field collapse over the season's final six weeks, while also threatening to rip the club apart at the seams.[20] It had started in spring training when outfielder Bobby Higginson and his $8.5 million salary made the roster over the more-deserving Marcus Thames. That decision created a rift in the Tigers' clubhouse that portended the ugliness yet to come. In early June, reliever Ugueth Urbina traded blows with teammates during a cross-country team charter, and was sent packing to Philadelphia just days later. His replacement as Trammell's closer in the bullpen, the hard-throwing Kyle Farnsworth, also exited via trade at the July 31 deadline. The team languished seven games in back of a wild card spot. The trade of Farnsworth, a pending free agent at season's end, seemingly disheartened a Tigers' team that interpreted the move as Detroit's front office waving a white flag on the remainder of the season.

Perhaps the most damaging incident that negatively impacted team morale, centered around the top star on the club. Rodriguez had received a four-game suspension from major league baseball for an altercation he had with umpire Ted Barnettin in early–August. Instead of accompanying the team on a road trip to Toronto while serving the suspension, however, Rodriguez spent his time on a puzzling international trip to Columbia. When Rodriguez failed to return in time to play on his first day after serving the suspension, another divisive wedge had been formed within a questioning Detroit clubhouse. As the hot summer wore on and the losing compounded, tempers flared. "I don't see any changes," spouted Rodriguez in a rant in which he bashed nearly everyone in the organization. "We stink," declared Ordonez, obviously discouraged over the losing culture that surrounded the team.[21]

The Tigers won just ten of their final 39 games, disintegrating down the stretch to finish a disappointing 28 games behind the division-winning Chicago White Sox. As the losses mounted and discontent intensified around the third-year manager, the frustration in Trammell's demeanor finally started to show. Umpires ejected him from games five different times that season (as compared to only a single time in the 119-loss 2003 season), and the good vibes that surrounded the club a year earlier disappeared. Despite a second-straight season of improved performances from the pitching staff, the team regressed offensively (11th in the American League in runs scored, last in walks) and defensively (third highest error total in the league). "It's almost too much to take," complained Trammell after yet another loss late in September. "We can't catch a break—in light of us struggling, it's not coming easy."[22]

The season's coup de grace may have come on September 23, when Young—the top home run threat on the Tigers in 2005–refused to pinch-hit in the ninth inning of a 2–1 loss to Seattle, citing a hamstring injury. The insubordination came just days after Young had reached the 500 at-bat plateau, which triggered an automatic $8 million club option he had in his contract for 2006, as well as an unpleasant exchange with Gibson afterwards.[23]

"I don't think anyone in the organization could be pleased with what our record was at the major league level," Dombrowski said ominously after the Tigers lost the last five games of the season to finish with a 71–91 record.[24] He met with Trammell the very next day. The exchange was brief as the Detroit general manager explained that the team would be going in a different direction. "As I continued to watch the club, I felt we need to make this change," stated Dombrowski when the firing was announced publicly. "We thought we had a chance to be a better ballclub."[25]

Despite finishing with only one less victory than the prior year, the tenor at the completion of the 2005 season was much different than it had been at the conclusion of 2004. "The manager is first and foremost primarily responsible for the clubhouse," explained Dombrowski when pressed about the off-field issues that had chipped away at the club's morale. "That's just the way it is."[26] While many of the players expressed sincere disappointment over the just-completed campaign and the fall Trammell had taken because of it, that viewpoint was not universal. "No comment," said Young when asked about the firing, before adding "It was a failed project. All parties failed. The players, the coaches, Trammell. That's why we lost."[27]

Trammell refused to blame anyone and quietly left Detroit for his off-season retreat in San Diego. "I thought we responded to everything well except for this last month," he said. "I think, looking back, it is fair to say that we hit a wall."[28]

"I'm saddened because you're dealing with somebody who has put their heart and soul into something," said Dombrowski, expressing the feelings of many. "For the organization, he's one of the greatest players of all time. If you've met Alan Trammell and you don't like him, you should probably look at yourself."[29]

"Oh, do I feel sorry for him," said Sparky Anderson while watching the situation play out from California. "I love the man, I really do. But you're only as good as your horses when you're a manager, and if your horses ain't running, you got problems."[30]

Whether Trammell ever had the horses is a question that can never be adequately answered. He certainly didn't in 2003. Clubhouse chemistry ruined any chance his team had to build on what it had started in 2004. What is certain is that a managerial regime that seemed so right at the time, and was greeted with so much enthusiasm, had failed miserably.

16

Legacy

The restoration of Alan Trammell's image did not take long to complete in the eyes of Tiger fans. Detroit's surprising 2006 season, in which they qualified for a wild-card berth and then made a post-season run all the way to the World Series, without doubt, softened the disappointment associated with Trammell's unsuccessful regime as manager. Instead of patrons harboring ill-feelings towards the failed three seasons that had been led by one of Detroit's favorite sons, there was a renewed interest and enthusiasm in Tiger Baseball. The newfound success brought back fans from an earlier period, including many that had followed the team throughout the successful years of the 1980s. Additionally, a whole new generation of fans were attracted to the game, soaking up not only the excitement of the contemporary team, but also the stories and heroes passed down to them by an earlier generation of Tiger followers. Prominent among those heroes from the past was the all-everything shortstop that played 20 years in a Tiger uniform.

The first public acknowledgment that Trammell's disappointing run as manager was far out-trumped by the many years of goodwill he had built up as player, came before Game Two of the 2006 World Series in Detroit. He was honored during first pitch ceremonies, and what could have been an awkward moment for a deposed manager, instead turned into a stirring tribute as Trammell received a rousing, standing ovation from the festive Comerica Park crowd. Barely more than a year since he had been sacked by the Tigers' brass, Trammell basked in adulation as his former team prepared to play on baseball's grandest stage.

He had spent the year away from the game, laying low in suburban San Diego with his family. That didn't prevent him from closely following the remarkable turnaround taking place in Detroit that summer. The team's new manager, Jim Leyland, was the antithesis of Trammell in many ways. He came to the job with an abundance of experience at the professional level, having served ten seasons in the Detroit organization as a minor league manager, before moving on to the major leagues where he had 18 years of experience, including serving as manager for Pittsburgh, Florida, and Colorado. Leyland brought a gruff, no-nonsense demeanor with him that didn't always endear him to the media and fans, but had a track record of results that did.

How much credit or blame should be attributed to Trammell for the Tigers' 2006 club that amassed 95 regular season victories and won an American League pennant—after winning only 71 games in 2005? The difference between the two teams was not as clear-cut as merely the person standing on the dugout's first step. Trammell never had the benefit of a full season of Placido Polanco at second base, Curtis Granderson in center field, or a healthy Magglio Ordonez in the outfield; key components, offensively and defensively, for the 2006 Detroit Tigers. Nor did he have the type of steadying influence in his starting rotation that veteran left-hander Kenny Rogers brought to the 2006 team, winning 17 games for the Tigers after signing as a free agent. Rookies Justin Verlander and Joel Zumaya had electrifying stuff on the mound, and brought an additional level of talent to the pitching staff that also didn't exist for Trammell.

Young players, like Granderson, Brandon Inge, Omar Infante, Craig Monroe, Jeremy Bonderman, Nate Robertson, and Fernando Rodney, among others, whose development was paramount to the fortunes of Detroit pennant-winning club, all cut their teeth in the big leagues under the tutelage of Trammell and his coaching staff. Whether those players would have blossomed following the painful lessons of 2003 through 2005, no matter who the manager was in 2006—or if those abilities were drawn out under the leadership of Leyland—is difficult to assess.

Unfortunately, history typically records only the cold, hard facts. Credit goes to those who have the numbers supporting them, and blame to those that don't. Trammell's managerial record is amongst the worst in baseball history, 187–302; a winning percentage of only .383. Fairly or unfairly, *The Sporting News* ranked Trammell as the worst manager in the last 30 years in a 2015 rating, citing his poor overall record and the 2003 team's flirtation with baseball infamy.[1] Perhaps a more objective analysis can be made using Bill James' Baseball Pythagorean Expectation which compares a team's actual won-loss record for a season against a complex statistical computation based on run differential. But even that paints a less than flattering portrayal. The Tigers' 2003, 2004, and 2005 teams finished under the projected number of wins by six, seven, and four victories for those three seasons based on the Pythagorean Expectation formula.

Trammell's dismal record dimmed any chance he had of landing another managerial position immediately, but his desire to be back in uniform remained strong. Having sat out the 2006 campaign, he joined Lou Piniella in Chicago as a member of the Cubs' coaching staff. There he served as Piniella's bench coach for four seasons, supporting the veteran manager not only as an active coach—willing to pitch batting practice or fungo balls to fielders, but also acting as a sounding board and resource for in-game strategy and lineup adjustments. While coaching under Piniella, Trammell contributed to a pair of National League Central Division title teams, including a 97-win Chicago club in 2008.

While in a Cubs' uniform, Trammell made his first visit to Detroit as a member of an opposing team. Despite wearing the traditional visiting grey jersey with the Cubs' trademark "C" on his blue cap, he still wore number "3" and was a magnet for autograph and picture-seeking fans anytime he stepped outside of Comerica Park's visitor's dugout. "I'm a Chicago Cub now, but I know that to a lot of people, I'll always be a Detroit Tiger, and that's fine with me and the people here."[2]

During that same late-June 2009 series in Detroit, Trammell was able to make an emotional, and aptly-timed visit just a few blocks away from where the Cubs and Tigers were doing battle. Tiger Stadium, the Tigers' home for 87 years including Trammell's entire 20-year playing career, was being demolished that summer. It had fallen into disrepair in the decade since the team had moved to Comerica Park, and despite the pleas of purists and ill-financed planners wanting to convert the site into a functional historic monument, Tiger Stadium finally met the wrecking ball that summer. Ever the baseball historian, Trammell wanted to make one final visit to the tradition-rich grounds that had been trod by the likes of Cobb, Ruth, Gehrig, DiMaggio, Williams, Kaline, and so many other great players.

"I talked to a few people and heard what was going on, I decided to go right away," he explained almost as if visiting the deathbed of a dear friend.[3]

What he saw as he peered through a restraining fence near the street, were the final remnants of what had once been a magnificent ballpark. Most of the stadium had already been knocked down. The first base dugout, part of a wall supported by the few remaining beams that were left, and the familiar infield grass was all that was recognizable. "The building isn't there anymore, but all of my memories of that place will last forever," he said. "It was a very special place, and I spent a large portion of my life there."[4]

As he walked away, a few reporters on hand to note the occasion didn't sense sadness from Trammell, but rather the opposite. "I'm smiling because the memories will never change. It was inevitable."[5]

"Call it closure or whatever," he said, unable perhaps to put into words his exact feelings. "I'm glad I got it over with."[6]

After Piniella retired following the 2010 season, Trammell was reunited with his long-time friend, Kirk Gibson, who had been hired as the manager of the Arizona Diamondbacks for the 2011 campaign. It was an ideal situation for Trammell, with Phoenix only a short flight away from his San Diego home. In a reversal of roles from their time spent leading the Tigers a half-decade earlier, Trammell was now Gibson's bench coach and most-trusted advisor. In their first season together in the desert, they oversaw a worst-to-first turnaround as the "D-backs," last place finishers in the National League West in 2010, won the division title. The turnaround was made even more impressive when considering the team fell 6½ games back in the early going, before storming back to win the title by eight games, accumulating 94 victories in the process.

Although Arizona fell to Milwaukee that season in the divisional round of the National League Playoffs, and failed to reach post-season in any of the next three seasons, the Diamondbacks were mostly competitive over that period. Injuries and a series of trades that didn't pan out depleted the club of the necessary talent to win more often in a highly-contested division that included the San Francisco Giants, winners of three World Series in a five year span between 2010 and 2014.

Donning the Sedona Red and Sonoran Sand colors of the D-backs, Trammell was near Gibson's side helping to direct traffic and in-game strategy while drawing on his nearly 40 years in professional baseball. Passing from his mid- to late-fifties, Trammell's thinning hair had turned completely grey and he was no longer as spry physically as he had once been. A total of five knee surgeries going back to his playing days, and a hip replacement procedure performed in 2006, had taken their toll. But the competitive fires still burned within him on the diamond, though sometimes they resulted in embarrassing outcomes.

On a June 2013 night in Los Angeles, Arizona's pitcher Ian Kennedy plunked Dodger's starting pitcher, Zack Greinke, with a pitch in the seventh inning of what had already been a bean ball-filled contest. The pitch triggered an emptying of both dugouts, with emotions running high between two teams that had a recent history of contentiousness. As the players pushed and shoved outside the first base line, there was Trammell confronting Los Angeles' manager, Don Mattingly, just outside the fray. Within seconds Trammell was on his back, having been thrown to the ground by Mattingly, who then stumbled over him before being pulled off by Arizona coach Matt Williams. In what was neither of the former AL East rivals' finest moments, Trammell and Mattingly's brief exchange became the focal point of highlight shows and Internet clips depicting the otherwise harmless scuffle.

By the end of the 2014 season, Gibson's run as manager of Arizona was coming to an end. When he and his staff were released at the end of the schedule, Trammell found himself without a position in baseball. By that point of his career, he could be very selective in the type of position or situation he would consider. Trammell certainly didn't need to work any longer; yet the desire to remain involved in the game remained.

His opportunity came quickly, and to some from a surprising party. Just weeks after the close of the 2014 season, the Detroit Tigers announced that Trammell had been appointed as a special assistant to Tigers' president, general manager, and chief executive officer Dave Dombrowski. The specially created position would entail on-field instruction at both the major and minor league levels, scouting at both the professional and amateur levels, as well as being an advisor on personnel and other baseball-related matters within the organization. "I'm thrilled about it," said Trammell about his new position. "I think everyone knows the special place in my heart that the Tigers have always occupied."[7]

By bringing Trammell back to the Detroit organization, the Tiger management closed a circle that had been broken nearly a decade earlier when he had been fired as field manager. After seemingly being in exile for the previous nine seasons, the club was bringing back one of the most celebrated and beloved personalities in team history. "Tram will forever be revered as one of the greatest Tigers to ever wear the Olde English 'D,'" said Dombrowski in announcing the appointment. "It's great to have him back."[8]

Trammell joined Tiger greats, Al Kaline and Willie Horton, who held similar posts in the organization. Kaline, who by the fall of 2014 had spent more than 60 years with the Detroit organization, remains the godfather of the Tigers and in many ways is still the face of the organization. More than 40 years since he played his last game, Kaline's stature is one of class and understated excellence—qualities that best represent the tradition-rich Detroit Tigers. His place at the head of the franchise is an honor that Trammell seems well-positioned to inherit someday.

Dombrowski's introduction of Trammell as "one of the greatest Tigers," followed a growing sentiment among Tigers' observers. By the late 1980s, barely halfway through his playing career, Trammell was already being named on informal lists as the greatest shortstop in franchise history. When he retired as a player, that honor was nearly indisputable, as only Donnie Bush and Billy Rogell from the early 1900s, or Harvey Kuenn from the 1950s, even stood out as longtime occupants of the shortstop position in Detroit. But as the years since the ending of Trammell's playing days passed by, his legacy began to separate from those of his peers.

Kirk Gibson, Lance Parrish, and Jack Morris might have been more dynamic players, and in the cases of Gibson and Morris, were certainly more outspoken. But they all left Detroit ostensibly for money and fame, and at a point when many people knew the peak years of the 1980s had passed by, and darker days were coming on the field. In contrast, Trammell had stayed in Detroit and played out the last seasons of his great career as the last remaining link to the glory days that had once been. When Trammell had been hired as manager of the club in October of 2002, *he* was the one person from Detroit's illustrious past that the people wanted to lead the franchise out of the darkness. *He* was the player fans could identify with. The "Huck Finn" in a baseball uniform that had come to town as a skinny, 19-year-old kid from California, and then stayed 20 years—making all the right plays in the field and at the plate.

The greatness that defined Alan Trammell as a player is difficult to pinpoint. He was never noted as being exceedingly above other "good" players in any specific phase of the game. Physically, there were certainly players at his position that were bigger, faster, quicker, and possessed better throwing arms. He often held a secondary role to other higher-profile players in Detroit during the years he played. Yet, 20 years after he had played his last game, Trammell's name holds a prominence in the Tigers' hierarchy of all-time great players that places him squarely in the conversation with the Gehringer's, Greenberg's, Heilmann's, Crawford's, and Newhouser's, just behind the franchise's Mount Rushmore figures of Ty Cobb, Al Kaline, and likely someday, Miguel Cabrera.

What Trammell was is the consummate baseball player. Pigeon-holed as a soft-hitting, solid-fielding infielder prospect when he came to the major leagues, he developed into one of the greatest all-around shortstops the game had seen up to that time. He could do everything, and do it all well. He could hit for average, he could draw a walk, he rarely stuck out, he hit with some power, he could steal a base, he was an excellent base runner, and he could field at the shortstop position at an elite level. A look at his placement on the Detroit Tigers all-time rankings displays the breadth of his abilities. His career totals place him in the Top 10 in franchise history in games played (5th), at-bats (5th), hits (7th), total bases (7th), extra-base hits (9th), runs scored (6th), doubles (6th), RBI's (10th), bases on balls (7th), stolen bases (5th), and even sacrifice flies (3rd). He lurks just outside the team's Top-10 in doubles and home runs, ranking 14th on both lists.

However, to describe Trammell based only on his statistical record is missing the essence of what he brought to the Tigers as a player and as a leader. He possessed intangibles that transcended physical skills. He was an exceptionally smart player, always ahead of the game in situations both in the field and at the plate. He could lay down a sacrifice bunt, take a pitch to the right side of the infield to advance a runner, or when the situation presented itself, hit the ball out of the ballpark. "Offensively, he developed into a great player, one who merited MVP consideration," said American League peer, Paul Molitor, whose own 21-year Hall of Fame career, mostly with the Milwaukee Brewers, overlapped that of Trammell. "He was a great situational hitter, who knew how to hit the ball to the opposite field. As his power numbers declined, he (still) found a way to be productive."[9]

Trammell also played with hustle and an enthusiasm that rubbed off on teammates, never better exemplified than when he and Whitaker formed such a potent 1–2 punch at the top of the Tigers' batting order in the early and mid–1980s. With those two on base with great regularity, and then running the bases with abandon, Detroit frequently found itself staked to an early lead. "He went 100 percent whether it was his first day, his 200th day, or his 2,000th day," said Phil Garner after Trammell's final game. "That's class."[10]

Yet, it was his play at the shortstop position that perhaps brought Trammell his greatest acclaim from those within the game. He had textbook fundamentals, whether fielding the ball with both hands off the proper hop, or unleashing a throw with his quick release and overhand motion, a strike to first base. Trammell seemed to instinctively know how a play was developing and where to go with the ball. He took command in the middle of the diamond and exuded a sense of control to the rest of the team. "To be a successful shortstop, you have to have the sixth sense on where all the guys should be," he said after his career had ended. "I always enjoyed the cat-and-mouse game ... where did the batter hit the ball before? We had to read the ball off the bat, pay attention, and be able to react quickly."[11]

"What I'll remember about him, other than the 1984 World Series and the homeruns he hit in it, is the way he played shortstop," explained Molitor. As someone who began at that position and was moved (to third base primarily), I marveled at the way he played it."[12]

Those strong fundamentals helped give Trammell a reputation as the type of player you would want the ball hit towards in a pressure situation, helping to build his image as a clutch player. "Alan had such sure, soft hands," said Sparky Anderson about his shortstop for all 17 of the years he managed in Detroit. "There was no one better picking up the baseball. He had such a quick and accurate release. Every time he threw the ball, regardless of where he was on the field, it was thrown overhand."[13]

"As a defensive shortstop, he was as solid fundamentally as could be," explained Molitor. "His footwork was ideal. He never panicked."[14]

"Trammell had great consistency," said the Tigers' radio broadcaster of five decades, Ernie Harwell. "In the clutch, you wanted the ball hit to Alan. Fundamentally he was so sound."[15]

A fitting tribute came from his long-time rival, Cal Ripken, Jr., who when asked to sign a bat for Trammell during the latter's last season wrote the inscription: "Thanks for being an inspiration. (Mark) Belanger was right: You were the one to watch."[16]

Trammell's reputation as a player is surpassed only by the respect he holds throughout the game. He is genuinely considered one of the most likeable people in the sport, respected by management, coaches, players, and the media.

"He brought a great passion," said Harwell. "He had great respect and love for baseball."[17]

"He's one of the great guys in the game and one of the greatest players," said his successor as manager of the Tigers, Jim Leyland. "It's none of my business, but I think he's a Hall of Famer. They don't come any finer than that guy."[18]

At the 2015 Hall of Fame induction ceremony in Cooperstown, New York, new inductee John Smoltz—a 213-game winner over his 22-season major league career—recalled a story from the days just after he had turned professional as a lowly 22nd round draft pick by the Detroit Tigers. Invited to come to Tiger Stadium in August 1985, in order to get the feel of a professional clubhouse, the then 18-year-old Smoltz admittedly felt like a "fish out of water," in the home of the defending World Champions. However, that all changed when a face familiar to the Lansing, Michigan, native approached him in the Tiger clubhouse. "Hello, I'm Alan Trammell," said one of Smoltz' boyhood heroes. "Anything I can do for you, don't hesitate to ask. This house is your house."[19]

Smoltz never forgot the gesture passed to him, a kid just out of high school from a star player fresh off a World Series MVP. That he mentioned this 15-second interaction in his Hall of Fame induction speech nearly 30 years later shows the amount of respect held for the former Tigers' shortstop. "I thank you, Alan Trammell, for teaching me what a professional baseball player is all about."[20]

Sparky Anderson may have summed it up best late in his stay in Detroit when he said: "The marvelous thing you can say about Alan Trammell is he's the same acting kid he was ten years ago. Never changed and that's unreal. And when he's done, there won't be a player that played with him that won't remember him. And they'll know that they were better off having played with him."[21]

17

Hall of Fame Bound?

Alan Trammell's candidacy for induction to baseball's National Baseball Hall of Fame is a polarizing topic among not only Detroit Tiger fans, but also among the growing number of pundits who debate such matters. It makes for fascinating discussion and debate; the merits of individual players and their career body of work, and the imprecise standards applied in order to receive baseball's highest honor.

As the clock runs out on his eligibility for election by the Baseball Writers Association of America (BBWAA), Trammell's case, for or against induction, remains one of the most hotly disputed of any former player eligible for election. His is usually listed among the ten most up for debate. Once you remove those cases for and against players whose career accomplishments are either clouded by the uncertainty of who and what took place during the performance-enhancing, drug-tainted 1990s, or are under lifetime bans from the game (Pete Rose, "Shoeless" Joe Jackson), Trammell typically makes the short list of players waiting just outside the exclusive club. There he joins such notables as Dick Allen, Jim Kaat, Tony Oliva, and Tim Raines as lightning-rod figures, all debated purely on career accomplishments, without the stigma of competitive advantages gained through either illegal or unethical means.

For his fans, Trammell's cause is an emotional one, fueled by the attachment formed watching a 19-year-old kid come to the major leagues and play 20 years at an extremely high level, while never causing waves off the field. He is the greatest shortstop in the Detroit Tigers' long history, and was an on-field extension of his manager, Sparky Anderson, for all but two of those years—some of the most successful the franchise has ever had. Trammell symbolized a time during the 1980s when the team was wildly popular with its constituents and winning consistently on the field. He joined Ty Cobb and Al Kaline, Tiger legends, as the only players in franchise history to play 20 seasons with the club. With his long-time keystone partner, Lou Whitaker, Trammell formed the longest tenured double-play combination in baseball history. He played nearly 2,300 games over his career and had over 2,300 base hits, 185 home runs, 1,003 RBI's, scored 1,231 runs, and stole 236 career bases. He batted over .300 seven times while compiling a career mark of .285. He was a key member of the 1984 World Championship team in Detroit, and turned in a World Series MVP performance that October. To his fans, voting against Trammell is the equivalent of a smear campaign against a favorite son, or spitting at a likeness of George Washington.

The rules for gaining entry to baseball's greatest shrine are fairly simple, even though criteria for inclusion is much more subjective. The voting is done on an annual basis by members of the BBWAA with at least ten years of membership. Five years after retirement, any player with ten years or more of major league experience can be included on the Hall of Fame election ballot for the first time. Electors can then vote for up to ten names from that list. A candidate must be named on 75 percent of the ballots in order to be enshrined as a Hall of Fame member. Any player who fails to garner at least five percent of the ballots is dropped from any future ballots and is no longer considered for election. Former players that receive more than the five percent minimum, but less than the 75 percent required for induction, are included on the next year's ballot up to a maximum of fifteen years in Trammell's case (since shortened to ten years). Should a former player go all fifteen years without being elected, they would be eligible for further consideration by the Hall of Fame's Veterans Committee, which is made up of living Hall of Fame members. That group meets every three years to consider candidates no longer eligible under the BBWAA guidelines for election.

Starting with Trammell's first year of eligibility in 2002, the vote totals he received by the BBWAA Hall of Fame balloting left him in a continual state of purgatory. His vote totals neither seriously closed the gap towards the total required for election, nor did they fall to levels that failed to keep him on future ballots. Trammell's first year of eligibility saw him gain votes on 15.7 percent of the ballots, which was 14th out of the 28 players under consideration in 2002. Though his first-year totals seemed relatively low, and perhaps even disappointing, they greatly exceeded the results of three of his former teammates who had dropped off of the ballot a year earlier. None from the group of Lance Parrish, Kirk Gibson, or Lou Whitaker, received more than 2.9 percent of the vote in their first year of eligibility in 2001, ending any consideration for their inclusion in astonishingly brief fashion. Over the next decade, Trammell's vote percentages fluctuated between 13.4 and 18.2 percent. At no time did there appear to be any serious momentum for his candidacy that would take his totals anywhere near the required 75 percent needed for induction.

The elements typically cited against Trammell's Hall-worthiness were varied, and not without some merit. It was difficult for many, especially outside of the Tiger Nation, to separate his career from that of Whitaker's, their career numbers being so similar and their identities so closely linked with that of the other. It certainly didn't help matters that Whitaker fell out of Hall of Fame consideration after his very first year on the ballot, diminishing any recognition the duo would have continued to receive in the two decades immediately following the close of their playing careers.

Many observers have recognized the 1984 Detroit Tigers as a great team from a historical perspective, made up of very good players, but with no truly great players. They were led by a Hall of Fame manager in Sparky Anderson, who was often recognized nationally as the real face of that ball club. Trammell is sometimes viewed as a key cog in those very successful Detroit teams from the 1980s, but only a cog—not a superstar. He batted second in the order for many of those years, and is remembered primarily as a table-setter for the big bats that came later in the lineup. He was more often recognized as being the Tigers' on-field leader from his shortstop position, where he was an excellent individual defender.

Trammell also suffered the misfortune of playing much of his career in the shadow of a handful of players that transformed the shortstop position; precursors to a whole generation of players that would later redefine what the shortstop position would become.[1] The Milwaukee Brewers' Robin Yount had a similar early-career path to that of Trammell. He too had been thrown into the lineup at shortstop as a slightly-built, 19-year-old regular in 1974, where he put up middling numbers offensively through his first five years in the majors. Through extensive weight training and physical maturation however, Yount converted himself into an offensive force for a Brewers team that won an American League pennant in 1982. That season saw Yount win the league's MVP award, the first shortstop to win the award in nearly two decades. His combination of average, power, and base running ability led to an eventual mid-career switch to the outfield, where he eventually won another MVP award in 1989. Yount would accumulate 3,142 hits over a 20-season, Hall-of-Fame career.

Cal Ripken, Jr., of the Baltimore Orioles started his major league career five years after Trammell, winning the American League's Rookie of the Year and MVP awards in his first two seasons, 1982 and 1983. Ripken would become the ideal prototype for future players at the shortstop position, 6-feet 4-inches in height and weighing well over 200 pounds, athletic enough to make the required plays in the field, but with the offensive clout to be a middle-of-the-lineup hitter. Ripken would belt over 20 home runs in each of his first ten season in the league, while never driving in less than 80 runs, and three times exceeding 100. More damagingly to Trammell, Ripken's peak years overlapped those of the overshadowed Detroit shortstop. Ripken was viewed as the American League's premiere player at the position for the better part of two decades, and was named *The Sporting News'* AL Shortstop on their end of season teams eight times between 1983 and 1995, including during two of Trammell's greatest years, 1983 and 1984. As the notoriety increased for Ripken while he chased, and eventually broke, the legendary Lou Gehrig's consecutive games played streak in 1995, the longtime Oriole was cemented as the greatest player at his position for that era, as well as one of the greatest of all time. He was a first ballot Hall-of-Fame inductee in 2007.

Yount and Ripken set a trend that would see the shortstop role changed from an "all-field, whatever you can get offensively" spot in the lineup that had traditionally been filled with smallish or slender body types, to a destination position for the greatest athletes in the game. Players such as Alex Rodriguez, Derek Jeter, Nomar Garciaparra, and Miguel Tejada took over the position a generation later, and put up previously unheard of offensive totals such as Jeter's 3,464 career hits (6th all-time), Rodriguez's 57 home runs in 2002, Garciaparra's .372 batting average in 2000, and Tejada's 150 RBI's in 2004. Those figures dwarfed anything that came before them at the shortstop position.[2]

While most baseball historians would give Trammell an edge as a fielder over his direct rivals, Yount and Ripken, as well as many of those other offensively-endowed players that followed, another damaging shadow had also been cast from a contemporary playing in the opposite league. Ozzie Smith's first season in the major leagues coincided with Trammell's rookie year of 1978. But, by the time he had been traded to the St. Louis Cardinals in time for the 1982 season, "The Wizard of Oz" as Smith was nicknamed, had already established himself as one of the most athletic and gifted fielders the game had ever seen. Smith won an astounding 13-consecutive NL Gold Gloves at shortstop, and would eventually be a 15-time National League All Star. He is considered by many, if not most, to be the greatest fielding player at the position in major league baseball history, certainly the flashiest. Smith's presence as the preeminent defensive shortstop of the era, stretching from the late 1970s and into the early 1990s , directly overlaps Trammell's career, and often causes the tremendous prowess and consistency that Trammell displayed with the glove to be undervalued.[3]

For most of his first ten years on the ballot, Trammell's vote totals suggested a candidacy and career that just didn't measure up to Hall of Fame credentials. Using traditional baseball statistics as a basis of comparison, Trammell's offensive career totals were never going to sway a large enough block of voting members of the BBWAA, many of whom were steeped in those traditional benchmarks. However around 2010, non-traditional measurements began to gain a foothold with a larger public following, as new methods of analysis emerged regarding seasonal and career productivity in baseball. Many of these measurements spurred a wave of increased appreciation for Trammell's career, as the Sabermetrics crowd recognized the unique skillset he brought as an elite defender and his well above the norm offensive, both for the position he performed at, as well as in the era he played.[4]

"Sabermetrics" is loosely defined as "the search for objective knowledge about baseball" and challenges the traditional measures of baseball skill and accomplishment that have existed for well over 100 years in some cases. One common metric used by this formerly obscure group of mathematicians, viewed largely as "geeks" by traditional baseball pundits, is the measurement of an individual's WAR. The advent of WAR (Wins Above Replacement), specifically, brought to light an entirely new perspective on the way Alan Trammell's career was viewed. WAR is an attempt to quantify the estimated value an individual player brings to his team. It is measured in "wins" a specific player provides, against the expected number of wins a team would gain if a replacement level player was substituted in that player's place. The mathematical basis for a WAR value is the estimated number of runs contributed by a player through offensive actions such as batting and base running, as well as runs denied to the opposition by the player through defensive actions such as fielding or pitching. The measurements are derived through advanced statistical comparisons with league averages for a given year or period, sometimes using non-traditional measurements. The accumulation of approximately ten additional runs produced or saved over a replacement level player, equates to 1.0 WAR, or one additional win above replacement. A full-season total that exceeds 5.0 is considered outstanding, and anything approaching double-digits will lead the major leagues most years.

Alan Trammell's career total of approximately 70.7 WAR places him somewhere within the 100 highest totals among players all time, and somewhere in the '60s among position players all time.[5] Because the specific calculations for WAR are not standardized, there are minor deviations in totals and placement among baseball's annual and career leaders. However, the variations are so slight that positioning on all-time lists fluctuates only by a placement or two. Trammell's ranking among all players to have played at the major league level ('90s), and position players all-time ('60s), as well as shortstops all time (11th), would appear to place him easily among the greatest players ever by this metric alone.[6]

Another changing view that has benefited the overall perception of Trammell is the valuation of peak years of a career, over raw career totals.[7] The theory is that by focusing on a five-to-ten-year stretch at the peak of a player's career, one can appreciate the greatness of a player in comparison to the rest of his league, versus just analyzing career totals that may have been racked up as the player performed at a mediocre level while outside of his peak period. The six-year period between 1983 and 1988 saw the Tigers achieve the best record in baseball over that stretch, including the major leagues' best record in two of those seasons. Trammell was arguably the most valuable player on those Detroit teams during that period, and has the numbers to support it. His offensive production during that period was well above the norm at the shortstop position. Trammell's WAR of approximately 35.0 during that six-year run is one of the remarkable stretches in baseball history and by itself, is a telling tribute to the value of player he was to the Tigers.[8] To add further perspective, Trammell's total WAR over that 6-season spell, surpasses the career WAR of many noteworthy players in baseball history. That Trammell was injury-plagued for many of the last seasons he played in the major leagues, which took away his opportunity to add to conventional statistical measurements, does not detract from the unique impact he had on his team and the American League race during the height of his career.

While WAR and other advanced statistical analyses should be used as only part of the overall evaluation of a player's career, they seem to support other comparisons that continue to irritate Trammell's supporters. His career WAR rating of roughly 70 is higher than Ozzie Smith's and approximately two points lower than former Cincinnati Reds shortstop Barry Larkin, who succeeded Smith as the National League's premier shortstop. Yet, while Smith was elected to the Hall of Fame in his very first year of eligibility (2002), and Larkin was elected in his third year (2012), Trammell remains an outsider looking in to the Halls at Cooperstown.

A comparison of traditional statistical benchmarks would show Larkin as having the better overall offensive numbers among the three (.295/.371/.444–198 HR's, 441 2B's, 379 SB's), which included an MVP award in 1995. However, Larkin also played the majority of his career (1986–2004) in a much more offense-friendly era than that in which Trammell and Smith played. The Trammell-Smith comparison gets even more curious. Trammell's career stat line of (.285/.352/.415–185 HR's, 1,003 RBI's, 1,231 R's, 236 SB's) seems to outshine Smith's (.261/.337/.328–28 HR's, 793 RBI's, 1,257 R's, 580 SB's) by a considerable margin, especially in the slugging and run production categories. Smith's defensive acrobatics and 13 NL Gold Glove Awards notwithstanding (in comparison to Trammell's four), do not seem to sufficiently explain how one player was a first-ballot selectee and the other has not been seriously considered.

"Ozzie Smith goes into the Hall on the first ballot and Trammell barely gets a mention?" asks longtime Detroit coach Dick Tracewski, who watched all but the final season of Trammell's 20-year career from the dugout and first base coaching box. "You've got to be kidding. If Whitey Herzog (St. Louis Cardinals manager from 1980 through 1990) had come to the Tigers when Smith was playing for him in St. Louis and offered to trade him for Tram even-up, we would have laughed at him. Alan was his equal defensively and he could even hit cleanup for us. The only thing he couldn't do was that backflip Ozzie used to make. And I bet if he really wanted to, Alan could have done that too."[9]

Unfortunately, the mathematical expression known as the Transitive Property of Equality where if a=b and b=c than it must be true that a=c, does not always apply when it comes to membership in Cooperstown. The pro–Trammell arguers will state that because the careers of Trammell, Smith, and Larkin were so comparable, and Smith and Larkin were early inductees, than Trammell certainly must be Hall of Fame worthy. That Trammell's career as a whole was undoubtedly better than current Hall of Fame shortstops such as Joe Tinker, Dan Bancroft, Hughie Jennings, Travis Jackson, Phil Rizzuto, and Rabbit Maranville—whether viewed by subjective or objective measures—has not been enough to sway the deciding voters.[10]

The reception for the advanced statistical analysis put out in recent years has grown considerably over the past decade, and is no longer viewed with the same disdain it had earlier engendered from many of those who work within the game. The popularity of Michael Lewis' book, *Moneyball*, followed by the movie starring Brad Pitt, certainly introduced the concepts to the mainstream. However, those analyses which seem to put Trammell's career accomplishments in a more enlightened context, have provided only a slight incline to the voting trajectory for his induction. He showed gains for three consecutive years starting in 2010, peaking at 36.8 percent in 2012, before regressing again in the years that followed.

What the voters seem to suggest is that Alan Trammell is a member of the "Hall of Very Good," a good, but not dominant player, for a long period of time that did many things very well, but nothing extraordinarily well.[11] In 20 seasons he was a six-time All-Star that won four American League Gold Gloves and three Silver Slugger awards. He played in the postseason twice, won a World Championship in 1984, and was the MVP of that season's World Series. Trammell received MVP votes in seven different seasons, finishing in the top ten three times, including the runner-up spot in 1987, when he lost out in a very tight vote to George Bell.

The greatest hindrance in Trammell's case for inclusion in the Hall may be just the fact that he wasn't the *best* at anything. He had the misfortune of playing in the shadow of, and being compared to, contemporaries such as Yount, Ripken, and Smith, players whose strengths by most accounts exceeded Trammell's. He didn't have the career numbers of Yount, didn't slug like Ripken, and wasn't acknowledged as being the fielder that Smith was.[12] In many circles, Trammell doesn't always get mentioned with other prominent players of his era. The names of Brett, Henderson, Winfield, Murray, Ripken, Mattingly, Rice, and Boggs frequently come to mind when reminiscence of the American League during the late '70s and 1980s takes place, a cache that Trammell doesn't always carry.[13] Even though for a short period in the late 1980s, an argument could have been made for him being the best player in the game.

What Trammell was, however, was a true all-around player. He was an outstanding defensive shortstop, the clear on-field leader from very early on in his career and lasting throughout the entire time he was in Detroit. Offensively, he brought a unique skillset to the lineup in which he batted .300 or better seven times, and amassed an impressive .352 career on-base percentage. He walked more than he struck out seven different seasons (with two other seasons where he had an equal number of walks and strikeouts). He also led the American League in sacrifice bunts two different times, and stole 236 bases in his career—indicative of a player capable of excelling in "small-ball," which was the offensive norm for the shortstop position during the era he played. Where Trammell differentiated himself from most other peers at the position, was in the run production he created. He had a career slugging percentage of .415, including an astounding .551 clip during his fabulous 1987 campaign. He swatted over 30 doubles in six different seasons, hit double-digit home runs eight times—including twice hitting over 20–and had 60 or more RBIs in eight different years. Less measureable, but equally important, Trammell was an outstanding base runner with good speed, awareness, and aggressiveness. He scored 70 or more runs eight different times in his career.

To truly appreciate Trammell as a player, you had to watch him every day—a point taken up by his sidekick, Lou Whitaker, when discussing one of the obstacles preventing their inclusion in Cooperstown. "The writers who covered the Tigers saw our excellence every day," he said in a 2011 interview. "Those writers who maybe saw us play once or twice, they're the voters."[14] With the proliferation of televised games on both regional and national cable outlets not taking place until later in Trammell's career, few outside the Tigers' local broadcast region were able to watch him play with any regularity. The same would have been true with game highlights which were rarely shown outside of the reach of Detroit's local news telecasts. To gain national notoriety during the era he played, one had to shine under the game's brightest lights—the All Star Game or in post-season play. Because of injury, however, Trammell appeared in only four All Star games. And while he was a World Series MVP, he had the misfortune of winning the award in a truncated series that was largely nondescript to much of the rest of the country, while also having his most notable game—the two home run day in Game Four of the 1984 World Series—largely overshadowed by Gibson's dramatic blasts in the clincher the following day. The upset at the hands of the Minnesota Twins in the 1987 American League playoffs robbed Trammell of another opportunity to play on baseball's biggest stage following what ended up being his greatest season.

With little momentum, and his candidacy for election by the BBWAA extinguished, Trammell's induction chances appear tied to a future review by the Veteran's Committee, specifically, the Expansion Era Committee that reviews candidates with bodies of work from 1973 to the present day. With Trammell having hit zero of the traditional statistical benchmarks (3,000 hits, 500 doubles, 1,500 RBI's or Runs Scored), nor placing highly on the career list for any prominent categories (not in top 100 in career hits, runs, doubles, total bases, walks, etc.), it will again take an enlightened view of the game Trammell played, for him to gain election from that group. The fact that the Veteran's Committee has recently passed on other players with high-end peak periods, but lower career totals, like Gil Hodges, Dick Allen, and Tony Oliva, make Trammell's future inclusion to Baseball's Hall of Fame far from a certainty.[15]

Regardless of what happens, Trammell remains content with his achievements on the field. "I'm proud of what I've accomplished," he said in early 2015. "But to the voters, obviously, they feel I'm a little short of that (election), and I'm OK with that." He does hold out hope, though, that if he ever is inducted, that it will come as joint recognition for what he accomplished with his long-time partner, Whitaker, over nearly two decades around the bag at second base. "I would like to think the Veteran's Committee could look at us together," he said. "If you look at what we accomplished, obviously, it would be great, and I hope they'll look at that."[16]

Appendix: Career Statistics

Alan Trammell Career Batting Record

Year	Club	Age	G	AB	R	H	2b	3b	HR	RBI	SB	CS	BA	OBP	SLG	OPS	WAR
1976	Brstl	18	41	140	27	38	2	2	0	9	11	6	.245	.354	.276	.629	—
1976	Mont	18	21	56	4	10	0	0	0	0	2	0	.179	.270	.179	.448	—
1977	Mont	19	134	454	78	132	9	19	3	50	4	4	.291	.365	.414	.779	—
1977	Det	19	19	43	6	8	0	0	0	0	0	0	.186	.255	.186	.441	-0.6
1978	Det	20	139	448	49	120	14	6	2	34	3	1	.268	.335	.339	.675	2.8
1979	Det	21	142	460	68	127	11	4	6	50	17	14	.276	.335	.357	.691	0.7
1980	Det	22	146	560	107	168	21	5	9	65	12	12	.300	.376	.404	.779	4.8
1981	Det	23	105	392	52	101	15	3	2	31	10	3	.258	.342	.327	.669	3.8
1982	Det	24	157	489	66	126	34	3	9	57	19	8	.258	.325	.395	.720	4.2
1983	Det	25	142	505	83	161	31	2	14	66	30	10	.319	.385	.471	.856	6.0
1984	Det	26	139	555	85	174	34	5	14	69	19	13	.314	.382	.468	.851	6.7
1985	Det	27	149	605	79	156	21	7	13	57	14	5	.258	.312	.380	.692	3.0
1986	Det	28	151	574	107	159	33	7	21	75	25	12	.277	.347	.469	.816	6.3
1987	Det	29	151	597	109	205	34	3	28	105	21	2	.343	.402	.551	.953	8.2
1988	Det	30	128	466	73	145	24	1	15	69	7	4	.311	.373	.464	.836	6.0
1989	Det	31	121	449	54	109	20	3	5	43	10	2	.243	.314	.334	.648	3.7
1990	Det	32	146	559	71	170	37	1	14	89	12	10	.304	.377	.449	.826	6.7
1991	Det	33	101	375	57	93	20	0	9	55	11	2	.248	.320	.373	.693	3.3
1992	Det	34	29	102	11	28	7	1	1	11	2	2	.275	.370	.392	.762	1.0
1993	Det	35	112	401	72	132	25	3	12	60	12	8	.329	.388	.496	.885	4.2
1994	Det	36	76	292	38	78	17	1	8	28	3	0	.267	.307	.414	.722	0.0
1995	Det	37	74	223	28	60	12	0	2	23	3	1	.269	.345	.350	.695	0.9
1996	Det	38	66	193	16	45	2	0	1	16	6	0	.233	.267	.259	.526	-1.0
MLB Totals			2293	8288	1231	2365	412	55	185	1003	236	109	.285	.352	.415	.767	70.7

6-Time MLB All Star: 1980, 1984, 1985, 1987, 1988, 1990
4-Time Gold Glove Award: 1980, 1981, 1983, 1984
3-Time Silver Slugger Award: 1987, 1988, 1990
7-Time MVP vote recipient: 1980 (20th), 1981 (21st), 1983 (15th), 1984 (9th), 1987 (2nd), 1988 (7th), 1990 (19th)
World Series MVP: 1984
Rookie-of-the-Year candidate: 1978 (4th)
AL Comeback Player of the Year: 1983

Post-Season Batting Record

Year	Club	Age	G	AB	R	H	2b	3b	HR	RBI	SB	CS	BA	OBP	SLG	OPS	WAR
1984	ALCS	26	3	11	2	4	0	1	1	3	0	0	.364	.500	.818	1.318	—
1984	WS	26	5	20	5	9	1	0	2	6	1	1	.450	.500	0.800	1.300	—
1987	ALCS	29	5	20	3	4	1	0	0	2	0	0	.200	.238	.250	.488	—

Chapter Notes

Introduction

1. Ken Rosenthal, "The Imperfect Science of the Perfect Ballot," *The Sporting News*, January 6, 2003, 54.
2. Richard Tracewski, interview, May 21, 2013.
3. Barry Janoff, *Alan Trammell: Tiger on the Prowl* (Chicago: Children's Press, 1985), 27.

Chapter 1

1. Steve Wulf, "Short to Second to None," *Sports Illustrated*, September 12, 1983.
2. Ibid.
3. Scott Harrison, "Yore Detroit Tigers," *Metrotimes*, March 26, 2003.
4. John Garrity, "Having a Monster of a Season," *Sports Illustrated*, May 28, 1984.
5. Harrison, "Yore Detroit Tigers," *Metrotimes*, March 26, 2003.
6. Buck Jersey, PolishSportsHallofFame.com, July 18, 1998.
7. Garrity, "Having a Monster of a Season," *Sports Illustrated*, May 28, 1984.
8. Jerry Green, "Trammell Is Back Home," *The Detroit News*, October 9, 1984, 3D.
9. Ibid.
10. Ron Fimrite, "A Son of San Diego Pounds the Padres," *Sports Illustrated*, October 22, 1984.
11. Steve Grooms, email communication, January 31, 2013.
12. Harrison, "Yore Detroit Tigers," *Metrotimes*, March 26, 2003.
13. Hugh McMillan, interview, January 31, 2013.
14. John Mafei, email communication, January 23, 2013.
15. McMillan interview.
16. Brad Griffith, interview, January 31, 2013.
17. Harrison, "Yore Detroit Tigers," *Metrotimes*, March 26, 2003.
18. McMillan interview.
19. Ibid.
20. Ibid.
21. Ibid.
22. Griffith interview.
23. *KHS Galaxy*, June 1976.
24. Ibid.
25. McMillan interview.
26. Nick Canepa, email exchange, September 16, 2015.
27. McMillan interview.
28. Wulf, "Short to Second to None," *Sports Illustrated*, September 12, 1983.
29. Harrison, "Yore Detroit Tigers," *Metrotimes*, March 26, 2003.
30. Maffei email exchange.
31. Wulf, "Short to Second to None," *Sports Illustrated*, September 12, 1983.
32. Ibid.
33. Ibid.
34. Harrison, "Yore Detroit Tigers," *Metrotimes*, March 26, 2003.
35. "Tigers Draft Lefthanded Pitcher," *The Detroit Free Press*, June 9, 1976, D3.
36. *KHS Galaxy*, June 1976.
37. Harrison, "Yore Detroit Tigers," *Metrotimes*, March 26, 2003.
38. Garrity, "Having a Monster of a Season," *Sports Illustrated*, May 28, 1984.
39. McMillan interview.

Chapter 2

1. Larry Corr, interview, January 16, 2013.
2. Corr interview.
3. Ibid.
4. Ibid.
5. Harrison, "Yore Detroit Tigers," *Metrotimes*, March 26, 2003.
6. Corr interview.
7. Ibid.
8. Jack Ellison, "Tigers Boast SS's," *The Sporting News*, November 13, 1976, 47.
9. Corr interview.

10. Terrance Lynch, interview, January 8, 2013.
11. Lynch interview.
12. Ibid.
13. Wulf, "Short to Second to None," *Sports Illustrated*, September 12, 1983.
14. Ibid.
15. Ibid.
16. Ibid.
17. Ibid.
18. Ibid.
19. Ibid.
20. Ibid.
21. Lynch interview.
22. A. Stacy Long, "2004 Story: Trammell, Whitaker met as Rebels," *Montgomery Advertiser*, May 20, 2014.
23. Lynch interview.
24. Ibid.
25. Corr interview.
26. Ibid.
27. Lynch interview.
28. Wulf, "Short to Second to None," *Sports Illustrated*, September 12, 1983.
29. Ibid.
30. Corr interview.
31. Lynch interview.
32. Long, "2004 Story: Trammell, Whitaker met as Rebels," *Montgomery Advertiser*, May 20, 2014.
33. Doane, Jack, "Trammell turns into Tiger for Triples," *The Sporting News*, July 16, 1977, 42.
34. Lynch interview.
35. Doane, "Trammell turns into Tiger for Triples," *The Sporting News*, July 16, 1977, 42.
36. Lynch interview.
37. Corr interview.
38. Long, "2004 Story: Trammell, Whitaker met as Rebels," *Montgomery Advertiser*, May 20, 2014.
39. Richard Bak, "Alan Trammell Remembers Tiger Stadium," *Detroit Athletic Co. Blog*, November 1, 2012.
40. Bak, "Alan Trammell Remembers Tiger Stadium," *Detroit Athletic Co. Blog*, November 1, 2012.
41. Bak, "Alan Trammell Remembers Tiger Stadium," *Detroit Athletic Co. Blog*, November 1, 2012.
42. Charlie Vincent, "Let's Make a Deal," *The Detroit Free Press*, August 27, 1977, C1.
43. "Trammell to Whitaker," *The Sporting News*, October 2, 1995, 18.
44. Jim Hawkins, "Tigers Belted by Bosox, 7-1," *The Detroit Free Press*, September 11, 1977, E1.
45. Jim Hawkins, "Are Tigers Looking at Medich?" *The Detroit Free Press*, September 12, 1977, D5.
46. Hawkins, "Tigers Belted by Bosox, 7-1," *The Detroit Free Press*, September 11, 1977, E1.

Chapter 3

1. Jim Hawkins, "Sweet Lou, Alan Ready to Anchor Tigers' Infield," *The Detroit Free Press*, March 9, 1978, D1.
2. Doane, "Trammell Turns Into Tiger for Triples," *The Sporting News*, July 16, 1977, 42.
3. Hawkins, "Sweet Lou, Alan Ready to Anchor Tigers' Infield," *The Detroit Free Press*, March 9, 1978, D1.
4. Ibid.
5. Tracewski interview.
6. Jerry Green, "Youthful Tigers a Year Away," *The Detroit News*, March 22, 1978, C1.
7. Hawkins, "Sweet Lou, Alan Ready to Anchor Tigers' Infield," *The Detroit Free Press*, March 9, 1978, D1.
8. Ibid.
9. Ibid.
10. Doug Bradford, "Kids Star in Tigers' Victory," *The Detroit News*, March 28, 1978, D1.
11. Doug Bradford, "Bird, Mankowski Thrill, Scare 52,528," *The Detroit News*, April 8, 1978, B1.
12. Larry Keith, "Roar? No, the Tigers Go 'Tweety!'" *Sports Illustrated*, April 24, 1978.
13. Ibid.
14. Ibid.
15. Ibid.
16. Ibid.
17. Joe Falls, "No One Shows More Poise Than Rookie Alan Trammell," *The Detroit News*, July 10, 1978, D6.
18. Ibid.
19. Ibid.
20. Jim Hawkins, "It Was a Very Good Year for Tigers—But Could Have Been a Lot Better," *The Detroit Free Press*, October 1, 1978, E11.

Chapter 4

1. Garrity, "Having a Monster of a Season," *Sports Illustrated*, May 28, 1984.
2. Brian Bragg, "Hot Tiger Bats Burn Angels, 10-7," *The Detroit Free Press*, June 11, 1979, D1.
3. *The Detroit Free Press*, June 15, 1979.
4. Jim Hawkins, "Sparky Promises a Pennant By '84," *The Detroit Free Press*, June 15, 1979), D1.
5. Ibid.
6. Ibid.
7. *The Detroit Free Press*, June 15, 1979.
8. Brian Bragg, "Tigers Infield: Solid as

Rock of Gibraltar," *The Detroit Free Press*, April 7, 1980, D1.
9. *The Detroit Free Press*, June 15, 1979.
10. Charlie Vincent, "Thrill of a Lifetime at 22—Trammell Trips with Stars," *The Detroit Free Press*, July 6, 1980, E1.
11. Ibid.
12. Ibid.
13. Brian Bragg, "Playoff-Bound Yankees Put Nowhere-Bound Tigers in 5th," *The Detroit Free Press*, October 6, 1980, D3.
14. Joe Falls, "Trammell: 7-Year, $2.8-Million Pact," *The Detroit News*, August 30, 1980, B1.
15. Ibid.
16. Ibid.
17. *The Detroit News*, October 5, 1981.
18. Ibid.
19. "Horseplay," *Ludington Daily News*, April 9, 1982, 6.
20. Ibid.
21. Ibid.
22. Garrity, "Having a Monster of a Season," *Sports Illustrated*, May 28, 1984.
23. Ibid.

Chapter 5

1. Tom Gage, "Tiger Notebook," *The Detroit News*, June 21, 1983, D4.
2. Ibid.
3. Lance Parrish, and Phil Pepe, *Few and Chosen: Defining Tigers Greatness Across Eras*, Chicago: Triumph Books, 2010.
4. Ibid.
5. Joe Falls, "Cabell ... Tigers Cheerleader But Tough—Jack Morris," *The Detroit News*, August 19, 1983, C1.
6. Wulf, "Short to Second to None," *Sports Illustrated*, September 12, 1983.
7. Garrity, "Having a Monster of a Season," *Sports Illustrated*, May 28, 1984.
8. Wulf, "Short to Second to None," *Sports Illustrated*, September 12, 1983.
9. Garrity, "Having a Monster of a Season," *Sports Illustrated*, May 28, 1984.
10. Gage, Tom, "Tiger Notebook," *The Detroit News*, July 11, 1983, D5.
11. Tom Gage, "Banner Day for Herndon Leads to Angels Downfall," *The Detroit News*, July 12, 1983, D1.
12. Garrity, "Having a Monster of a Season," *Sports Illustrated*, May 28, 1984.
13. Lynn Henning, "Trammell's Bat Turns Burly," *The Detroit News*, August 14, 1983, C1.
14. Wulf, "Short to Second to None," *Sports Illustrated*, September 12, 1983.
15. Ibid.
16. Garrity, "Having a Monster of a Season," *Sports Illustrated*, May 28, 1984.

17. Henning, "Trammell's Bat Turns Burly," *The Detroit News*, August 14, 1983, C1.
18. Ibid.
19. Ibid.
20. Garrity, "Having a Monster of a Season," *Sports Illustrated*, May 28, 1984.
21. Henning, "Trammell's Bat Turns Burly," *The Detroit News*, August 14, 1983, C1.
22. Garrity, "Having a Monster of a Season," *Sports Illustrated*, May 28, 1984.
23. Joe Falls, "Cabell Hails Team Spirit While Tigers Welcome Day Off," *The Detroit News*, August 19, 1983, C3.
24. Ibid.
25. Tom Gage, "Tiger Notebook," *The Detroit News*, September 21, 1983, H4.
26. "Orioles Clinch Division," *The Detroit News*, September 23, 1983.
27. Ibid.
28. Tom Gage, "Tigers Deserve to Smile Despite Brewers Sweep," *The Detroit News*, October 3, 1983, C1.

Chapter 6

1. George Cantor, *Wire to Wire*, Chicago, Triumph Books, 2004.
2. Garrity, "Having a Monster of a Season," *Sports Illustrated*, May 28, 1984.
3. Ibid.
4. Ibid.
5. Ibid.
6. Sparky Anderson, *Bless You Boys*, Chicago: Contemporary Books, 1984, 34.
7. Garrity, "Having a Monster of a Season," *Sports Illustrated*, May 28, 1984.
8. Ibid.
9. Ibid.
10. Ibid.
11. Anderson, *Bless You Boys*, 54.
12. Garrity, "Having a Monster of a Season," *Sports Illustrated*, May 28, 1984.
13. Ron Fimrite, "When Will the Bubble Burst," *Sports Illustrated*, May 14, 1984.
14. Garrity, "Having a Monster of a Season," *Sports Illustrated*, May 28, 1984.
15. Ibid.
16. Ibid.
17. Ibid.
18. Peter Gammons, "Surprise, Bosox, Texas have Pitching," *The Sporting News*, May 16, 1983, 15.
19. Anderson, *Bless You Boys*, 113.
20. *The Roar of '84*, *The Detroit Free Press*, 1985.
21. Jerry Green, "Can Tigers Survive Loss of Trammell?" *The Detroit News*, July 12, 1984, C1.
22. Tom Gage, "Verdict on Trammell: 'Bad, Good,'" *The Detroit News*, July 14, 1984, B1.

23. Tom Gage, "Shutout Places East Crown on Magic Season," *The Detroit News*, September 19, 1984, D1.

Chapter 7

1. Jerry Green, "Same Formula—Trammell Leads the Way," *The Detroit News*, October 3, 1984, H1.
2. Jerry Green, "Solid Second Half Play Gives Royals Some Reason for Hope," *The Detroit News*, October 2, 1984, C3.
3. Green, "Same Formula—Trammell Leads the Way," *The Detroit News*, October 3, 1984, H1.
4. Ibid.
5. Ibid.
6. Ibid.
7. *The Detroit News*, October 4, 1984.
8. Jerry Green, "Tigers Thrive on Attention," *The Detroit News*, October 6, 1984, B1.
9. Cantor, *Wire to Wire*, 139.
10. Jerry Green, "Trammell Proves He's Tiger Heart," *The Detroit News*, October 14, 1984, C1.
11. Mike O'Hara, "Are Padres Close to Their Last Supper?" *The Detroit News*, October 14, 1984, C3.
12. Green, "Trammell Proves He's Tiger Heart," *The Detroit News*, October 14, 1984, C1.
13. Ibid.
14. "Trammell Powers Tigers to Victory over Padres," *The Detroit News*, October 14, 1984, A1.
15. Ibid.
16. Ibid.
17. Tom Gage, "Tiger Magic: It's Real," *The Detroit News*, October 15, 1984, C1.
18. Ibid.
19. Ibid.
20. Ibid.
21. Ibid.
22. Ibid.
23. Ibid.
24. Ibid.
25. Tom Gage, "Tigers' Secret of 1984: A New MVP Each Week," *The Detroit News*, October 16, 1984, E1.
26. "Alan Trammell Remembers (1995)"—YouTube video clip: https://www.youtube.com/watch?v=hEpFo_kgQVo.
27. Cantor, *Wire to Wire*, 139.

Chapter 8

1. Jerry Green, "Predicting Lineup for Opening Day," *The Detroit News*, March 25, 1985, F1.
2. Ibid.
3. Tom Gage, "Whitaker Goes to Third in Tiger Spring Shuffle," *The Detroit News*, March 23, 1985, D1.
4. Tom Gage, "Where Did the Years Go?" *The Detroit News*, February 22, 1985, C1.
5. Tom Gage, "Whitaker Goes to Third in Tiger Spring Shuffle," *The Detroit News*, March 23, 1985, D1.
6. Joe Falls, "Sparky Turns to Trammell for Some Help," *The Detroit News*, July 15, 1985, D1.
7. Ibid.
8. Joe Falls, "Game is Debacle for Tiger Players," *The Detroit News*, July 17, 1985, G1.
9. Joe Falls, "Yankees Raise Fear in Sparky," *The Detroit News*, July 18, 1985, F1.
10. Joe Falls, "Tigers Lackluster Play Raises Sparky's Dander," *The Detroit News*, August 30, 1985, C1.
11. Corky Meinecke, "Tigers Spin 5-1 defeat on Boyd," *The Detroit News*, September 28, 1985, D1.
12. Tom Gage, "The Tigers: Story of a Lost Season," *The Detroit News*, October 6, 1985, C1.
13. John Lowe, "Trammell's Not Short on Effort," *The Detroit Free Press*, June 17, 1986, D5.
14. Ibid.
15. Ibid.
16. Ibid.
17. Ibid.
18. John Lowe, "Late Hit Fells Tigers Again," *The Detroit Free Press*, September 1, 1986, D1.
19. Ibid.
20. John Lowe, "Evans Helps Trammell's Attitude, Bat," *The Detroit Free Press*, September 4, 1986, D7.
21. Tracewski interview.
22. "Tiger Corner," *The Detroit Free Press*, September 3, 1986, D5.
23. Lowe, "Trammell's Not Short on Effort," *The Detroit Free Press*, June 17, 1986, D5.
24. "Even Tender Elbow Can't Dim Trammell's Fine '86 Season," *The Detroit Free Press*, October 2, 1986.
25. Ibid.
26. Ibid.

Chapter 9

1. Corky Meinecke, "Tigers Fifth? That's What 'Experts' Predict," *The Detroit News*, March 1, 1987.
2. Tom Gage, "Experiment Becomes Plan," *The Detroit News*, March 23, 1987, F3.
3. Tracewski interview.
4. Jerry Green, "Trammell Still Gains Despite the Pain," *The Detroit News*, June 7, 1987, D5.

5. Ibid.
6. Ibid.
7. Tom Gage, "Tigers Survive Red Sox," *The Detroit News*, June 13, 1987, D1.
8. Ibid.
9. Tom Gage, "Tigers Stuff Themselves at Plate 18–8," *The Detroit News*, June 8, 1987, F1.
10. *The Detroit News* (June 23, 1987).
11. Ibid.
12. "Quotable Lineup," *The SunSentinel*, June 10, 1987.
13. John Garrity, "Revving Up in Motown," *Sports Illustrated*, August 17, 1987.
14. Ibid.
15. Tom Gage, "Trammell Hits HR Century Mark," *The Detroit News*, June 21, 1987, C8.
16. Lynn Henning, "Trammell Shrugs Off Star Vote Snub," *The Detroit News*, June 20, 1987, D5.
17. Tom Gage, "Trammell's Near Hit Ruled Short-Hop Error," *The Detroit News*, July 16, 1987, F5.
18. Garrity, "Revving up in Motown," *Sports Illustrated*, August 17, 1987.
19. Lynn Henning, "Kell Enjoying Second Career with Tigers," *The Detroit News*, June 22, 1987, F5.
20. Tom Gage, "Trammell's Hot June No Threat to Record," *The Detroit News*, June 25, 1987, F5.
21. Ibid.

Chapter 10

1. Tommy George, "Success in Cleanup Spot Makes the Tigers Shine," *The Detroit Free Press*, September 24, 1987, D9.
2. Peter Gammons, "Birds on the Wing," *Sports Illustrated*, October 5, 1987.
3. Gene Guidi, "The Matchup," *The Detroit Free Press*, September 24, 1987, D1.
4. Peter Gammons, "Birds on the Wing," *Sports Illustrated*, October 5, 1987.
5. Mitch Albom, "One Awful Inning Leaves a Terrible Sinking Feeling," *The Detroit Free Press*, September 26, 1987, D1.
6. Joe Lapointe, "Tigers Could Get Left at Gate," *The Detroit Free Press*, September 25, 1987, D5.
7. Gammons, "Birds on the Wing," *Sports Illustrated*, October 5, 1987.
8. John Lowe, "Tigers Get Reliever Noles," *The Detroit Free Press*, September 22, 1987, D5.
9. Mitch Albom, "Tigers Reeling in Haunted House," *The Detroit Free Press*, September 27, 1987, D11.
10. Kirk Gibson and Lynn Henning, *Bottom of the Ninth*, Chelsea, MI, Sleeping Bear Press, 1997, 108.
11. "Tigers Beat Jays in 13th, 3–2," *The Detroit Free Press*, September 28, 1987, E12.
12. Ibid.
13. Jerry Green, "Junk Food Fuels Trammell's Firepower," *The Detroit News*, June 23, 1987, D5.
14. "Tram: Time Running Out," *The Detroit Free Press*, September 29, 1987.
15. Gene Guidi, "Sparky, Williams Aren't Birds of a Feather," *The Detroit Free Press*, September 24, 1987, D7.
16. "Jays' 'Big Guy' Quiet, But Carries a Big Stick," *The Detroit Free Press*, September 24, 1987.
17. Tommy George, "Success in Cleanup Spot Makes the Tigers Shine," *The Detroit Free Press*, September 24, 1987, D9.
18. "Tram: Time Running Out," *The Detroit Free Press* (September 29, 1987).
19. Mitch Albom, "Redhead and Reliever Are Unlikely Heroes," *The Detroit Free Press*, October 3, 1987, D2.
20. Peter Gammons, "Out!" *Sports Illustrated*, October 12, 1987.
21. Ibid.
22. Mitch Albom, "This Team Pulled It Off Perfectly," *The Detroit Free Press*, October 5, 1987, A14.
23. Gammons, "Out!" *Sports Illustrated*, October 12, 1987.
24. Albom, "This Team Pulled It Off Perfectly," *The Detroit Free Press*, October 5, 1987, A14.

Chapter 11

1. "1987 ALCS Game 5," NBC Television broadcast, October 10, 1987.
2. Charlie Vincent, "One Swing Sweeps Gloom for Tigers," *The Detroit Free Press*, October 11, 1987, D8.
3. Joe Lapointe, "A Philosophical Sparky Gives Credit Where it is Due," *The Detroit Free Press*, October 13, 1987, D3.
4. Mitch Albom, "Trammell Misses MVP But the Big Prize is His," *The Detroit Free Press*, November 18, 1987, D1.
5. Ibid.
6. Ibid.
7. George, "Success in Cleanup Spot Makes the Tigers Shine," *The Detroit Free Press*, September 24, 1987, D9.
8. Ibid.
9. Ibid.
10. John Valerino, "It Was a Match Made in Baseball Heaven," The Baseball Page.com, April 14, 2011.
11. Steve Crowe, "MVP: Bell Nips Tram-

mell," *The Detroit Free Press*, November 18, 1987, D1.

Chapter 12

1. Tom Gage, "Tigers: Shades of '87—Trammell HR Beats Red Sox," *The Detroit News*, April 4, 1988, E6.
2. Moss Klein, "George and Billy Act V Fall Flat," *The Sporting News*, July 4, 1988, 20.
3. Richard Goldstein, "Thomas T. Roberts Dies at 84; Rules That Baseball Owners Engaged in Collusion," *The New York Times*, February 19, 2008.
4. Gibson and Henning, *Bottom of the Ninth*, 113.
5. Tom Gage, "Tigers' Hopes are High for a Repeat," *The Detroit News*, April 4, 1988, D5.
6. Tom Gage, "Trammell's Slam in 9th Stuns Yanks," *The Detroit News*, June 21, 1988, H1.
7. Steve Wulf, "Too Hot Not to Cool Down," *Sports Illustrated*, August 15, 1988.
8. Ibid.
9. Tom Gage, "By George, Tigers End Skid," *The Detroit News*, September 8, 1988, D6.
10. Mitch Albom, "Mitch Flashback: Alan Trammell Negotiated His Own Contract," Pro Sports Group http://prosportsgroup.com/sports-agent-news/mitch-flashback-alan-trammell-negotiated-his-own-contract/ (2015).
11. "Sports People: Trammell in Accord," *The New York Times*, March 5, 1989.
12. Tom Gage, "No More Long Term Deals for Tigers," *The Detroit News*, March 17, 1989, C3.
13. Joe Lapointe, "Anderson Adjusts to (Ugh) Losing," *The New York Times*, July 31, 1989.
14. Tom Gage, "Injury Typical of Trammell's Season," *The Sporting News*, September 18, 1989, 20.
15. *The Sporting News*, October 2, 1989, 27.
16. Tom Gage, "Injury Typical of Trammell's Season," *The Sporting News*, September 18, 1989, 20.

Chapter 13

1. Jerry Green, "Making Dreams Come True," *The Detroit News*, July 3, 1988, D4.
2. Dave Dye, "Something to Prove," *The Detroit News*, April 9, 1990, E1.
3. Ibid.
4. "Trammell Proves '89 Wasn't Typical Year," *The Detroit News*, September 3, 1990.
5. Dave Dye, "Team's Slump Has Trammell Concerned," *The Detroit News*, August 17, 1990, C5.
6. https://www.detroitathletic.com/blog/2015/01/22/big-daddy-came-detroit/.
7. Neil MacCarl, "Most Indispensable Players," *The Sporting News*, April 1, 1991, 50.
8. Jennifer Frey, "Renaissance Man," *The Detroit News*, August 25, 1990, B3.
9. Ibid.
10. Reid Creager, "Baseball: AL East," *The Sporting News*, July 29, 1991, 22.
11. Ibid.
12. Reid Creager, "Baseball: AL East," *The Sporting News*, May 25, 1992, 23.
13. Cantor, *Wire to Wire*, 149.
14. Albom, "Mitch Flashback: Alan Trammell Negotiated His Own Contract," Pro Sports Group http://prosportsgroup.com/sports-agent-news/mitch-flashback-alan-trammell-negotiated-his-own-contract/ (2015).
15. Ibid.
16. Reid Creager, "Baseball: AL East," *The Sporting News*, April 12, 1993, 19.
17. Tracewski interview.
18. Reid Creager, "Baseball: AL East," *The Sporting News*, September 6, 1993, 30.
19. Ibid.
20. Bob Wojinowski, "If Season Ends With Strike, Loss to Brewers Might Have Been the End for Three Tigers," *The Detroit News*, August 12, 1994, F1.

Chapter 14

1. Cliff Corcoran, "The Strike: Who was Right, Who was Wrong and How it Helped Baseball," SI.com, http://www.si.com/mlb/2014/08/12/1994-strike-bud-selig-orel-hershiser, August 12, 2014.
2. Jerry Green, *The Detroit News*, August 11, 1994.
3. John Heyman, *The Sporting News*, December 16, 1994.
4. Tom Gage, "Tigers Create Space for Trammell, Gibson," *The Detroit News*, April 9, 1995, E1.
5. Gibson and Henning, *Bottom of the Ninth*, 158.
6. "Whitaker, Trammell Hold Off on Decision," *The Detroit News*, September 14, 1995.
7. Mitch Albom, "It's Been Nice Working with You," *The Detroit Free Press*, March 8, 1987.
8. Valerino, "It Was a Match Made in Baseball Heaven," The Baseball Page.com, http://www.thebaseballpage.com/community/articles/it-was-match-made-baseball-heaven, April 14, 2011.
9. Albom, "It's Been Nice Working with You," *The Detroit Free Press*, March 8, 1987.
10. "Trammell to Whitaker," *The Sporting News*, October 2, 1995, 18.
11. Valerino, "It Was a Match Made in Base-

ball Heaven," The Baseball Page.com, http://www.thebaseballpage.com/community/articles/it-was-match-made-baseball-heaven, April 14, 2011.
12. Ibid.
13. Ibid.
14. "Whitaker, Trammell Hold Off on Decision," *The Detroit News*, September 14, 1995.
15. Tom Gage, "Sparky, Lou, Tram Near End of Their Tiger Stripes?" *The Detroit News*, October 1, 1995, C3.
16. "I Ain't Here No More," *The Detroit News*, October 3, 1995, D1.
17. Gene Guidi, "Tram Will Be All for 20th Tiger Season," *The Detroit Free Press*, January 25, 1996, D2.
18. Ibid.
19. Ibid.
20. Ibid.
21. Bob Nightengale, "There Clearly is no Die in This Sprouting Dynasty," *The Sporting News*, April 8, 1996, 24.
22. Tom Gage, "Ankle Injury Might Signal End of Road for Trammell," *The Detroit News*, July 28, 1996, D5.
23. Craig Carter and Mark Newman, "A Starter of Different Stripes," *The Sporting News*, September 30, 1996, 5.
24. John Lowe, "Final Curtain for Tram, Class Act," *The Detroit Free Press*, September 30, 1996, D1.
25. Ibid.
26. Ibid.
27. Charlie Vincent, "We'll Miss Tram, Not '96 Tigers," *The Detroit Free Press*, September 30, 1996, A1.
28. Steve Kornacki, "Trammell Lost it Where He Found His Greatest Joy," *Detroit Free Press*, September 30, 1996, D3.
29. Lowe, "Final Curtain for Tram, Class Act," *The Detroit Free Press*, September 30, 1996, D1.
30. Ibid.
31. Ibid.
32. Kornacki, "Trammell Lost it Where He Found His Greatest Joy," *Detroit Free Press*, September 30, 1996, D3.

Chapter 15

1. Tom Gage, "Search is Set to Start for Tigers," *The Detroit News*, October 2, 2002, E1.
2. Tom Gage, "Trammell Likes What He Sees from Tigers," *The Detroit News*, October 6, 2002, C7.
3. Gage, "Search is Set to Start for Tigers," *The Detroit News*, October 2, 2002, E1.
4. "Baseball Roundup: Tigers Bring Back Trammell, as Manager," *The New York Times*, October 2, 2010.
5. Ibid.
6. Tom Gage, "Hometown Heroes Rally Wings, Tigers," *The Detroit News*, October 10, 2002, A1.
7. Ibid.
8. "Welcome Home, Alan Trammell," *The Detroit Free Press*, October 10, 2002.
9. Rob Parker, "Trammell's Hiring is About Public Relations, Not Winning," *The Detroit News*, October 10, 2002, F1.
10. Ibid.
11. Harrison, "Yore Detroit Tigers," *Metrotimes*, March 26, 2003.
12. Ibid.
13. Matt Crossman, "Hard Knocks," *The Sporting News*, May 26, 2003, 16.
14. Ibid.
15. "Tigers Fall into Tie With '62 Mets," *The Detroit News*, September 21, 2003.
16. Tom Gage, "Tigers Stay Out of Record Book," *The Detroit News*, September 29, 2003, D1.
17. Crossman, "Hard Knocks," *The Sporting News*, May 26, 2003, 16.
18. Ken Rosenthal, "All the Right Moves," *The Sporting News*, October 28, 2002, 18.
19. Tom Gage, "Now Trammell Has Seen it All," *The Detroit News*, September 28, 2003.
20. Lynn Henning, "Lynn Henning Breaks Down the Tigers Season of Turmoil," *The Detroit News*, October 4, 2005, D1.
21. Ibid.
22. John Lowe, "Tigers Limping, Not Walking to End," *The Detroit News*, October 1, 2005, B5.
23. Henning, "Lynn Henning Breaks Down the Tigers Season of Turmoil," *The Detroit News*, October 4, 2005, D1.
24. Tom Gage, "Tigers Sloppy Right to End," *The Detroit News*, October 3, 2005, D5.
25. Bob Wojinowski, "Dombrowski Can Get Tough Guy, But Onus Now on Him, Ilitch," *The Detroit News*, October 4, 2005, D1.
26. Chris Silva, "Tigers Fire 'Fine Man,'" *The Detroit Free Press*, October 4, 2005, E10.
27. Rob Parker, "Young Says Players are to Blame for Trammell's Firing," *The Detroit News*, October 4, 2005, D6.
28. *ESPN.go* (October 3, 2005) http://espn.go.com/mlb/news/story?id=2179572.
29. Ibid.
30. Wojinowski, "Dombrowski Can Get Tough Guy, But Onus Now on Him, Illitch," *The Detroit News*, October 4, 2005, D1.

Chapter 16

1. "SN Ranking: Trammell Worst Manager in Last 30 Years," *The Detroit News*, May 22, 2015.

2. "Detroit Legend Trammell Makes Last Visit to Tiger Stadium," USAToday.com, June 24, 2009.
3. Ibid.
4. Ibid.
5. Steve Kornacki, "Former Tigers Great Alan Trammell Visits Tigers Stadium, Says Hello to Jim Leyland," mlive.com, June 23, 2009.
6. Ibid.
7. Tom Gage, "Alan Trammel Returning to Tigers as Assistant," *The Detroit News*, November 3, 2014.
8. Ibid.
9. John Lowe, "Gentleman Enriched Game: Molitor's Tribute to a Friend," *The Detroit Free Press*, September 30, 1996, D3.
10. Lowe, "Final Curtain for Tram, Class Act," *The Detroit Free Press*, September 30, 1996, D1.
11. John Valerino, "It Was a Match Made in Baseball Heaven," The Baseball Page. http://www.thebaseballpage.com/community/articles/it-was-match-made-baseball-heaven (April 14, 2011).
12. John Lowe, "Final Curtain for Tram, Class Act," *The Detroit Free Press* (September 30, 1996), p. D1.
13. John Valerino, "It Was a Match Made in Baseball Heaven," The Baseball Page. http://www.thebaseballpage.com/community/articles/it-was-match-made-baseball-heaven (April 14, 2011).
14. John Lowe, "Final Curtain for Tram, Class Act," *The Detroit Free Press* (September 30, 1996), p. D1.
15. Valerino, "It Was a Match Made in Baseball Heaven," The Baseball Page.com, http://www.thebaseballpage.com/community/articles/it-was-match-made-baseball-heaven, April 14, 2011.
16. Vincent, "We'll Miss Tram, Not '96 Tigers," *The Detroit Free Press*, September 30, 1996, A1.
17. Valerino, "It Was a Match Made in Baseball Heaven," The Baseball Page.com, http://www.thebaseballpage.com/community/articles/it-was-match-made-baseball-heaven, April 14, 2011.
18. Kornacki, "Former Tigers Great Alan Trammell Visits Tigers Stadium, Says Hello to Jim Leyland," mlive.com, June 23, 2009.
19. Tony Paul, "Smoltz Has High Praise for Trammell in Fame Speech," *The Detroit News*, July 27, 2015.
20. Ibid.
21. George, "Success in Cleanup Spot Makes the Tigers Shine," *The Detroit Free Press*, September 24, 1987, D9.

Chapter 17

1. David Tokarz, "Taking a Look at Alan Trammell's Hall of Fame Case," blessyouboys.com, January 4, 2011.
2. Ibid.
3. Jeff Sackmann, "The Hall of Fame Case for Alan Trammell," hardballtimes.com, January 5, 2010.
4. Matt Snyder, "'Lucky 13' Breaking Down Alan Trammell's Hall of Fame Case," cbssports.com, December 27, 2013.
5. Sackmann, "The Hall of Fame Case for Alan Trammell," hardballtimes.com, January 5, 2010.
6. Snyder, "'Lucky 13' Breaking Down Alan Trammell's Hall of Fame Case," cbssports.com, December 27, 2013.
7. Dave Cameron, "Trammell, Yount, and the Value of Career Length," fangraphs.com, December 27, 2011.
8. Sackmann, "The Hall of Fame Case for Alan Trammell," hardballtimes.com, January 5, 2010.
9. Cantor, *Wire to Wire*, 93.
10. "The Alan Trammell Debate: 2015," notinhalloffame.com, March 19, 2015.
11. Sackmann, "The Hall of Fame Case for Alan Trammell," hardballtimes.com, January 5, 2010.
12. Ibid.
13. Snyder, "'Lucky 13' Breaking Down Alan Trammell's Hall of Fame Case," cbssports.com, December 27, 2013.
14. Valerino, "It Was a Match Made in Baseball Heaven," The Baseball Page.com, http://www.thebaseballpage.com/community/articles/it-was-match-made-baseball-heaven, April 14, 2011.
15. "The Alan Trammell Debate: 2015," notinhalloffame.com, March 19, 2015.
16. Peter J. Wallner, "Alan Trammell Doubts Hall of Fame Will Happen—Unless It's with Lou Whitaker," Mlive.com, January 26, 2015.

Bibliography

Books

Anderson, Sparky. *Bless You Boys*. Chicago: Contemporary, 1984.

Cantor, George. *Wire to Wire*. Chicago: Triumph, 2004.

Gibson, Kirk, and Lynn Henning. *Bottom of the Ninth*. Chelsea, MI: Sleeping Bear Press, 1997.

Janoff, Barry. *Alan Trammell: Tiger on the Prowl*. Chicago: Children's Press, 1985.

Parrish, Lance, and Phil Pepe. *Few and Chosen: Defining Tigers Greatness Across Eras*. Chicago: Triumph, 2010.

Articles

Albom, Mitch. "It's Been Nice Working with You." *The Detroit Free Press*, March 8, 1987.

Cameron, Dave. "Trammell, Yount, and the Value of Career Length." Fangraphs.com, December 27, 2011.

Corcoran, Cliff. "The Strike: Who Was Right, Who Was Wrong and How It Helped Baseball." SI.com, http://www.si.com/mlb/2014/08/12/1994-strike-bud-selig-orel-hershiser, August 12, 2014.

Fimrite, Ron. "A Son of San Diego Pounds the Padres." *Sports Illustrated*, October 22, 1984.

Gammons, Peter. "Birds on the Wing." *Sports Illustrated*, October 5, 1987.

———. "Out!" *Sports Illustrated*, October 12, 1987.

Garrity, John. "Having a Monster of a Season." *Sports Illustrated*, May 28, 1984.

Harrison, Scott. "Yore Detroit Tigers." *Metrotimes*, March 26, 2003.

Sackmann, Jeff. "The Hall of Fame Case for Alan Trammell." Hardballtimes.com, January 5, 2010.

Snyder, Matt. "'Lucky 13' Breaking Down Alan Trammell's Hall of Fame Case." CBSsports.com, December 27, 2013.

Tokarz, David. "Taking a Look at Alan Trammell's Hall of Fame Case." Blessyouboys.com, January 4, 2011.

Valerino, John. "It Was a Match Made in Baseball Heaven." *The Baseball Page.com*, April 14, 2011.

Wulf, Steve. "Short to Second to None." *Sports Illustrated*, September 12, 1983.

"The Alan Trammell Debate: 2015." Notinhalloffame.com, March 19, 2015.

Newspapers and Magazines

Detroit Free Press
Detroit News
KHS Galaxy
Ludington Daily News
Montgomery Advertiser
The New York Times
The Sporting News
Sports Illustrated

Interviews

Canepa, Nick. Phone interview with author. September 16, 2015.

Corr, Larry. Phone interview with author. January 16, 2013.

Griffith, Brad. Phone interview with author. January 31, 2013.

Grooms, Steve. Email exchange with author. January 31, 2013.

Lynch, Terrance. Phone interview with author. January 8, 2013.

Maffei, John. Email exchange with author. January 23, 2013.

McMillan, Hugh. Phone interview with author. January 31, 2013.

Tracewski, Richard. Phone interview with author. May 21, 2013.

Websites

"Alan Trammell Remembers (1995)"—YouTube video clip: https://www.youtube.com/watch?v=hEpFo_kgQVo

Retrosheet.org

Baseballreference.com

Index

Abbott, Glen 85
ABC *Monday Night Baseball* 87
ABC's Good Morning America 85
Ackerman, Carl 22
Alexander, Doyle 130–132, 137, 139, 144–145, 151
Allen, Dick 205, 213
Altobelli, Joe 74, 88
Anderson, Sparky 9–10, 49–55, 58–64, 69–72, 74–75, 82–86, 88–89, 92, 96, 103–105, 109–114, 116–118, 120–126, 129, 131, 135–137, 139–140, 144–145, 147, 149, 155–156, 160–161, 163–168, 171, 173–176, 178–180, 186, 188–189, 196, 203–205, 207
Angelos, Peter 171
Aparicio, Luis 177
Appalachian League 2, 22
Arizona (University of) *see* University of Arizona
Arizona Diamondbacks 200–201
Arizona State University 19
Atlanta Braves 29, 98, 130
Auker, Eldon 6

Bair, Doug 85, 111
Balboni, Steve 82, 96
Baltimore Orioles 31–33, 43, 48, 52–53, 64–65, 71–74, 76, 79, 87–90, 92, 106, 108, 111, 118, 127, 138, 161, 166, 171, 178–179, 181, 185, 194, 207
Bancroft, Dan 211
Bannister, Floyd 19
Barbarino, Vinnie 16
Barfield, Jesse 133, 136–137, 142
Barnettin, Ted 195
Barrett, Tom 18
Baseball America 65, 173
Baseball Digest 79
Bautista, Danny 174
Baylor, Don 34
Beckert, Glen 177
Belanger, Mark 53, 87, 204
Bell, Buddy 180, 183–184, 186
Bell, George 133, 137, 139, 141, 146–147, 211
Belmont University 21

Beniquez, Juan 136–137
Berenguer, Juan 84–85, 90, 110, 124, 144–145
Bergman, Dave 79, 84, 87, 90, 111, 118, 126, 159
Berra, Yogi 18
Bertoia, Reno 6
Bevacqua, Kurt 100
Billingham, Jack 41–42, 178
Black, Bud 82, 94–95
Blackburn, Wayne 37
Bochy, Bruce 187
Boddicker, Mike 73–74
Boggs, John 173
Boggs, Wade 121–122, 212
Bonderman, Jeremy 193, 198
Boros, Steve 87
Boston Red Sox 7, 32–34, 37–39, 43, 52–53, 59, 61, 64, 71, 80, 79, 82, 90, 112–115, 117–118, 121–122, 132, 134, 149, 152–154, 161, 166, 174, 181, 183
Brett, George 94–95, 177, 212
Bridgeport (PA) 11
Brinkman, Ed 24–27, 29–30, 33, 46, 51, 87
Bristol, VA (Flying Tigers) 20–22, 28
Brookens, Tom 6, 22, 67, 84, 115, 126, 136, 155
Brooklyn Dodgers 92, 177
Brown, Bobby 99
Brown, Chris 155
Brown, Gates 6, 68, 70
Brumley, Rick 155
Bunning, Jim 6
Burleson, Rick 53
Burnside, Sheldon 31
Bush, Donnie 201

Cabell, Enos 61, 66, 68, 73
Cabrera, Miguel 202
California Angels 34, 48, 51, 67, 84, 122, 124, 152, 174
Camden Yards 178
Campbell, Bill 34
Campbell, Jim 24–25, 39–40, 47–49, 56, 77–78, 164
Canepa, Nick 17
Carey, Paul 79
Carlton, Steve 183

227

Index

Carter, Craig 183
Carter, President Jimmy 7
Castillo, Marty 67, 96, 100–101, 111
The CBS Morning News 85
Cedeno, Andujar 180
Chattanooga (TN) Lookouts 23, 29
Chicago Cubs 97–98, 136, 177–178, 199
Chicago White Sox 33, 47, 61, 64, 80, 88, 150, 160, 177, 181, 195
Christenson, Gary 30
Cincinnati Reds 41, 49–52, 71, 83–84, 92, 110, 161–162, 174, 177–178, 210
Clancy, Jim 62, 132, 137
Clemons, Roger 121, 132, 149
Cleveland, Reggie 32
Cleveland Indians 38, 61–62, 65, 97, 116, 118, 122, 161, 173, 181
Clinton, President Bill 7, 171
Cluck, Bob 189
Cobb, Ty 7, 146, 199, 202, 205
Codiroli, Chris 67
Colbert, Nate 13
Coles, Darnell 116, 120, 126
Collins, Dave 114
Colorado Rockies 198
Columbus (GA) Astros 27
Comerica Park 9, 186, 197, 199
Comiskey Park 80
Concepcion, Dave 51–52, 83, 177–178
Concepcion, Onix 96
Cooperstown, New York 204
Corcoran, Tim 22
Cornwall (England) 11
Corr, Larry 21–22, 27–28, 31
Coscarart, Pete 18
Cowens, Al 54
Cox, Bobby 132
Craig, Roger 102
Crawford, Sam 202

Davis, Eric 172
Davis, Ron 58
Davis, Storm 74
Deer, Rob 166
Dent, Bucky 53
Dent, Dick 78
Detroit (city) 7, 9, 56–57, 75
Detroit Catholic Central High School 37
Detroit Free Press 19, 45, 188
Detroit News 39
Detroit Pistons 121
Detroit Red Wings 121, 186
Detroit Tigers: 1934 team 6; 1935 team 6; 1968 team 1, 6, 13, 18, 54, 74, 97, 105; 2006 team 197, 198
Dickerson, Dan 9
Dietz, Jim 17
Dillard, Steve 37–39, 42
DiMaggio, Joe 6, 175, 178, 199
Dodger Stadium 53
Dombrowski, Dave 187–188, 193, 196, 201

Dravecky, Dave 103
Driessen, Ken 51
Drysdale, Don 175

Eichhorn, Mark 132, 140
Ellis Island 20
Engle, Dave 90
Evans, Darrell 1, 6, 77, 79–80, 84–85, 96, 103, 111, 116, 122–123, 125, 127, 135–137, 142, 145, 147, 153, 155
Evans, Dwight 113
Evansville (IN) Triplets 32, 37, 39, 48, 51
Evers, Johnny 175, 177
Exhibition Stadium (Toronto) 134, 136

Falls, Joe 188
Farnsworth, Kyle 195
Fenway Park 32, 45, 80, 132, 149
Fernandez, Tony 116, 128, 133–134, 139
Ferrell, Rick 18
Fetters, Mike 183
Fetzer, John 49, 77
Fidrych, Mark "The Bird" 6, 36, 40–42, 48–49, 54, 65
Field of Dreams 5
Fielder, Cecil 6, 133, 142, 159–162, 166
Fields, Bruce 187, 189
Fingers, Rollie 59
Flanagan, Mike 74, 132, 134, 140
Florida Instructional League 23–25
Florida Marlins 193, 198
Florida State League 24
Foster, George 51, 161
Fox, Nellie 177
Freehan, Bill 6, 56
Fryman, Travis 162, 164, 166–167, 172–174, 184
Fuentes, Tito 33, 35, 37

Gaetti, Gary 144
Gale, Rich 46
Garbey, Barbaro 82, 84, 111
Garcia, Pedro 33
Garciaparra, Nomar 3, 183, 208
Garner, Phil 184, 186–187, 203
Garvey, Steve 97, 99, 102
Gaston, Cito 13
Gehrig, Lou 171, 175, 199, 208
Gehringer, Charlie 146, 174, 202
German, Franklyn 191
Geronimo, Caesar 51
Gibson, Kirk 1, 6, 52, 58–59, 65, 68, 71, 84–85, 88–90, 95, 100, 103–106, 110–111, 117, 119–122, 125–126, 134–137, 140, 149–150, 152, 154, 166–167, 169, 172, 174–175, 189, 192, 196, 200–202, 206, 213
Gillick, Pat 132
Gomez, Chris 167–168, 174, 174, 180
Gossage, Rich "Goose" 98, 104, 112
Grammas, Alex 103
Granderson, Curtis 198
Greenberg, Hank 146, 202

Index

Greinke, Zack 200
Grich, Bobby 34
Griffey, Ken 51
Griffith, Brad 14
Grubb, John 68, 90, 96, 111, 118, 126, 136, 155
Gruber, Kelly 133, 137
Guante, Cecilio 151
Gubicza, Mark 94
Guidry, Don 45
Guillen, Carlos 193–194
Gullett, Don 34
Gullickson, Bill 172
Gulliver, Glenn 23
Gura, Larry 94
Gwynn, Tony 97, 99–100

Habyan, John 138
Hairston, Jerry 64
Halter, Shane 190
Hanshin Tigers (Japan) 159
Harper, Terry 120
Harwell, Ernie 164, 189, 203–204
Havens, Brad 61
Hawkins, Andy 100
Heath, Mike 119, 122, 126, 135
Hebner, Richie 54
Heilmann, Harry 202
Hemond, Roland 33
Henderson, Ricky 2, 118, 161, 212
Hendon, Larry 6, 61, 67–68, 71, 73, 84, 94, 99, 101, 122, 126
Henke, Tom 132, 134, 137, 140
Henneman, Mike 124, 135, 139–140, 144, 174
Hernandez, Enzo 13
Hernandez, Guillermo "Willie" 6, 79, 85, 89–91, 94–96, 101, 109–112, 118, 124, 135, 155, 141, 153
Herzog, Whitey 8, 211
Higginson, Bobby 174, 195
Hiller, John 54
Hodges, Gil 213
Hoover High School 16
Horton, Willie 6, 41, 187, 201
Houk, Ralph 32–33, 35–36, 38–40, 42–44, 47
Houston Astros 73, 174
Howell, Roy Lee 87
Howser, Dick 82–83, 94, 96
Hunter, Jim "Catfish" 34
Huson, Jeff 179
Hutton, Tom 40

Illitch, Mike 164, 175, 186
Infante, Omar 190, 194, 198
Inge, Brandon 190, 194, 198
Iorg, Dane 95
Iorg, Garth 133, 142

Jack Murphy Stadium 13, 78, 99, 100–101, 105
Jackson, Reggie 29, 34
Jackson, "Shoeless" Joe 205
Jackson, Travis 211

Jacksonville (FL) Suns 30
James, Bill 198
Jefferson, Jesse 41
Jennings, Hughie 211
Jeter, Derek 3, 173, 182–183, 208
Johnson, Howard 84, 87
Johnson, Jason 193
Jones, Jeff 67
Jones, Ruppert 84, 88, 96
Jones, Tracy 155
Jurges, Billy 25

Kaat, Jim 205
Kaline, Al 6–7, 45, 146, 187–188, 199, 201–202, 205
Kansas City Royals 5, 43, 52, 60, 80, 82, 93–99, 101, 105, 132, 143, 156, 177, 166, 181, 191, 194
Kauffman Stadium 82, 94, 163
Kearny High School 14–19
Kell, George 6, 45, 129
Kelleher, Mick 189
Kelly, Pat 166
Kemp, Steve 6, 22, 36, 41, 48, 50, 54, 59, 61
Kennedy, Ian 200
Kennedy, Terry 99, 138
Keough, Dave 42
Keough, Matt 71
Kessinger, Don 177
Key, Jimmy 132, 141
KHS Galaxy 16
King, Eric 124
Kingman, Dave 121
Kirkwood, Don 43
Klein, Joe 174
Klein, Moss 149
Knight, Ray 152
Knotts, Gary 193
Koegel, Pete 30
Koufax, Sandy 175
Kreuter, Chad 166
Kubek, Tony 145
Kuenn, Harvey 201

Lachemann, Rene 87
Lajoe, Bill 25, 77, 118, 130, 152, 154, 164
Lakeland, FL 26, 37–39, 40, 47, 109, 120, 154, 165, 180, 189
Lakeland Tigers 24
Lansford, Carney 46
Larkin, Barry 3, 162, 210
LaRoche, Dave 48
La Russa, Tony 8
Laudner, Tim 145
Law, Rudy 69
Leach, Rick 68, 135–136
Lee, Manny 135–136, 139–140, 142
Lefferts, Craig 100
LeFlore, Ron 6, 36, 41, 46, 51, 54, 82
Lemon, Chet 1, 6, 61, 69, 73, 84, 96, 117, 126, 142, 144, 159

230　　　　　　　　　　Index

Leno, Jay 191
Lewis, Joe 20
Lewis, Michael 211
Leyland, Jim 197, 204
Liebrandt, Charlie 94, 97
Livingstone, Scott 166
Lolich, Mickey 6, 105
Lollar, Tim 55, 101
Long Beach (CA) 11
Lopes, Davey 178
Lopez, Aurelio 54, 79, 85, 90, 96, 111
Los Angeles Dodgers 98–99, 102, 126, 150, 178, 200
Los Angeles Lakers 66
Lowenstein, John 73
Lusader, Scott 139
Lynch, Terry 23, 27–28, 30–31
Lynn, Fred 39

Macha, Ken 187
Madlock, Bill 126, 134, 138, 140, 152
Magnum, P.I. 75
Major League Scouting Bureau 17–18
Mankowski, Phil 40
Mantle, Mickey 2, 58, 183
Maranville, Rabbit 211
Marchant Stadium (Lakeland, FL) 154
Marion, Marty 18
Maroth, Mike 190, 193
Martin, Billy 151
Martinez, Carmelo 99–100
Martinez, Dennis 74
Martinez, Jesse 15
Mattingly, Don 118, 200, 212
Maxie, Larry 18
May, Milt 34, 45
May, Rudy 58
Mayberry, John 43
Mays, Willie 183
McAuliffe, Dick 6, 33
McGregor, Scott 74, 87
McGriff, Fred 133
McGuire, Mark 2, 8, 125
McHale, John 184
McKeon, Jack 98
McMillan, Hugh 14–17, 19
McNamara, John 128, 134
McRae, Hal 82, 94–95
McReynolds, Kevin 99
Mears, Chris 191
Melvin, Bob 191
Memphis, Tennessee 21
Mendoza, Mario 18
Mercado, Orlando 119
Metro, Charlie 18
Metro Airport (Detroit) 31
Metrodome, Hubert H. Humphrey 79, 143
Michael, Gene 58
Michigan (University of) *see* University of Michigan
Michigan State University 58

Milwaukee Brewers 41, 52–53, 59–60, 62, 64, 71–72, 79, 87, 91, 108, 116, 118, 121–122, 131–132, 138, 161, 168, 174, 183, 200, 203, 207
Minnesota Twins 38, 61, 64, 79, 80, 88, 90, 122, 131, 139, 143–146, 155, 180–181, 191–194, 213
Molitor, Paul 46, 52, 122, 203
Monaghan, Tom 77–78, 150, 164, 186
Moneyball 211
Monge, Sid 85
Monroe, Craig 190, 194, 198
Montgomery, Alabama (Rebels) 22–23, 26–, 38, 40, 48, 87, 176
Moore, Charlie 138
Moreland, Keith 155
Morgan, Joe 51, 177–178
Morris, Jack 1, 6, 22, 45, 52, 54, 59, 65–66, 68, 73–74, 79–80, 82–85, 94–95, 99, 103, 105, 110, 112–113, 115, 119, 123, 131, 135, 140, 144, 147, 149, 151, 154, 157, 159, 169, 201–202
Moseby, Lloyd 133, 135, 141–142, 159
Moss, Les 22, 47–49, 51
Mulliniks, Dave 133, 139
Munson, Eric 190
Murray, Dale 71
Murray, Eddie 73–74, 212
Musial, Stan 12
Musselman, Jeff 132, 140
Myers, Greg 138

NBC *Game of the Week* 80, 121
NBC *Tonight Show* 191
Nettles, Craig 98–99
New York Mets 92; 1962 team 191–192
New York Yankees 7, 32–34, 41, 43, 45, 52–55, 58, 64, 71, 79, 91, 93, 108, 118, 120–123, 126–127, 131, 150–151, 157, 161, 166, 170, 173, 181–182
Newhauser, Hal 202
Newman, Mark 183
Nokes, Matt 122, 125, 135, 153
Noles, Dickie 135
Northrup, Jim 6, 57

Oakland-Alameda County Stadium 42
Oakland A's 9, 67, 85, 87, 121, 123, 125, 161, 180, 190
Oliva, Tony 205, 213
O'Neal, Randy 91
Ordonez, Magglio 194–195, 198
Orlando (FL) Twins 23, 27
Oyler, Ray 18

Palmer, Jim 32, 45, 74
Parker, Rob 188
Parrish, Lance 1–2, 6, 22, 32, 34, 45, 50, 53–54, 61, 65–67, 69, 71, 73, 84–85, 94–95, 99, 103, 106, 109–111, 117, 119–120, 125–126, 150, 154, 189, 201, 206
Parrish, Larry 186–187
Pena, Carlos 190, 194

Index

Penn, Shannon 183–184
Percival, Troy 194
Perez, Tony 84
Peters, Ricky 30, 54
Petry, Dan 6, 54, 59, 61, 68, 73–74, 84–85, 100, 110, 112–113, 117, 123, 131, 136, 152
Pettis, Gary 149, 152
Philadelphia Phillies 79, 98, 119, 195
Phillips, Tony 159–160, 162, 166–167
Piniella, Lou 199
Pitt, Brad 211
Pittaro, Chris 109, 111
Pittsburgh Pirates 54, 126, 198
Polanco, Placido 198
Puckett, Kirby 146
Pujols, Luis 186

Quisenberry, Dan 83, 94, 96

Raines, Tim 205
Randolph, Willie 71, 187
Rasmussen, Dennis 116
Reagan, President Ronald 85
Reardon, Jeff 144
Reese, Pee Wee 177
Reich, Tom 119
Rice, Jim 212
Righetti, Dave 151
Rightnowar, Ron 174
Ripken, Cal, Jr. 74, 84, 86, 88, 112, 128, 152, 162–163, 171, 179, 185, 204, 207–208, 212
Rizzuto, Phil 211
Robertson, Nate 193, 198
Robinson, Jackie 177
Robinson, Jeff 124, 131, 151
Rodney, Fernando 198
Rodriguez, Alex 3, 182, 208
Rodriguez, Aurelio 6, 24
Rodriguez, Ivan "Pudge" 193–195
Rogell, Billy 6, 201
Rogers, Kenny 198
Rose, Pete 22, 205
Rozema, Dave 6, 22–23, 36, 41–42, 54, 60, 84–85
Rudi, Joe 34
Russell, Bill 178
Ruth, Babe 175, 199
Ryan, Nolan 48

Saberhagen, Brett 94–95
St. Louis (MO) 98, 211
St. Louis Cardinals 18, 91, 98, 125, 139, 143, 208, 211
St. Petersburg, FL 23–25
Salazar, Luis 152
Samuel, Juan 189
San Diego (CA) 9, 11, 13–15, 20, 29, 31, 43, 49, 100–101, 104, 137, 141, 146, 187, 196, 197–198, 200
San Diego Evening Tribune 17
San Diego Padres 13, 97–105, 158, 173, 187

San Diego State University 17
San Francisco Giants 40, 139, 200
Sanchez, Alex 194
Sandberg, Ryne 97
Santana (Sultans) High School 16
Santiago, Ramon 190
Santo, Ron 178
Savannah (GA) Braves 30
Schatzeder, Dan 54
Schembechler, Bo 164
Scherrer, Bill 85
Schmidt, Dave 128
Schu, Rick 155
Scott, George 39
Scrivener, Chuck 37
Seattle Mariners 54, 85, 165, 182, 191
Selig, Bud 169, 171
Selleck, Tom 75
Sheridan, Pat 120, 126, 144
Show, Eric 102
Singleton, Ken 74
Slaton, Jim 41
Slaught, Don 82, 95
Smith, Lee 97, 149
Smith, Ozzie 128, 208, 210–212
Smith, Randy 184
Smoltz, John 204
Sotomayor, Sonia 172
Sparks, Steve 190
Spezio, Ed 13
Spikes, Charlie 38
The Sporting News 65, 118, 149, 162, 183, 198, 208
Sports Illustrated 58, 65, 86, 152
Stanley, Mickey 6, 57
Staub, Rusty 36, 41, 48, 54, 120
Stegman, Dave 22
Steib, Dave 87, 132
Stottlemyre, Todd 152–153
Straker, Les 144
Summers, Champ 54
Sutherland, Gary 33
Suttcliffe, Rick 97, 128

Tanana, Frank 6, 37, 124, 131, 141–142, 151, 159
Taylor, Jack 15–16
Tejada, Miguel 190, 208
Templeton, Gary 99
Terrell, Walt 124, 131, 135, 151, 155
Tettleton, Mickey 166–167, 172
Texas Rangers 43, 62, 80, 88, 174, 180
Thames, Marcus 194–195
Thomas, Robert 149
Thompson, Jason 6, 36, 40–41, 48, 50, 54
Thurmond, Mark 99, 104, 124
Tiger Stadium 5, 31–32, 40–41, 43, 46, 58, 60, 67, 69, 71, 73, 80, 85, 87, 96, 100–101, 103, 121, 124, 127, 141–142, 144–145, 147, 151, 153, 164, 176–177, 179, 183–186, 199
Time Magazine 85
Tinker, Joe 175, 177, 211

Tobik, Dave 22
Toledo (Mudhens) 111, 187, 189
Toronto Blue Jays 40–41, 43, 57, 62, 79–80, 87–91, 110, 112, 116, 118, 123, 126–127, 159, 164, 167, 171, 174, 181
Torres, Andres 190
Torrez, Mike 45
Tracewski, Richard 8, 39, 116, 120, 211
Trammell, Alan: Al-Star appearances 53, 88–89, 112, 128, 152; Arizona Diamondbacks coach 200–201; boyhood 12–19; Chicago Cubs coach 199; contract negotiations 56–57, 154–155, 164–165, 172–173, 179; draft prospects 17–19; Florida Instructional League 23–25; *Magnum, P.I.* appearance 75; marriage 47; Southern League 22–23, 26–31; sports fan 65–66
Trammell, Anne 11–12
Trammell, Barbara (Leverett) 47, 78, 109
Trammell, Forrest 11
Trammell, Jade 137
Trammell, Kyle 109, 185
Trammell, Lance 109

UCLA 17
Underwood, Pat 19
University of Arizona 17
University of Michigan 164
Upshaw, Willie 133, 136, 139
Urbina, Ugueth 193, 195

Verlander, Justin 198
Veryzer, Tom 33–34, 37–38
Vizcaino, Sebastian 11
Vuckovich, Pete 59

Wagner, Honus 37
Wagner, Mark 37–39, 42
Walbeck, Matt 190
Walewander, Jim 137, 140
Walker, Jamie 191

Walker, Jerry 164–165
Ward, Gary 155, 159
Washington, George 206
Washington, U.L. 94
Washington Senators 26
Wathan, John 94
Weaver, Earl 53
Wells, David 132, 174
Whitaker, Lou 1, 6–9, 24–35, 37, 39–40, 42–43, 45–46, 50–52, 54, 56, 61, 65, 67, 69–76, 79, 82–85, 90, 94–95, 99–103, 109–112, 114, 120, 124–125, 134–135, 137, 139–140, 147, 157, 159–160, 162, 166–168, 175–180, 205–207, 212–213
White, Frank 80, 82, 94–95, 177
White, Rondell 193–194
Whitson, Ed 100
Whitt, Ernie 133, 138–139
Wiencek, Dick 18
Wiggins, Alan 99, 102
Wilcox, Milt 54, 64, 84–85, 96, 101, 110
Williams, Billy 178
Williams, Dick 99, 105
Williams, Jimy 155, 132, 136–137, 140
Williams, Ken 155
Williams, Matt 200
Williams, Ted 175, 199
Willoughby, Jim 32
Wilson, Glenn 68, 79
Wilson, Willie 2, 94, 96
Winfield, Dave 71, 212
Wise, Rick 32
Wockenfuss, John 54, 66, 68, 79
Wrigley Field 97

Yankee Stadium 161
Yastrzemski, Carl 32
Young, Dmitri 190, 194–196
Yount, Robin 53, 72, 84, 86, 207–208, 212

Zumaya, Joel 198

www.ingramcontent.com/pod-product-compliance
Lightning Source LLC
Chambersburg PA
CBHW030106170426
43198CB00009B/511